BLACK HAMMER ™

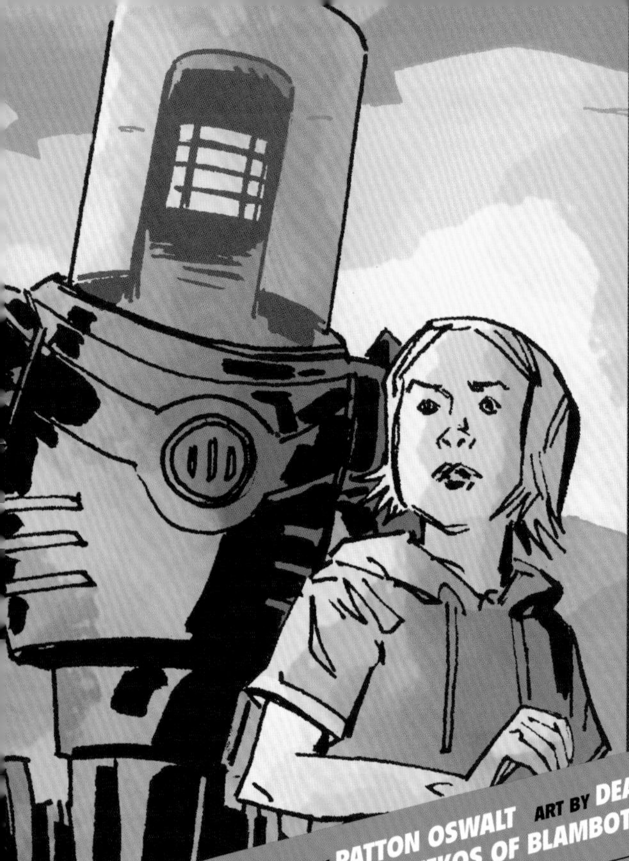

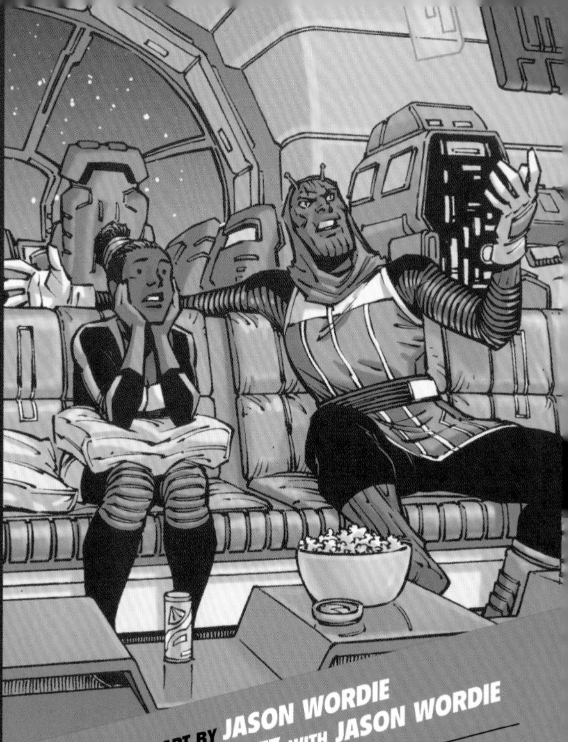

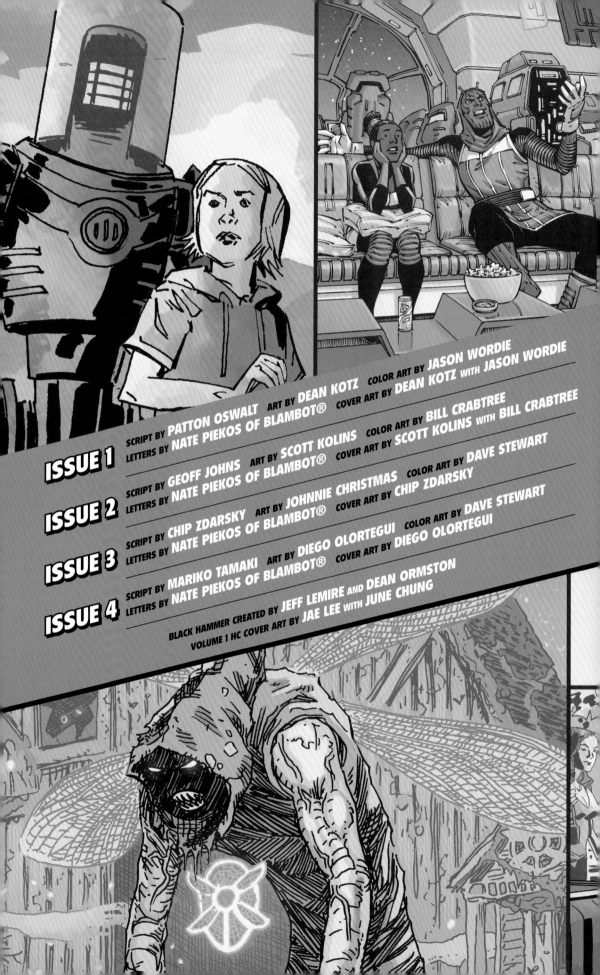

ISSUE 1
SCRIPT BY PATTON OSWALT ART BY DEAN KOTZ COLOR ART BY JASON WORDIE
LETTERS BY NATE PIEKOS OF BLAMBOT® COVER ART BY DEAN KOTZ WITH JASON WORDIE

ISSUE 2
SCRIPT BY GEOFF JOHNS ART BY SCOTT KOLINS COLOR ART BY BILL CRABTREE
LETTERS BY NATE PIEKOS OF BLAMBOT® COVER ART BY SCOTT KOLINS WITH BILL CRABTREE

ISSUE 3
SCRIPT BY CHIP ZDARSKY ART BY JOHNNIE CHRISTMAS COLOR ART BY DAVE STEWART
LETTERS BY NATE PIEKOS OF BLAMBOT® COVER ART BY CHIP ZDARSKY

ISSUE 4
SCRIPT BY MARIKO TAMAKI ART BY DIEGO OLORTEGUI COLOR ART BY DAVE STEWART
LETTERS BY NATE PIEKOS OF BLAMBOT® COVER ART BY DIEGO OLORTEGUI

BLACK HAMMER CREATED BY JEFF LEMIRE AND DEAN ORMSTON
VOLUME 1 HC COVER ART BY JAE LEE WITH JUNE CHUNG

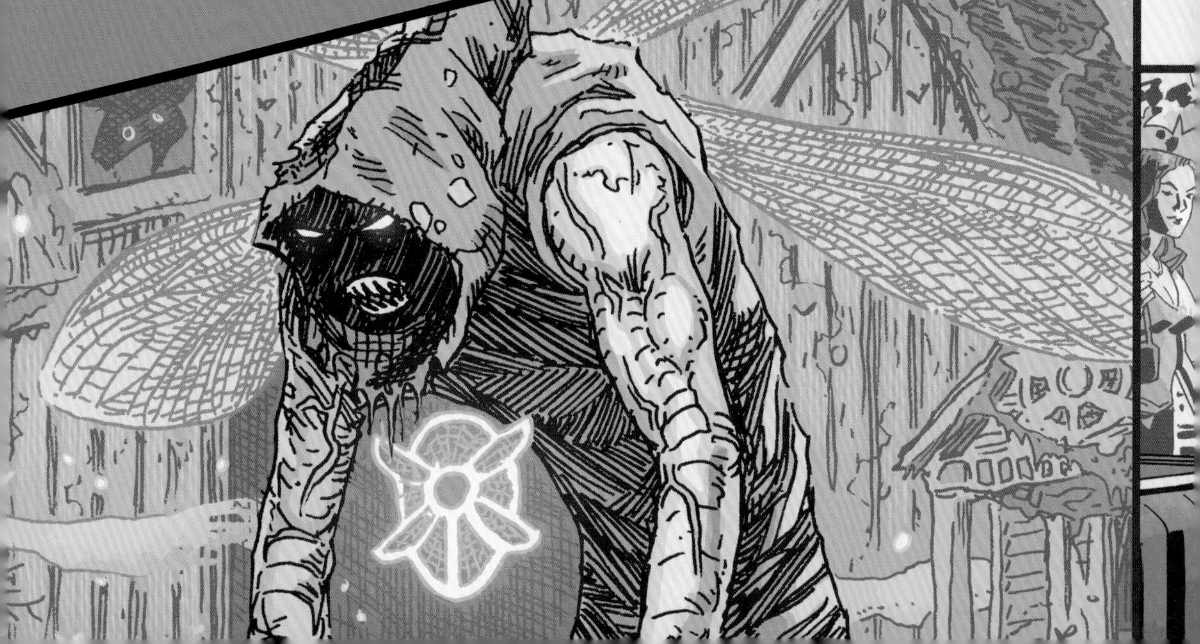

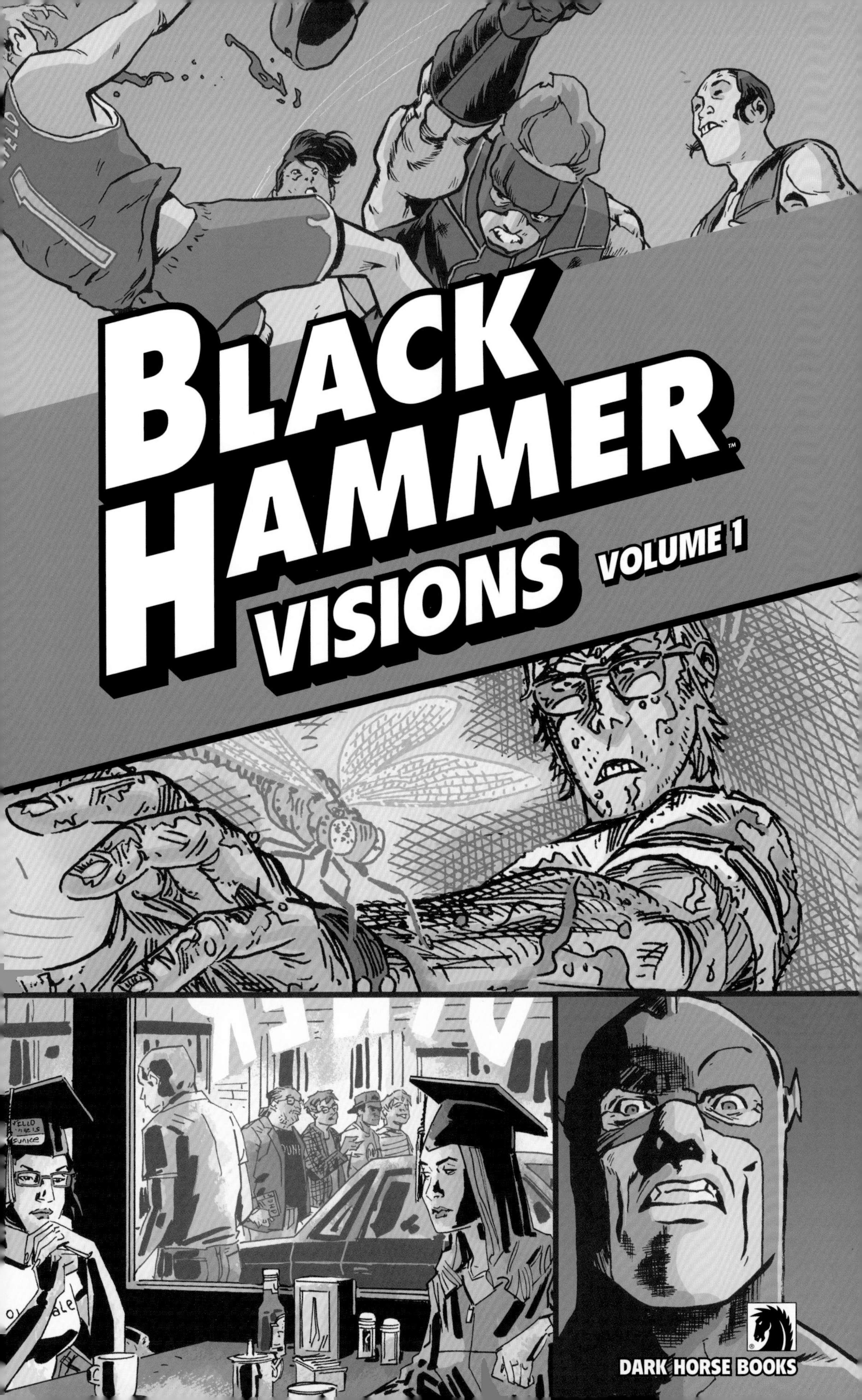
BLACK HAMMER™
VISIONS
VOLUME 1
DARK HORSE BOOKS

PUBLISHER
MIKE RICHARDSON

EDITOR
DANIEL CHABON

ASSISTANT EDITORS
CHUCK HOWITT
AND KONNER KNUDSEN

DESIGNER
ETHAN KIMBERLING

DIGITAL ART TECHNICIAN
JOSIE CHRISTENSEN

BLACK HAMMER: VISIONS VOLUME 1

Collects issues #1–#4 of the Dark Horse Comics series *Black Hammer: Visions*.

Library of Congress Cataloging-in-Publication Data

Names: Lemire, Jeff, author. | Ormston, Dean, artist. | Oswalt, Patton,
  1969- author. | Johns, Geoff, 1973- author. | Zdarsky, Chip, author. |
  Tamaki, Mariko, author. | Kotz, Dean, artist. | Kolins, Scott, artist. |
  Christmas, Johnnie, artist. | Olortegui, Diego, artist. | Stewart, Dave,
  colourist. | Wordie, Jason (Colorist), colourist. | Crabtree, Bill
  (Comic book colorist), colourist. | Piekos, Nate, letterer.
Title: Black Hammer : visions / Jeff Lemire, Dean Ormston, Patton Oswalt,
  Geoff Johns, Chip Zdarsky, Mariko Tamaki, Dean Kotz, Scott Kolins,
  Johnnie Christmas, Diego Olortegui, Dave Stewart, Jason Wordie, Bill
  Crabtree, Nate Piekos.
Other titles: Visions
Description: First edition. | Milwaukie, OR : Dark Horse Books, 2021. |
  "Black Hammer Created by Jeff Lemire and Dean Ormston"
Identifiers: LCCN 2021015089 (print) | LCCN 2021015090 (ebook) | ISBN
  9781506723266 (hardcover) | ISBN 9781506723273 (ebook)
Subjects: LCSH: Comic books, strips, etc.
Classification: LCC PN6728.B51926 L396 2021 (print) | LCC PN6728.B51926
  (ebook) | DDC 741.5/973--dc23
LC record available at https://lccn.loc.gov/2021015089
LC ebook record available at https://lccn.loc.gov/2021015090

Published by
Dark Horse Books
A division of Dark Horse Comics LLC
10956 SE Main Street
Milwaukie, OR 97222

DarkHorse.com

To find a comics shop in your area, visit comicshoplocator.com

First edition: September 2021
Ebook ISBN 978-1-50672-327-3
Hardcover ISBN 978-1-50672-326-6

10 9 8 7 6 5 4 3 2 1
Printed in China

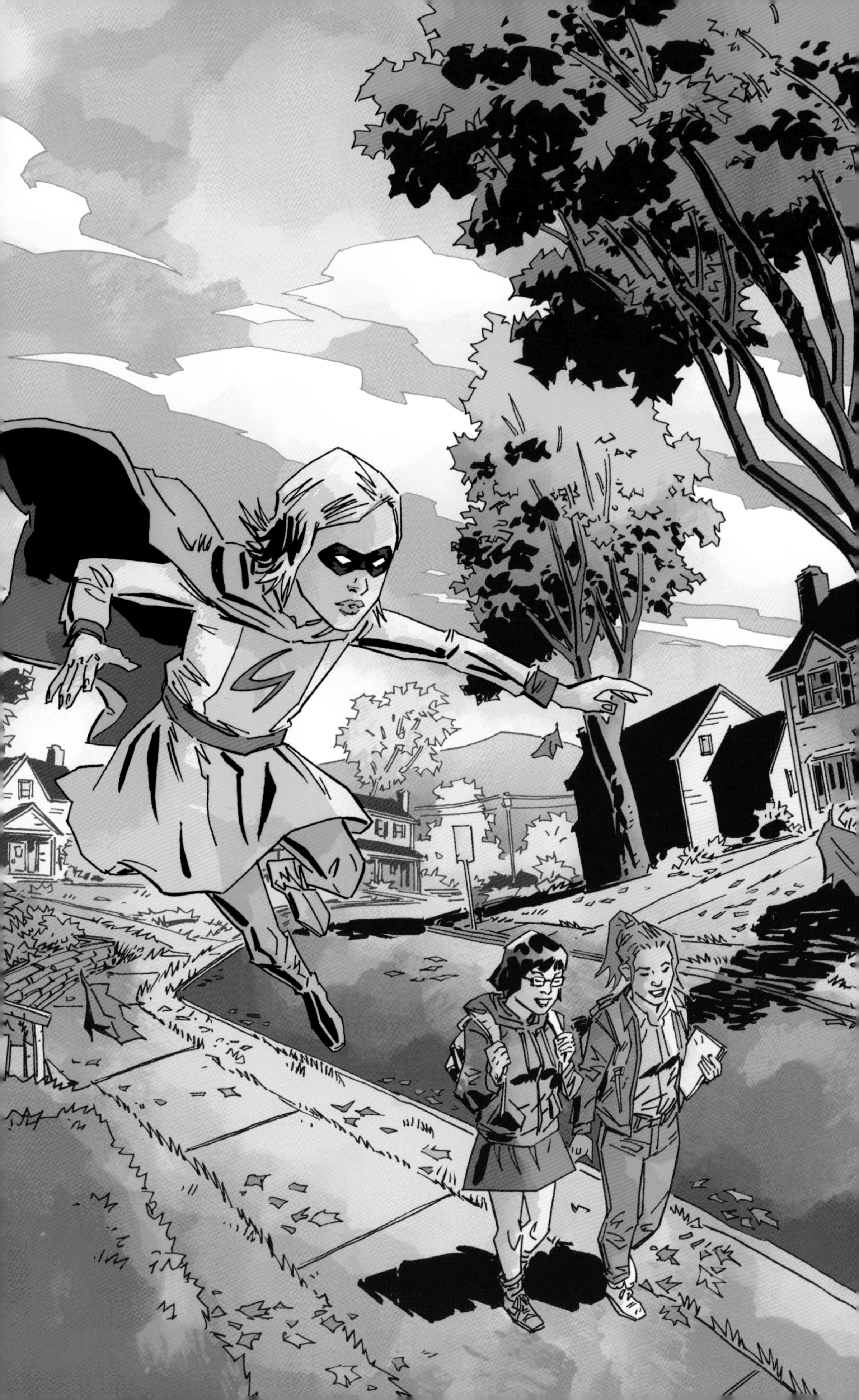

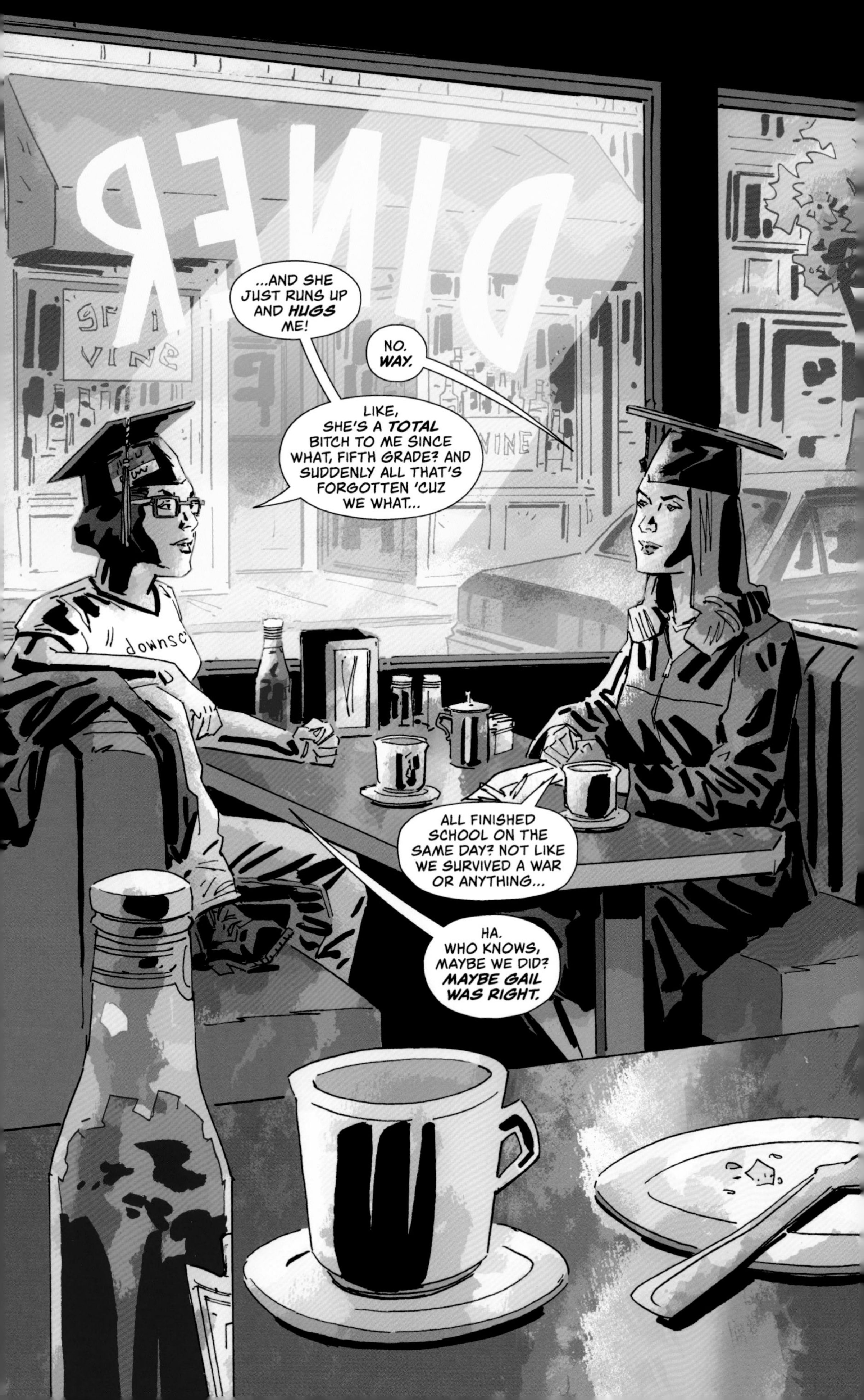
DINER
...AND SHE JUST RUNS UP AND **HUGS** ME!
NO. **WAY.**
LIKE, SHE'S A **TOTAL** BITCH TO ME SINCE WHAT, FIFTH GRADE? AND SUDDENLY ALL THAT'S FORGOTTEN 'CUZ WE WHAT...
ALL FINISHED SCHOOL ON THE SAME DAY? NOT LIKE WE SURVIVED A WAR OR ANYTHING...
HA. WHO KNOWS, MAYBE WE DID? **MAYBE GAIL WAS RIGHT.**

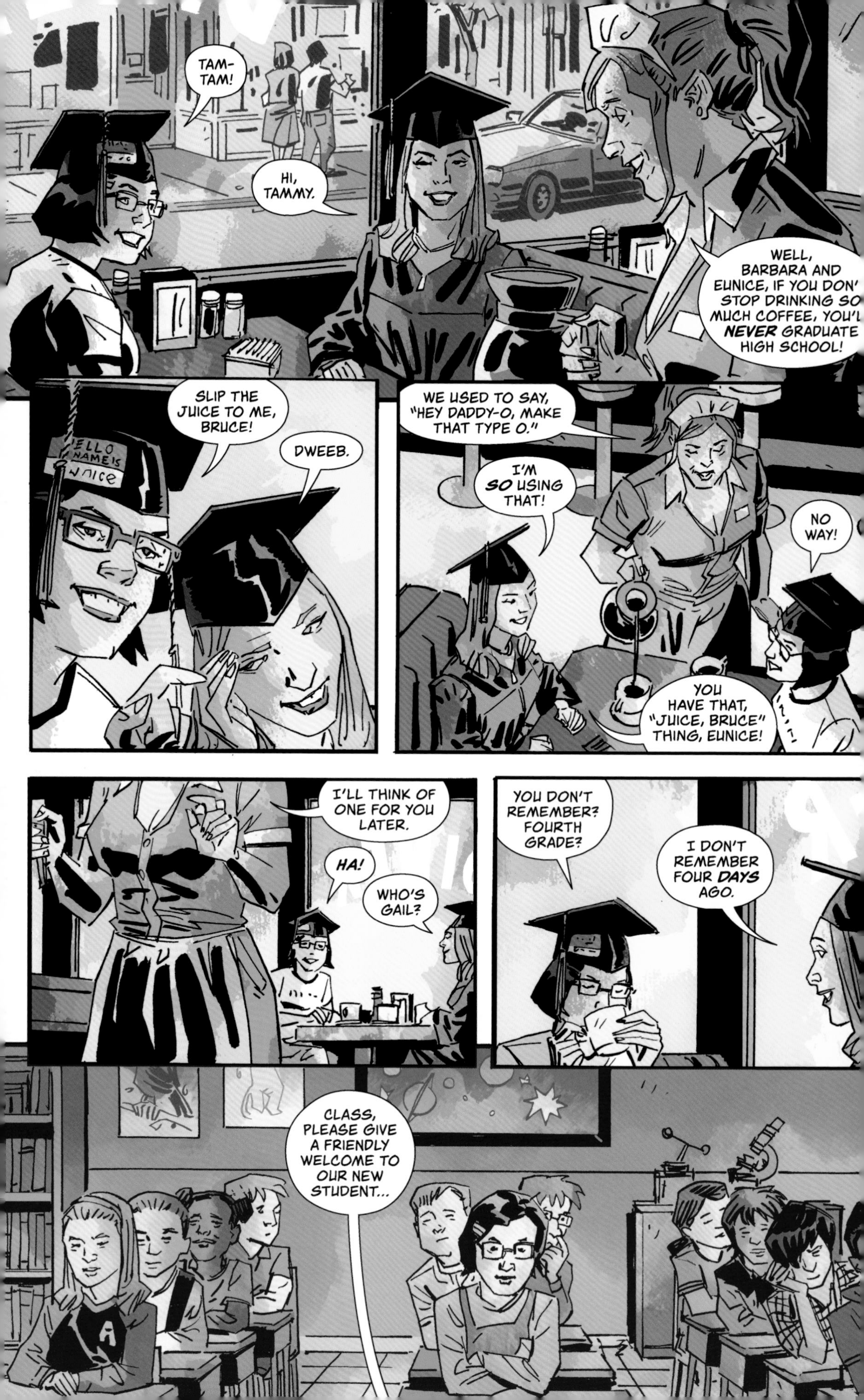
TAM-TAM!
HI, TAMMY.
WELL, BARBARA AND EUNICE, IF YOU DON'T STOP DRINKING SO MUCH COFFEE, YOU'LL NEVER GRADUATE HIGH SCHOOL!
SLIP THE JUICE TO ME, BRUCE!
DWEEB.
WE USED TO SAY, "HEY DADDY-O, MAKE THAT TYPE O."
I'M SO USING THAT!
NO WAY!
YOU HAVE THAT, "JUICE, BRUCE" THING, EUNICE!
I'LL THINK OF ONE FOR YOU LATER.
HA!
WHO'S GAIL?
YOU DON'T REMEMBER? FOURTH GRADE?
I DON'T REMEMBER FOUR DAYS AGO.
CLASS, PLEASE GIVE A FRIENDLY WELCOME TO OUR NEW STUDENT...

TRANSFER STUDENT

Written by Patton Oswalt • Art by Dean Kotz

Color Art by Jason Wordie • Lettering by Nate Piekos of Blambot®

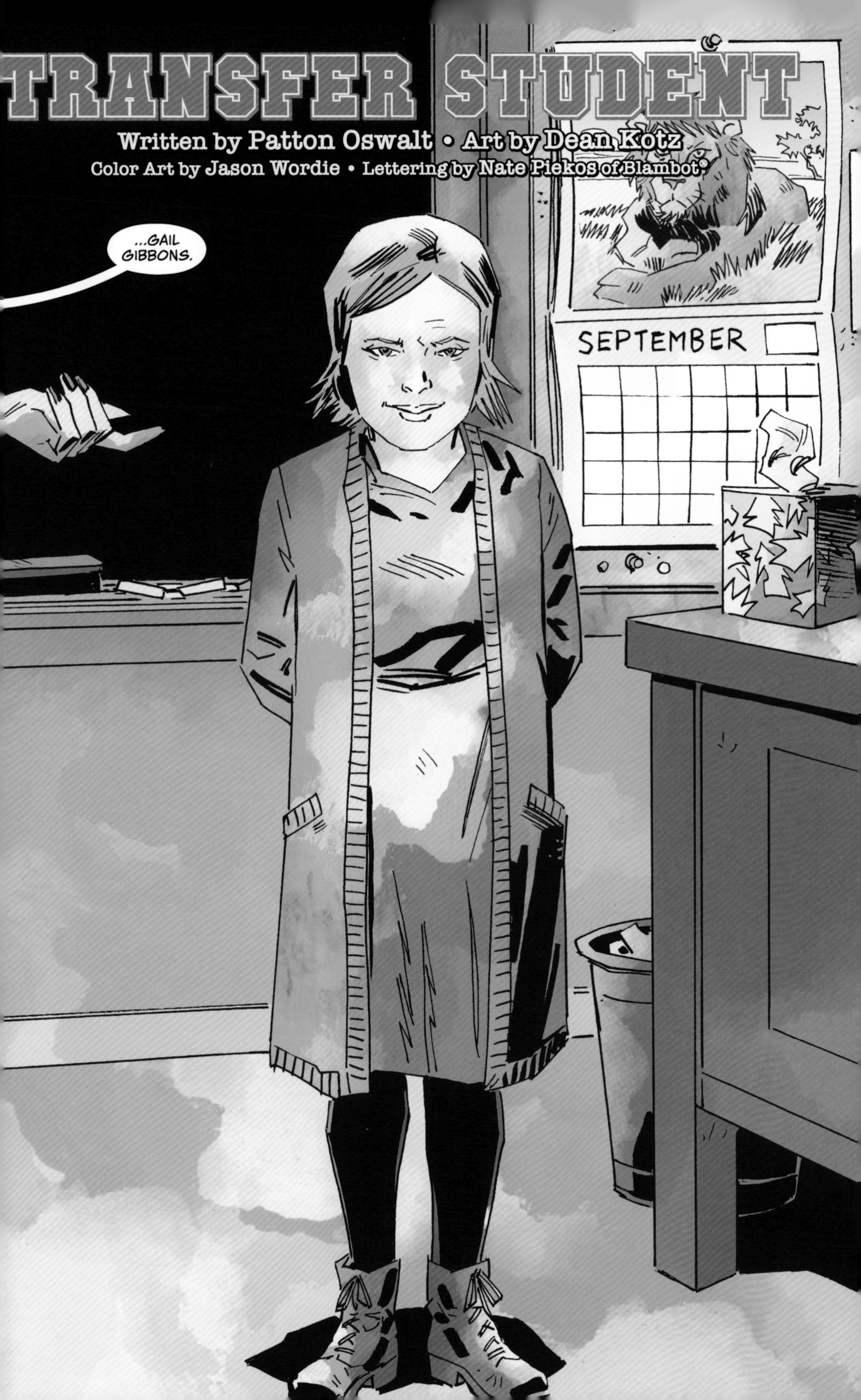

...GAIL GIBBONS.
SEPTEMBER

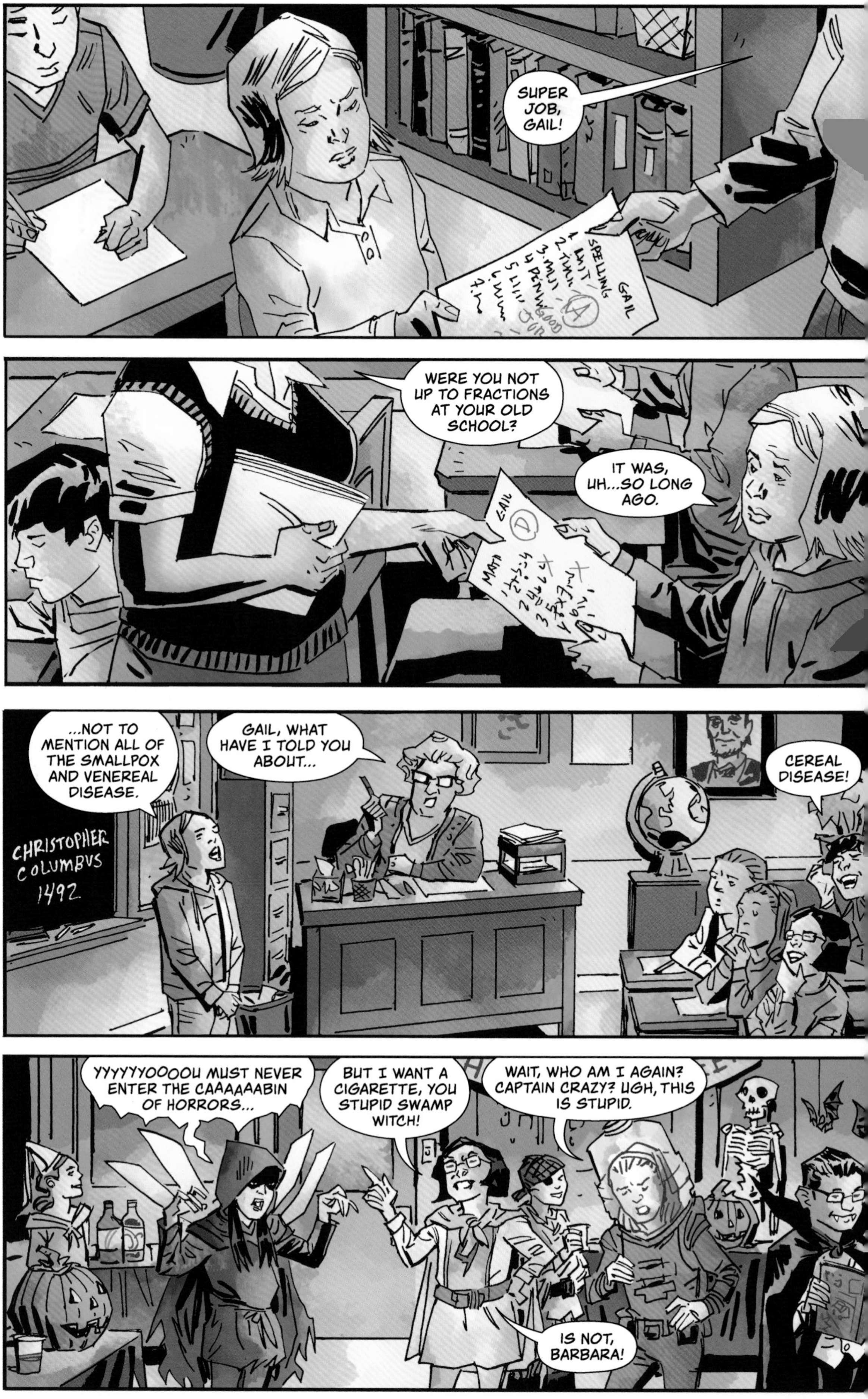
SUPER JOB, GAIL!
GAIL
SPELLING
WERE YOU NOT UP TO FRACTIONS AT YOUR OLD SCHOOL?
IT WAS, UH...SO LONG AGO.
GAIL
MATH
...NOT TO MENTION ALL OF THE SMALLPOX AND VENEREAL DISEASE.
CHRISTOPHER COLUMBUS 1492
GAIL, WHAT HAVE I TOLD YOU ABOUT...
CEREAL DISEASE!
YYYYYYOOOOU MUST NEVER ENTER THE CAAAAAABIN OF HORRORS...
BUT I WANT A CIGARETTE, YOU STUPID SWAMP WITCH!
WAIT, WHO AM I AGAIN? CAPTAIN CRAZY? UGH, THIS IS STUPID.
IS NOT, BARBARA!

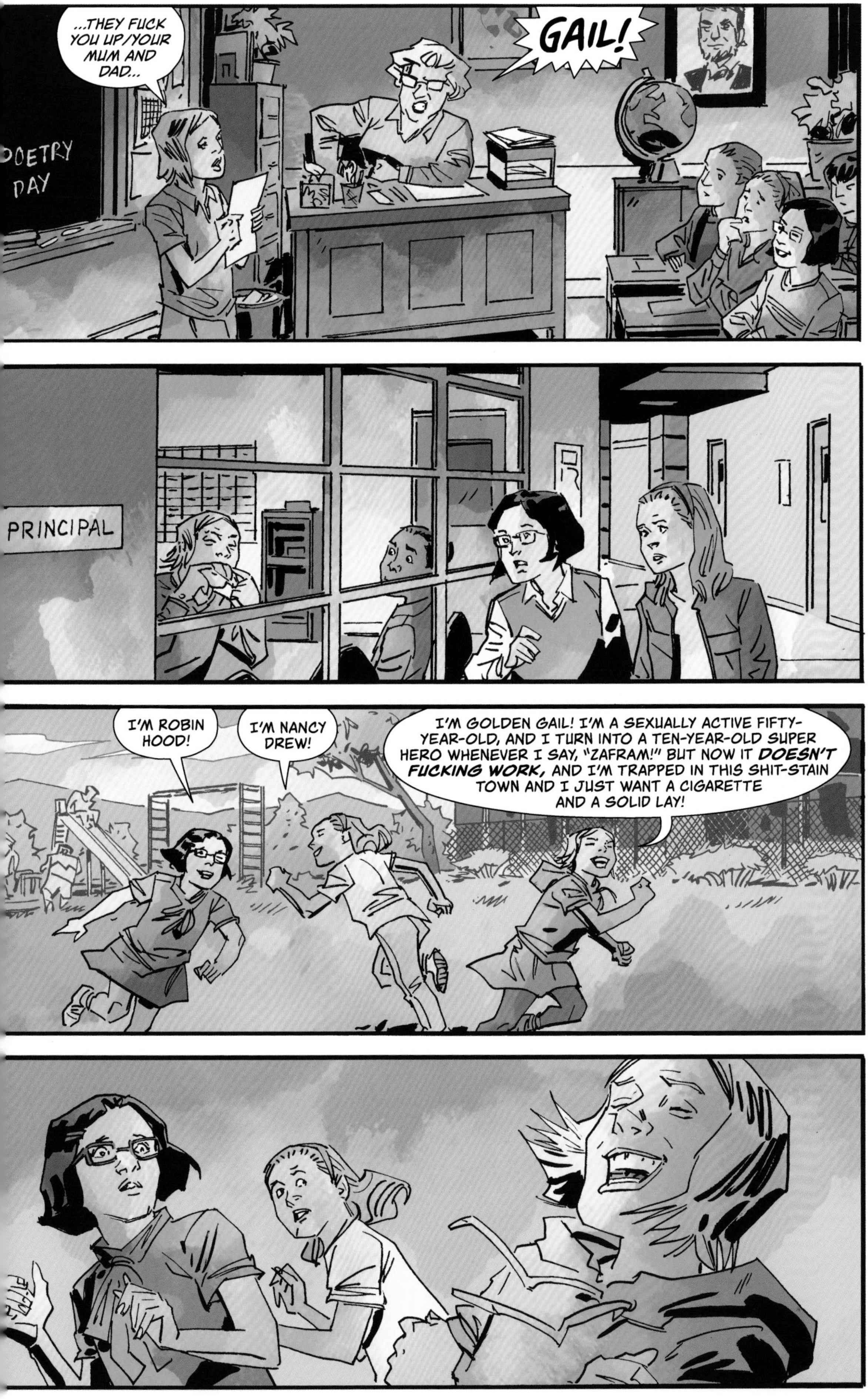
...THEY FUCK YOU UP/YOUR MUM AND DAD...
GAIL!
POETRY DAY
PRINCIPAL
I'M ROBIN HOOD!
I'M NANCY DREW!
I'M GOLDEN GAIL! I'M A SEXUALLY ACTIVE FIFTY-YEAR-OLD, AND I TURN INTO A TEN-YEAR-OLD SUPER HERO WHENEVER I SAY, "ZAFRAM!" BUT NOW IT DOESN'T FUCKING WORK, AND I'M TRAPPED IN THIS SHIT-STAIN TOWN AND I JUST WANT A CIGARETTE AND A SOLID LAY!

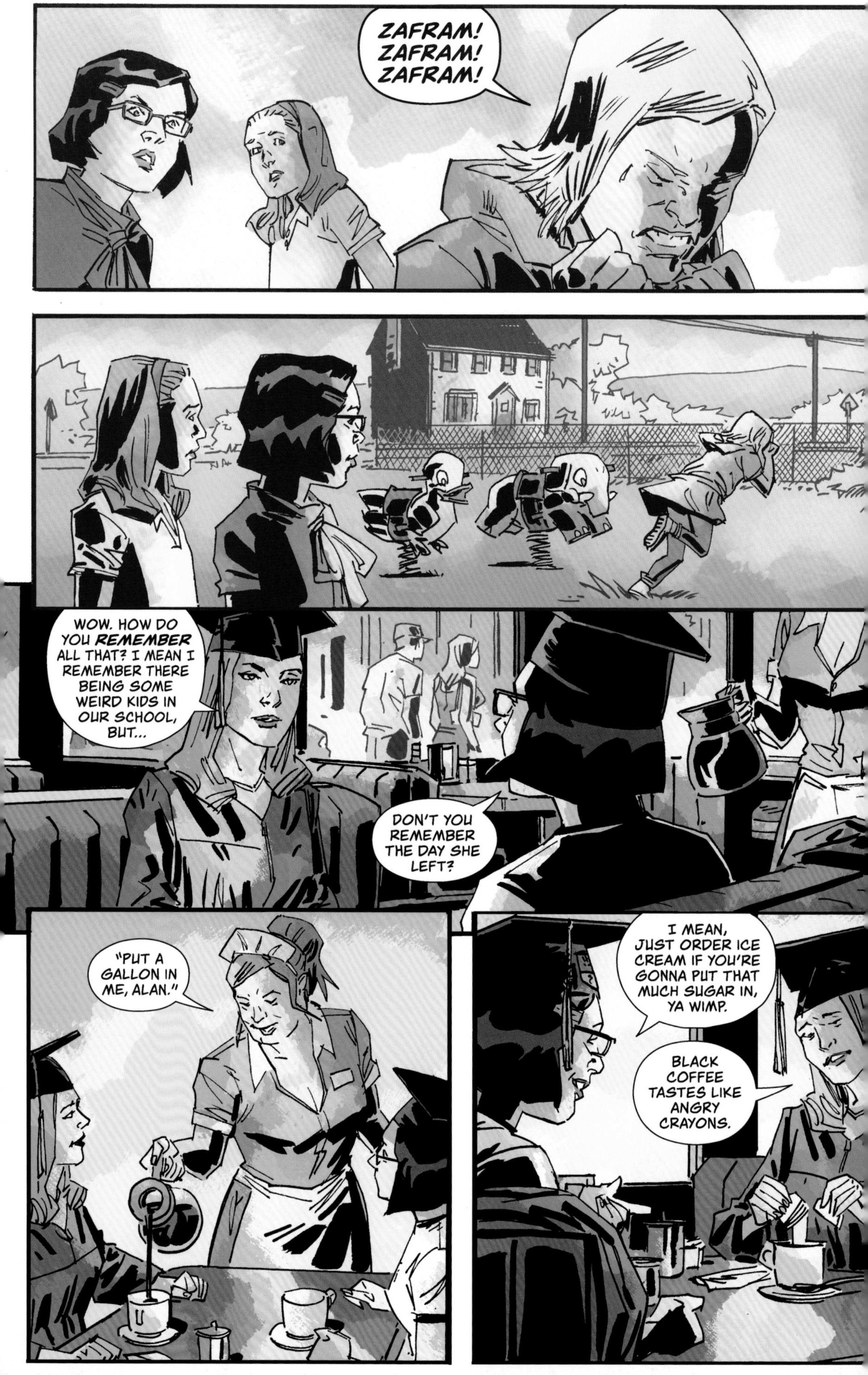
ZAFRAM! ZAFRAM! ZAFRAM!
WOW. HOW DO YOU REMEMBER ALL THAT? I MEAN I REMEMBER THERE BEING SOME WEIRD KIDS IN OUR SCHOOL, BUT...
DON'T YOU REMEMBER THE DAY SHE LEFT?
"PUT A GALLON IN ME, ALAN."
I MEAN, JUST ORDER ICE CREAM IF YOU'RE GONNA PUT THAT MUCH SUGAR IN, YA WIMP.
BLACK COFFEE TASTES LIKE ANGRY CRAYONS.

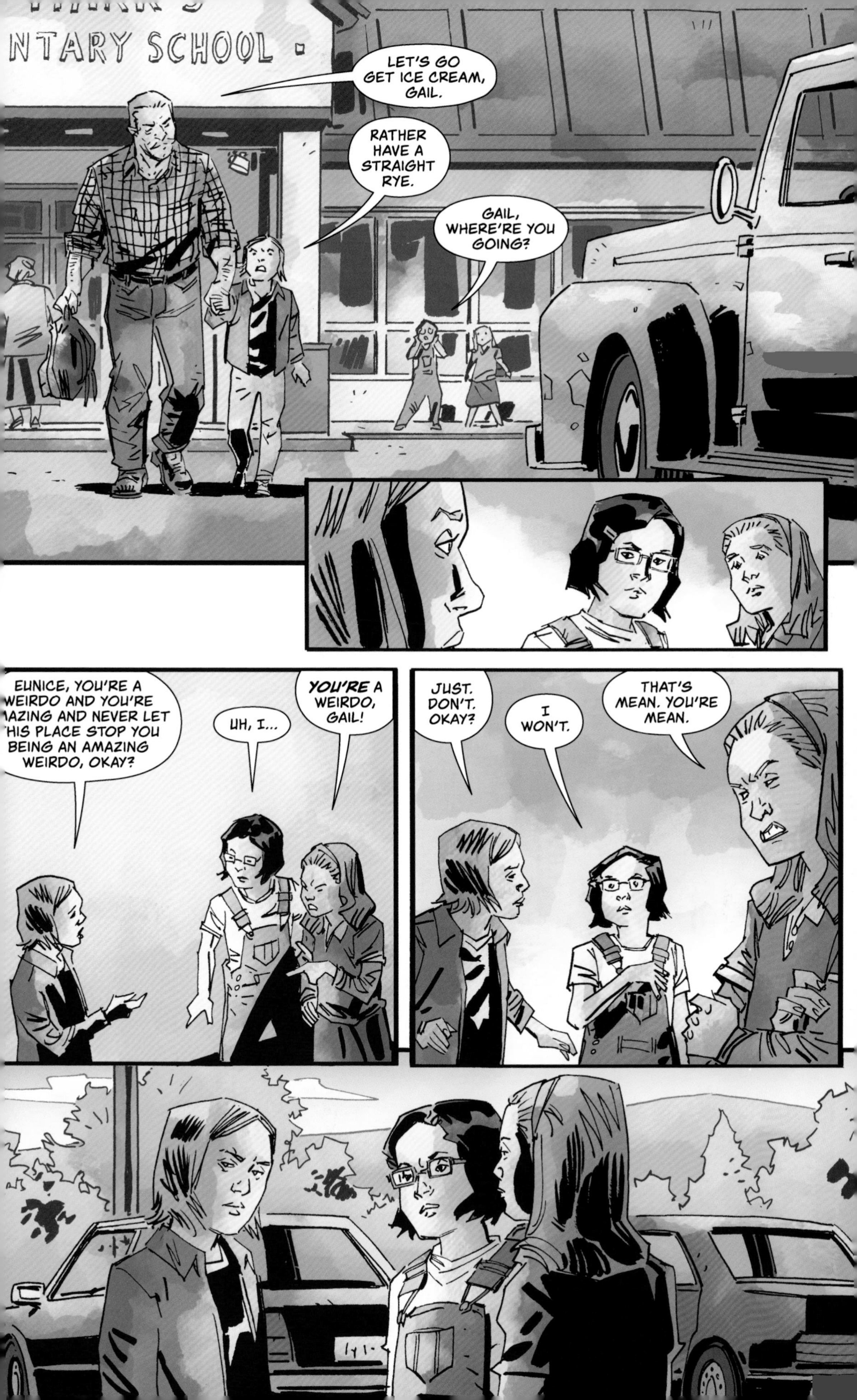
NTARY SCHOOL
LET'S GO GET ICE CREAM, GAIL.
RATHER HAVE A STRAIGHT RYE.
GAIL, WHERE'RE YOU GOING?
EUNICE, YOU'RE A WEIRDO AND YOU'RE AZING AND NEVER LET HIS PLACE STOP YOU BEING AN AMAZING WEIRDO, OKAY?
UH, I...
YOU'RE A WEIRDO, GAIL!
JUST. DON'T. OKAY?
I WON'T.
THAT'S MEAN. YOU'RE MEAN.

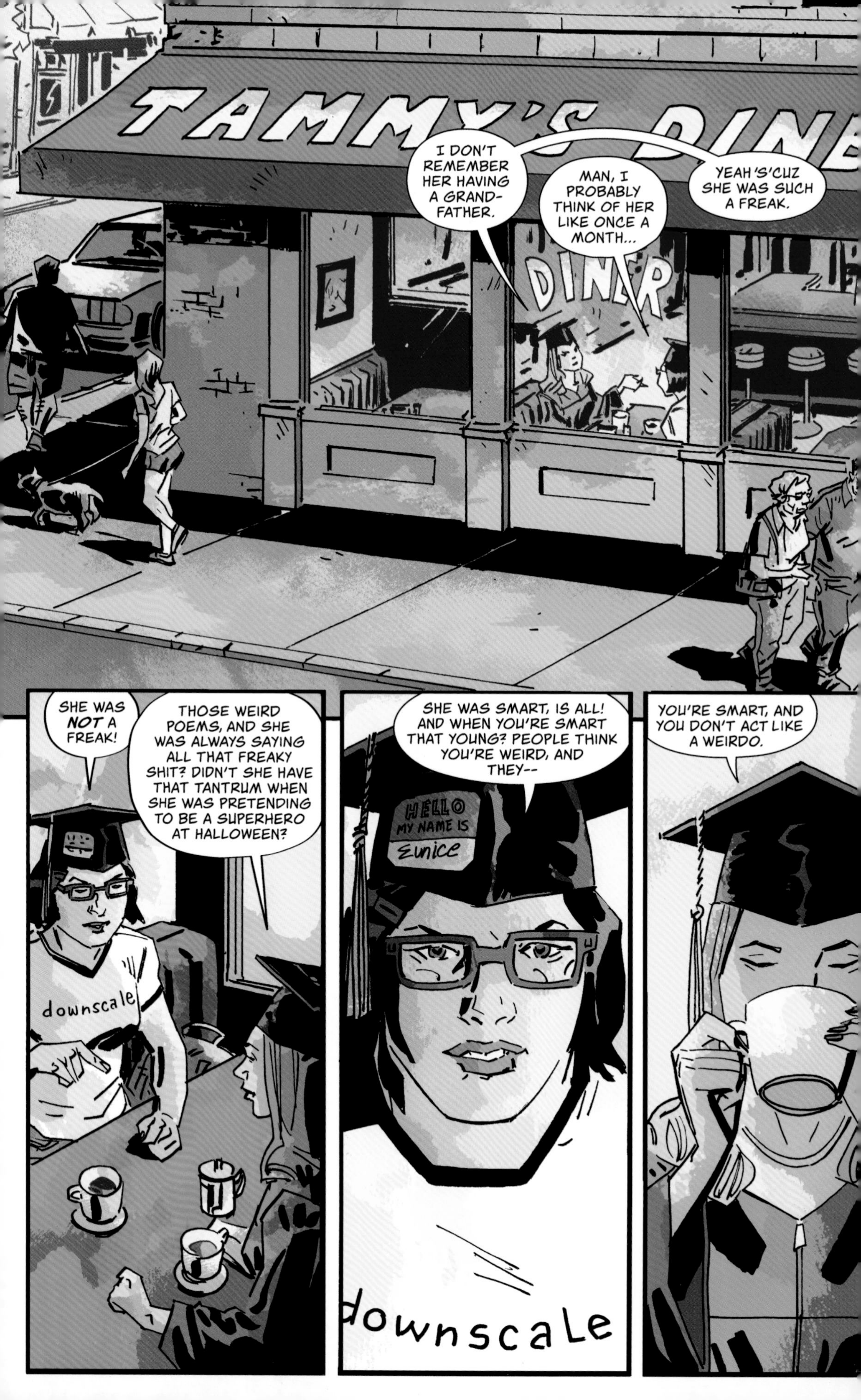
TAMMY'S DINE
I DON'T REMEMBER HER HAVING A GRAND-FATHER.
MAN, I PROBABLY THINK OF HER LIKE ONCE A MONTH...
YEAH 'S'CUZ SHE WAS SUCH A FREAK.
DINER
SHE WAS NOT A FREAK!
THOSE WEIRD POEMS, AND SHE WAS ALWAYS SAYING ALL THAT FREAKY SHIT? DIDN'T SHE HAVE THAT TANTRUM WHEN SHE WAS PRETENDING TO BE A SUPERHERO AT HALLOWEEN?
downscale
SHE WAS SMART, IS ALL! AND WHEN YOU'RE SMART THAT YOUNG? PEOPLE THINK YOU'RE WEIRD, AND THEY--
HELLO MY NAME IS Eunice
downscale
YOU'RE SMART, AND YOU DON'T ACT LIKE A WEIRDO.

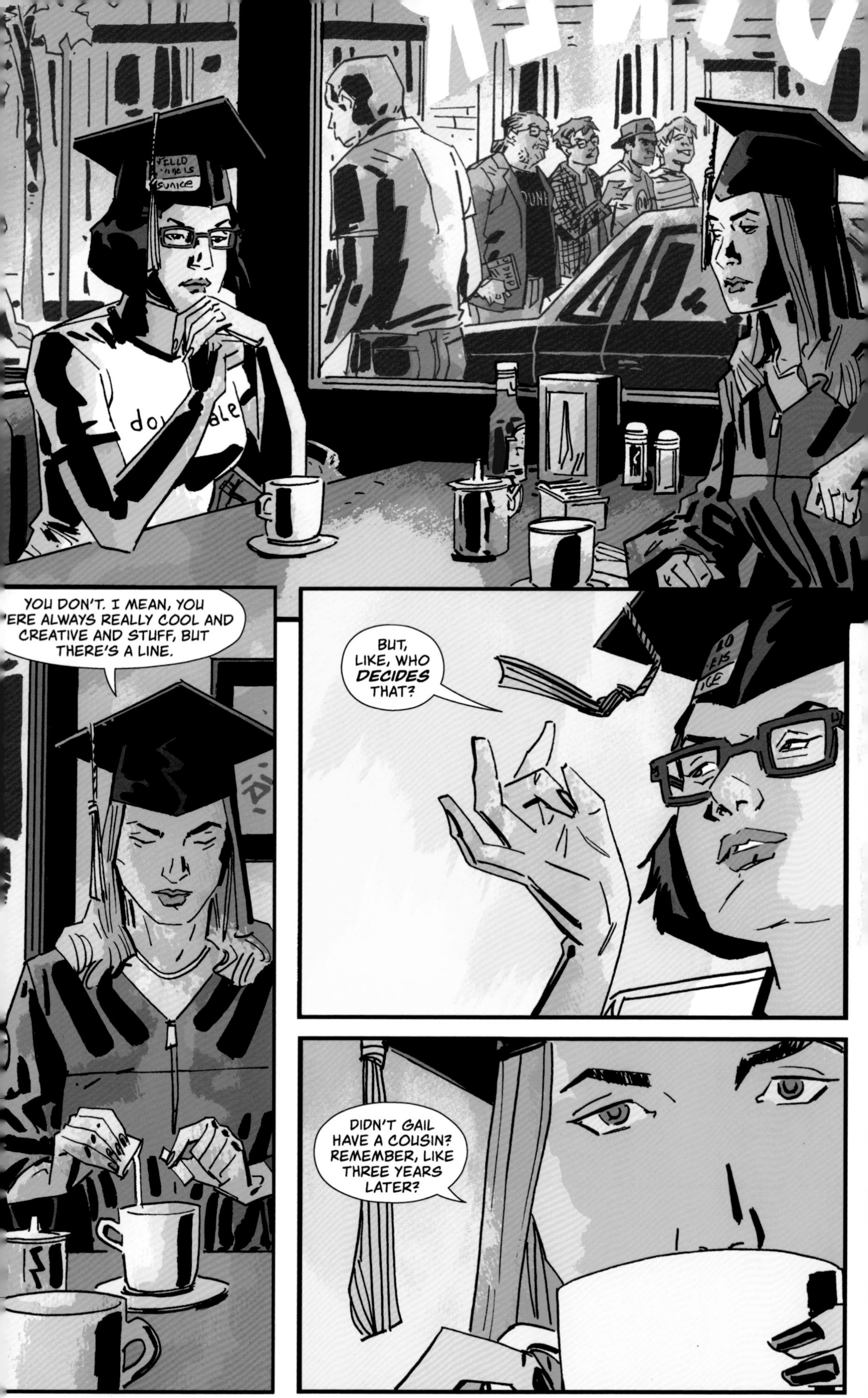

YOU DON'T. I MEAN, YOU 'ERE ALWAYS REALLY COOL AND CREATIVE AND STUFF, BUT THERE'S A LINE.
BUT, LIKE, WHO DECIDES THAT?
DIDN'T GAIL HAVE A COUSIN? REMEMBER, LIKE THREE YEARS LATER?

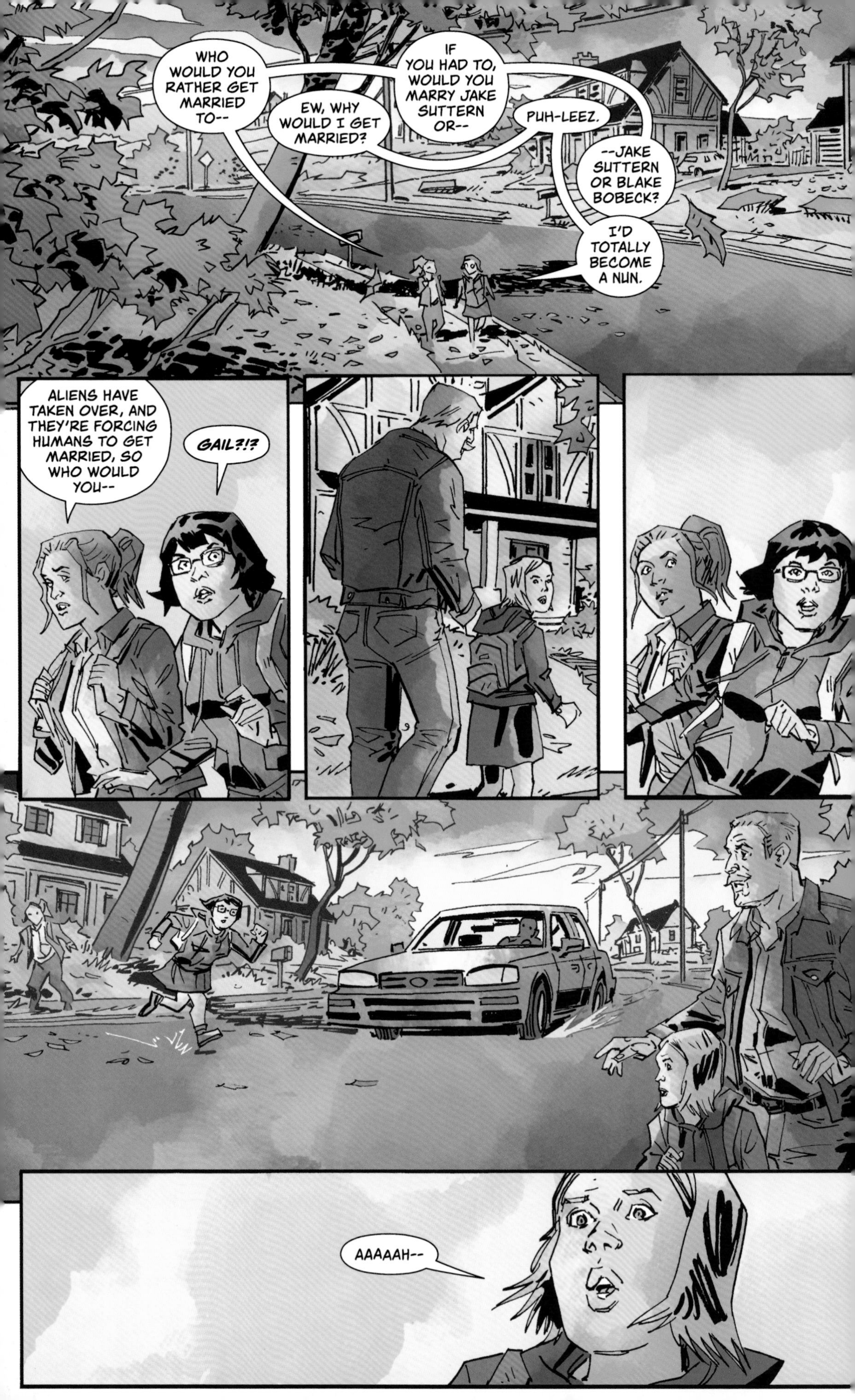
WHO WOULD YOU RATHER GET MARRIED TO--
EW, WHY WOULD I GET MARRIED?
IF YOU HAD TO, WOULD YOU MARRY JAKE SUTTERN OR--
PUH-LEEZ.
--JAKE SUTTERN OR BLAKE BOBECK?
I'D TOTALLY BECOME A NUN.
ALIENS HAVE TAKEN OVER, AND THEY'RE FORCING HUMANS TO GET MARRIED, SO WHO WOULD YOU--
GAIL?!?
AAAAAH--

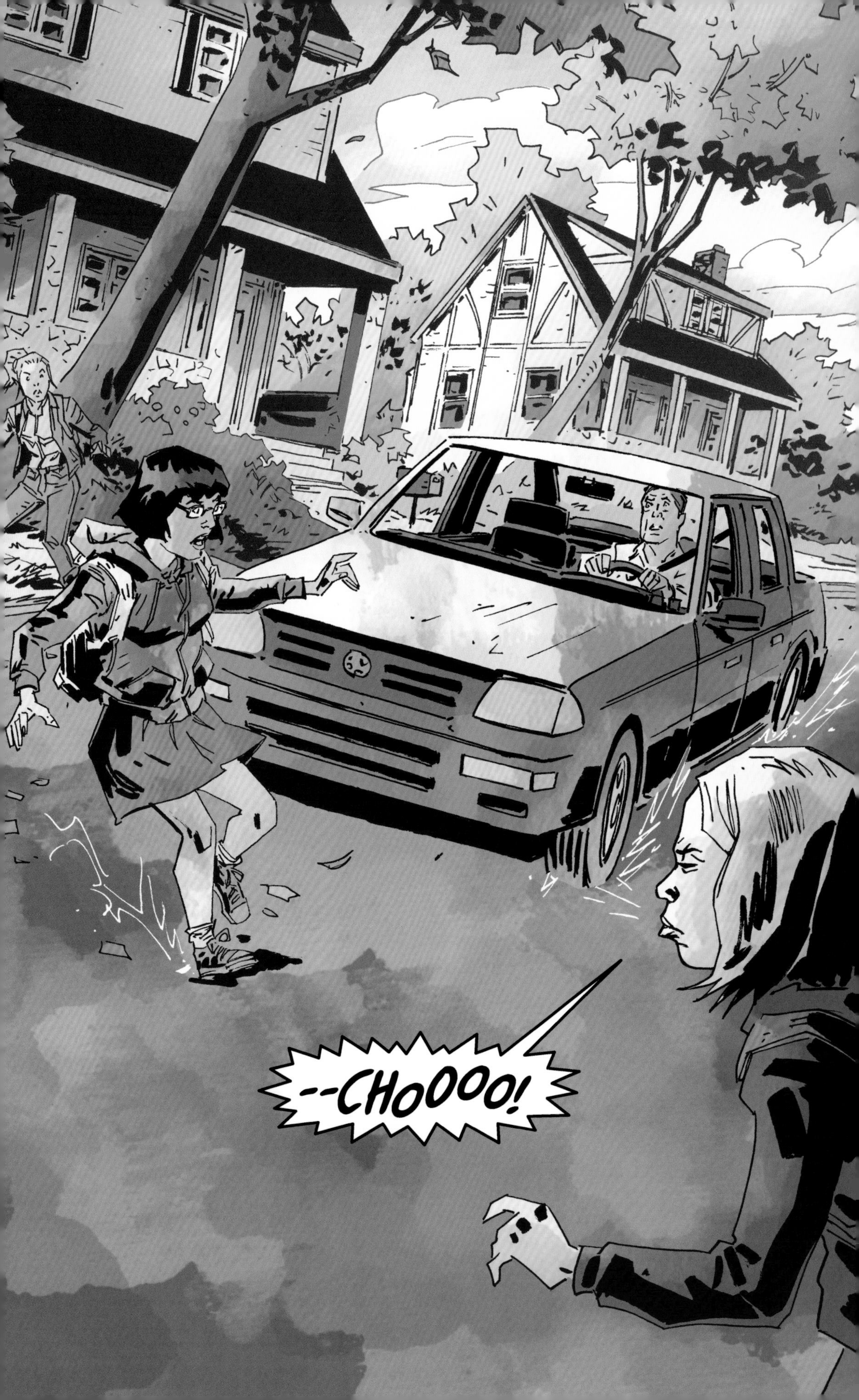
--CHOOOO!

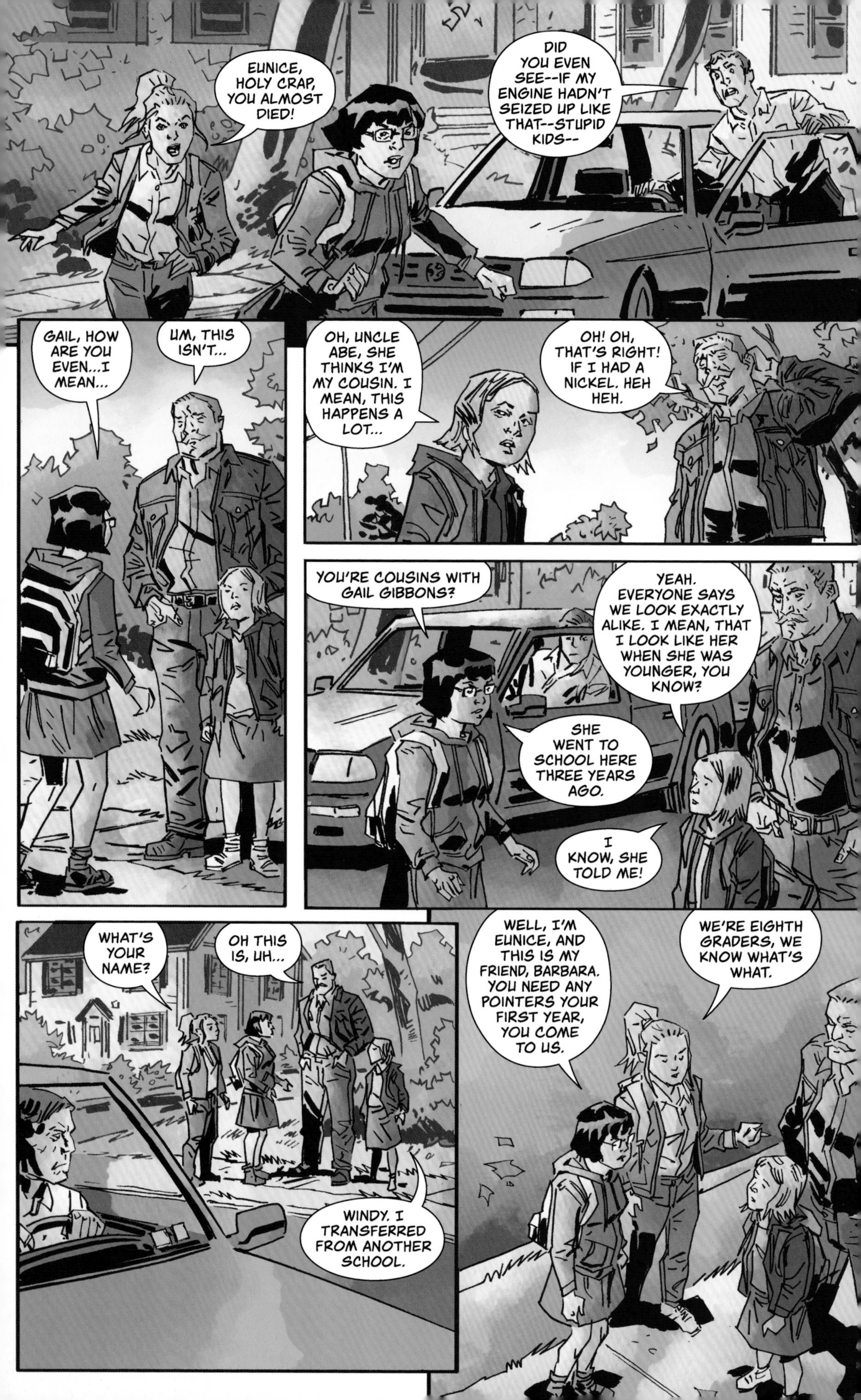
EUNICE, HOLY CRAP, YOU ALMOST DIED!
DID YOU EVEN SEE--IF MY ENGINE HADN'T SEIZED UP LIKE THAT--STUPID KIDS--
GAIL, HOW ARE YOU EVEN...I MEAN...
UM, THIS ISN'T...
OH, UNCLE ABE, SHE THINKS I'M MY COUSIN. I MEAN, THIS HAPPENS A LOT...
OH! OH, THAT'S RIGHT! IF I HAD A NICKEL. HEH HEH.
YOU'RE COUSINS WITH GAIL GIBBONS?
YEAH. EVERYONE SAYS WE LOOK EXACTLY ALIKE. I MEAN, THAT I LOOK LIKE HER WHEN SHE WAS YOUNGER, YOU KNOW?
SHE WENT TO SCHOOL HERE THREE YEARS AGO.
I KNOW, SHE TOLD ME!
WHAT'S YOUR NAME?
OH THIS IS, UH...
WINDY. I TRANSFERRED FROM ANOTHER SCHOOL.
WELL, I'M EUNICE, AND THIS IS MY FRIEND, BARBARA. YOU NEED ANY POINTERS YOUR FIRST YEAR, YOU COME TO US.
WE'RE EIGHTH GRADERS, WE KNOW WHAT'S WHAT.

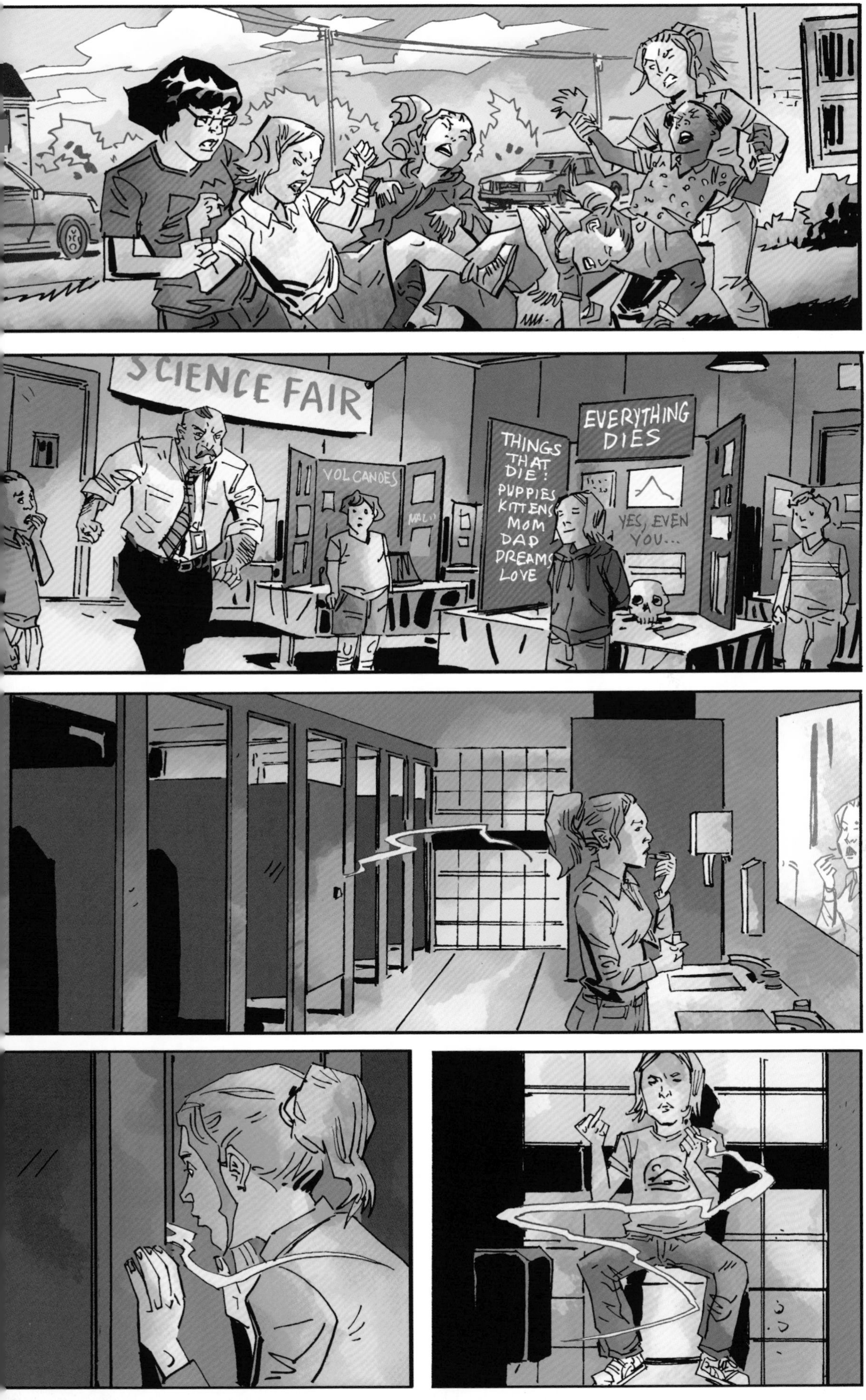
SCIENCE FAIR
VOLCANOES
THINGS THAT DIE:
PUPPIES
KITTENS
MOM
DAD
DREAMS
LOVE
EVERYTHING DIES
YES, EVEN YOU...

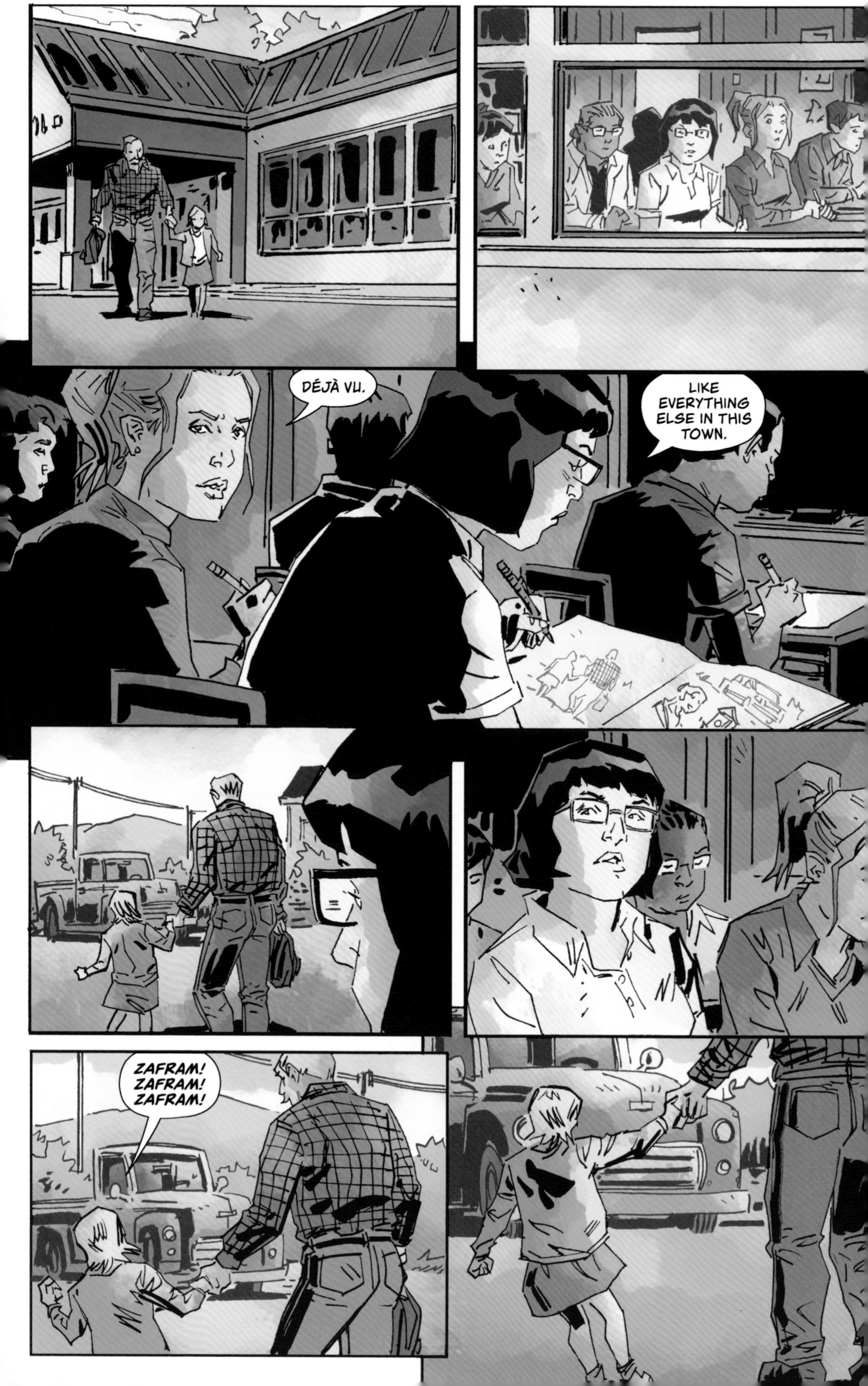
DÉJÀ VU.
LIKE EVERYTHING ELSE IN THIS TOWN.
ZAFRAM! ZAFRAM! ZAFRAM!

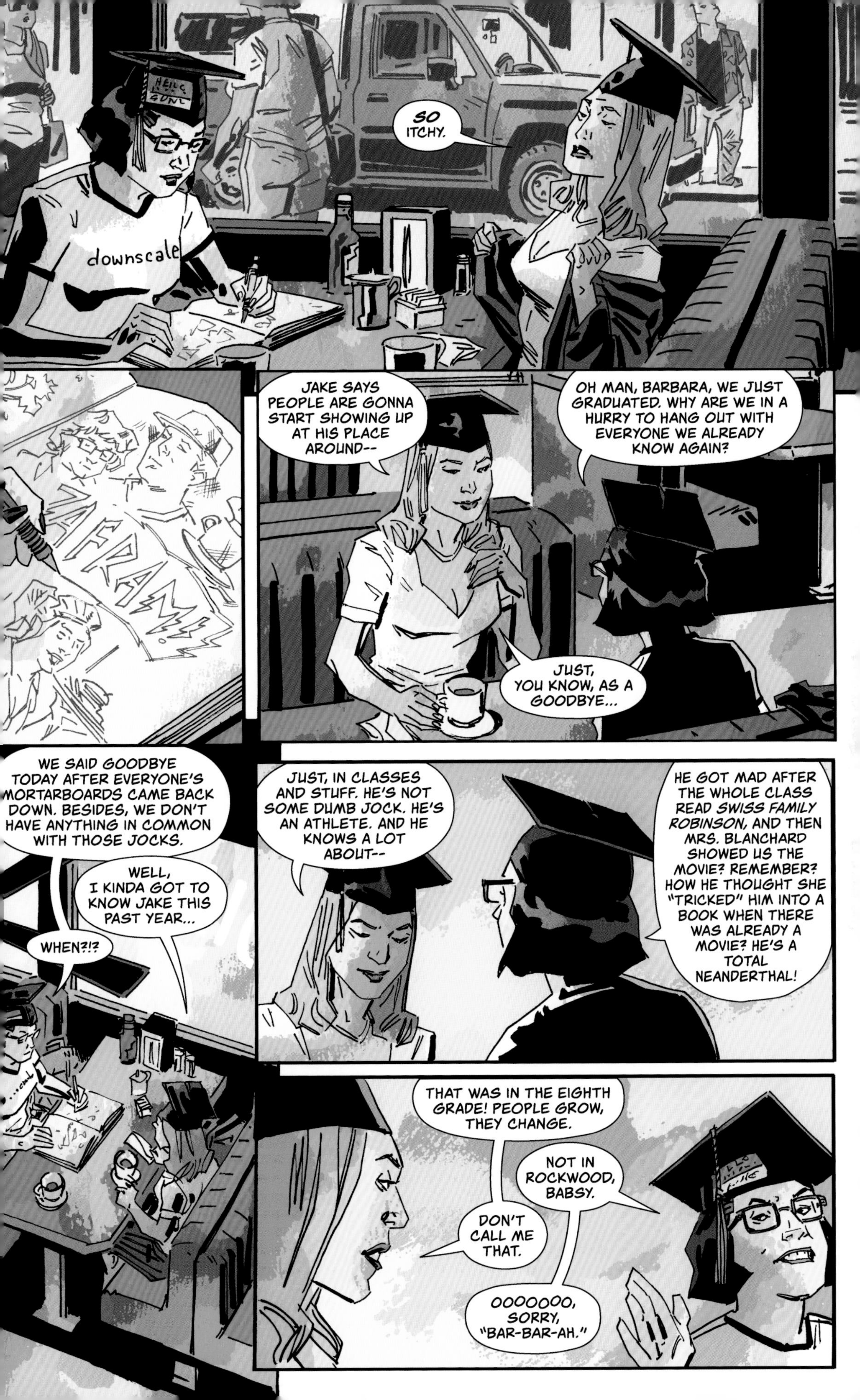
HEILC GUNL
SO ITCHY.
downscale
JAKE SAYS PEOPLE ARE GONNA START SHOWING UP AT HIS PLACE AROUND--
OH MAN, BARBARA, WE JUST GRADUATED. WHY ARE WE IN A HURRY TO HANG OUT WITH EVERYONE WE ALREADY KNOW AGAIN?
JUST, YOU KNOW, AS A GOODBYE...
WE SAID GOODBYE TODAY AFTER EVERYONE'S MORTARBOARDS CAME BACK DOWN. BESIDES, WE DON'T HAVE ANYTHING IN COMMON WITH THOSE JOCKS.
WELL, I KINDA GOT TO KNOW JAKE THIS PAST YEAR...
WHEN?!?
JUST, IN CLASSES AND STUFF. HE'S NOT SOME DUMB JOCK. HE'S AN ATHLETE. AND HE KNOWS A LOT ABOUT--
HE GOT MAD AFTER THE WHOLE CLASS READ *SWISS FAMILY ROBINSON*, AND THEN MRS. BLANCHARD SHOWED US THE MOVIE? REMEMBER? HOW HE THOUGHT SHE "TRICKED" HIM INTO A BOOK WHEN THERE WAS ALREADY A MOVIE? HE'S A TOTAL NEANDERTHAL!
THAT WAS IN THE EIGHTH GRADE! PEOPLE GROW, THEY CHANGE.
NOT IN ROCKWOOD, BABSY.
DON'T CALL ME THAT.
OOOOOOO, SORRY, "BAR-BAR-AH."

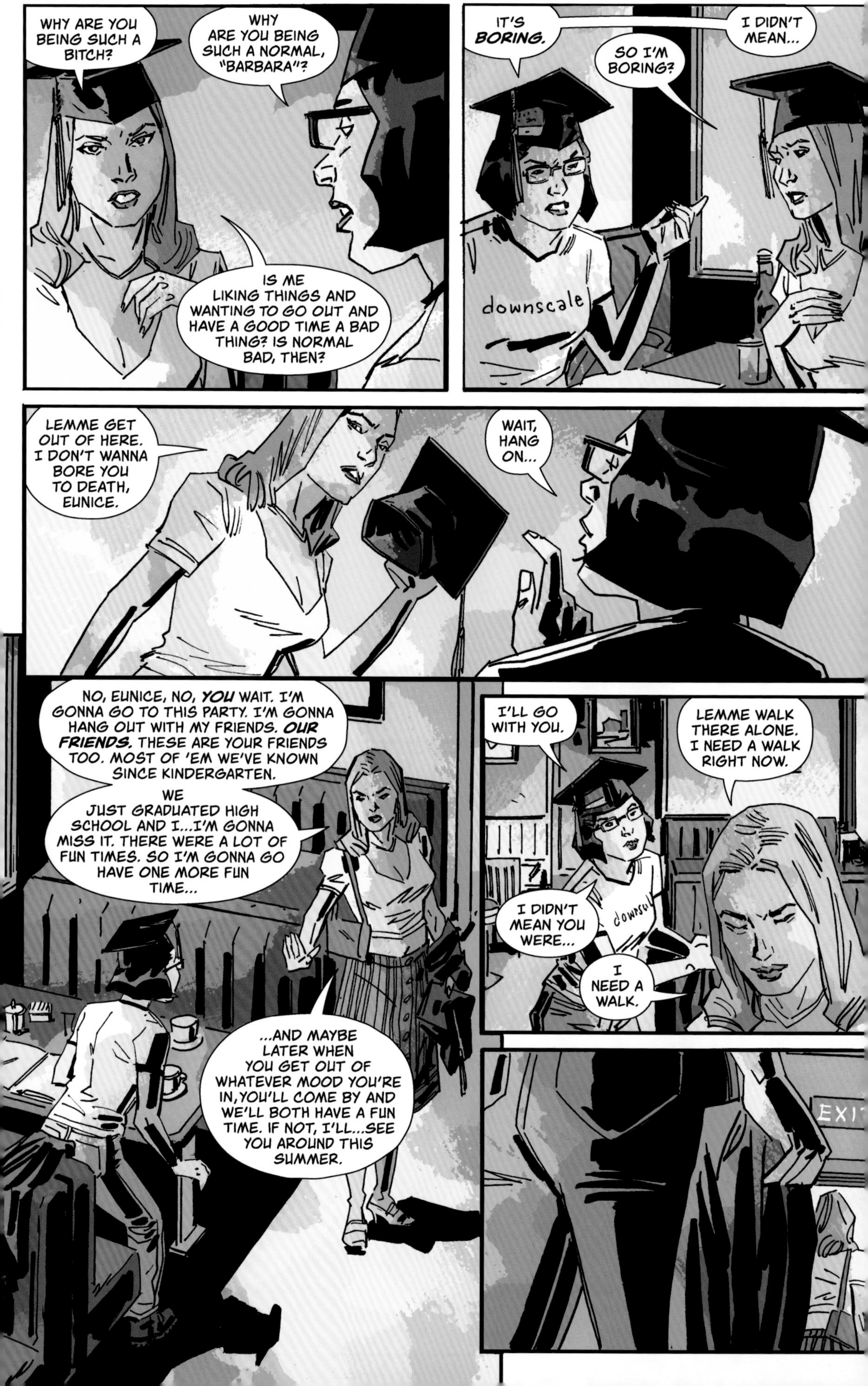
WHY ARE YOU BEING SUCH A BITCH?
WHY ARE YOU BEING SUCH A NORMAL, "BARBARA"?
IS ME LIKING THINGS AND WANTING TO GO OUT AND HAVE A GOOD TIME A BAD THING? IS NORMAL BAD, THEN?
IT'S *BORING.*
I DIDN'T MEAN...
SO I'M BORING?
downscale
LEMME GET OUT OF HERE. I DON'T WANNA BORE YOU TO DEATH, EUNICE.
WAIT, HANG ON...
NO, EUNICE, NO, *YOU* WAIT. I'M GONNA GO TO THIS PARTY. I'M GONNA HANG OUT WITH MY FRIENDS. *OUR FRIENDS.* THESE ARE YOUR FRIENDS TOO. MOST OF 'EM WE'VE KNOWN SINCE KINDERGARTEN.
WE JUST GRADUATED HIGH SCHOOL AND I...I'M GONNA MISS IT. THERE WERE A LOT OF FUN TIMES. SO I'M GONNA GO HAVE ONE MORE FUN TIME...
...AND MAYBE LATER WHEN YOU GET OUT OF WHATEVER MOOD YOU'RE IN, YOU'LL COME BY AND WE'LL BOTH HAVE A FUN TIME. IF NOT, I'LL...SEE YOU AROUND THIS SUMMER.
I'LL GO WITH YOU.
LEMME WALK THERE ALONE. I NEED A WALK RIGHT NOW.
I DIDN'T MEAN YOU WERE...
I NEED A WALK.
EXIT

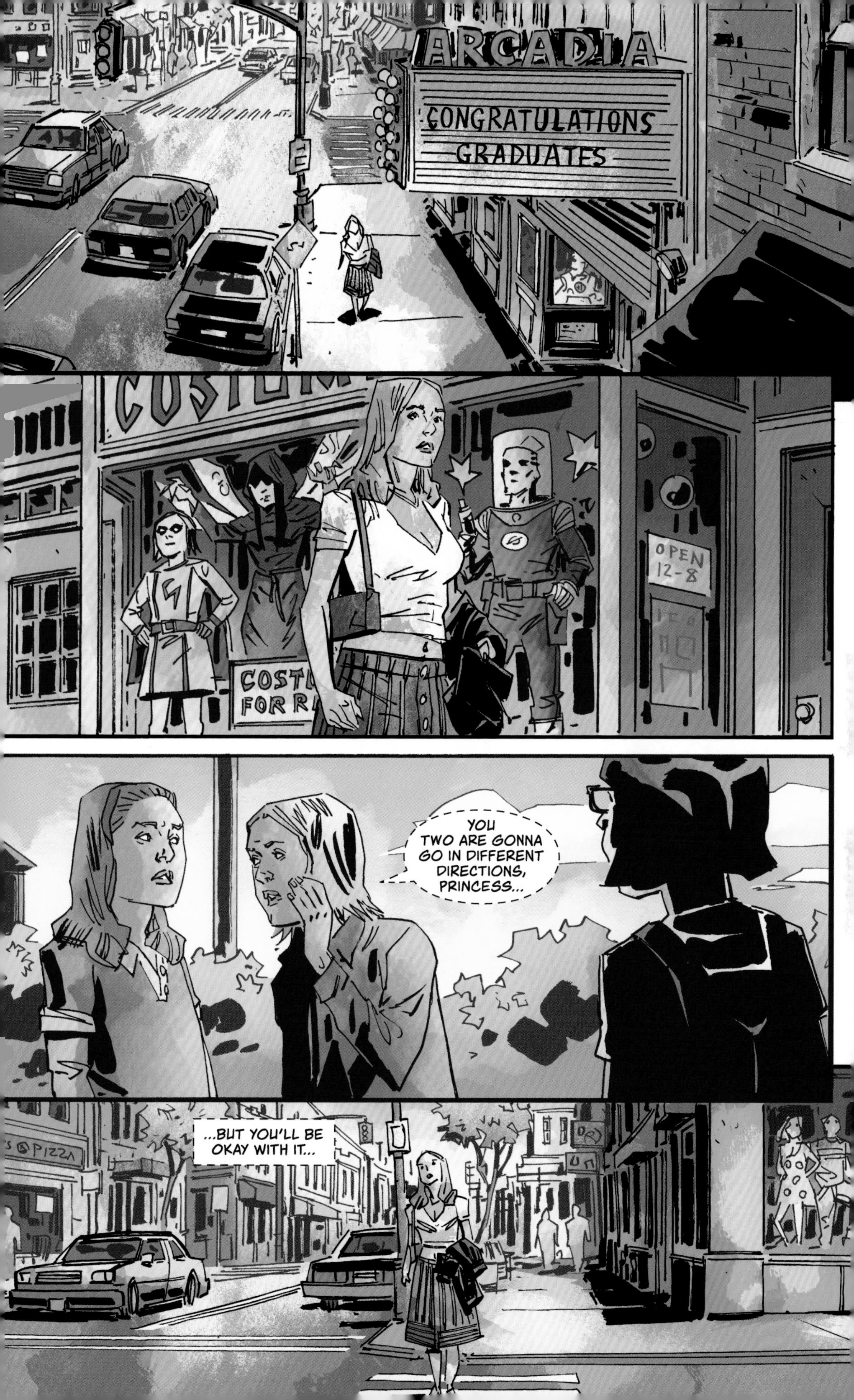
ARCADIA
CONGRATULATIONS GRADUATES
OPEN 12-8
YOU TWO ARE GONNA GO IN DIFFERENT DIRECTIONS, PRINCESS...
...BUT YOU'LL BE OKAY WITH IT...

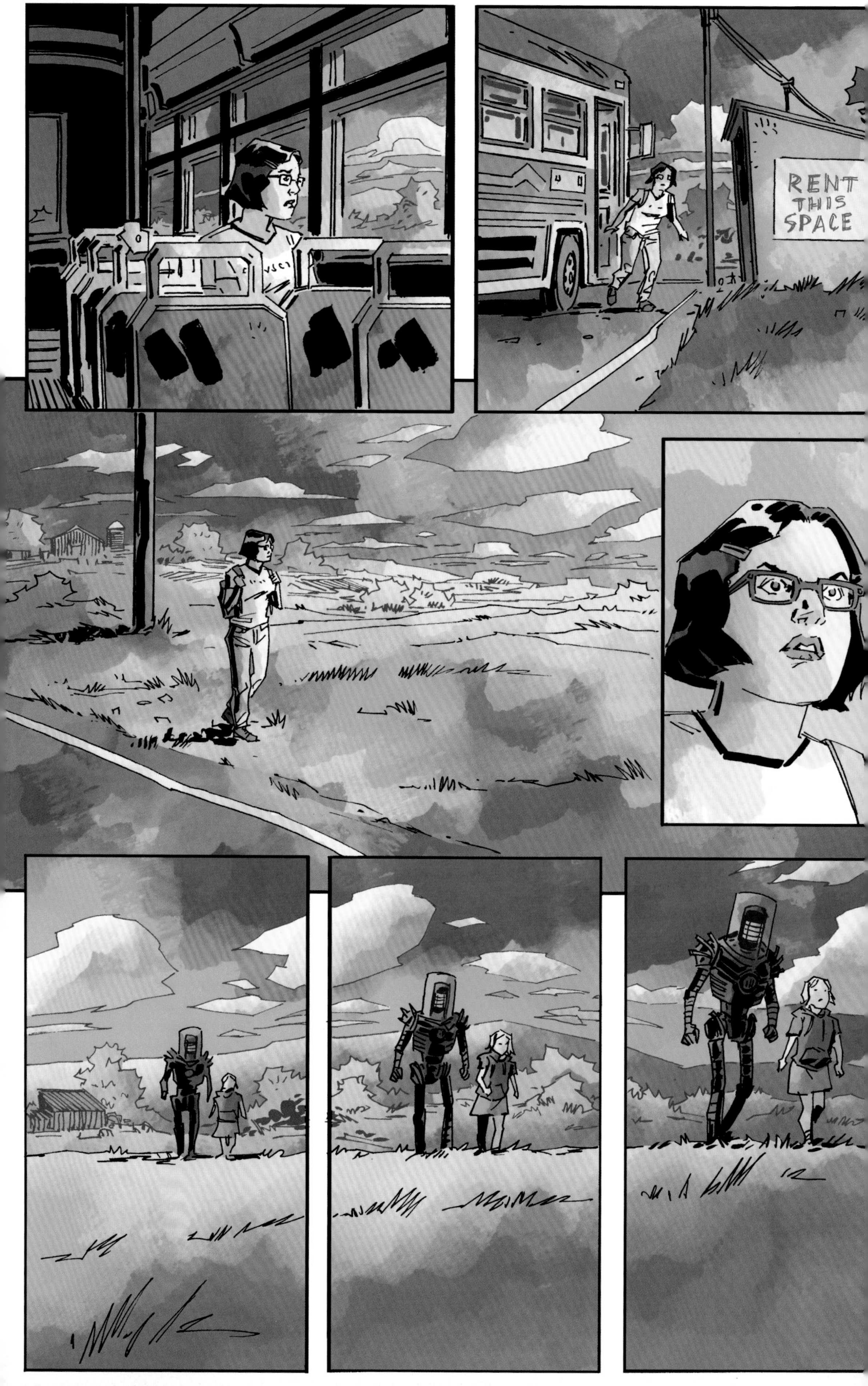
RENT THIS SPACE

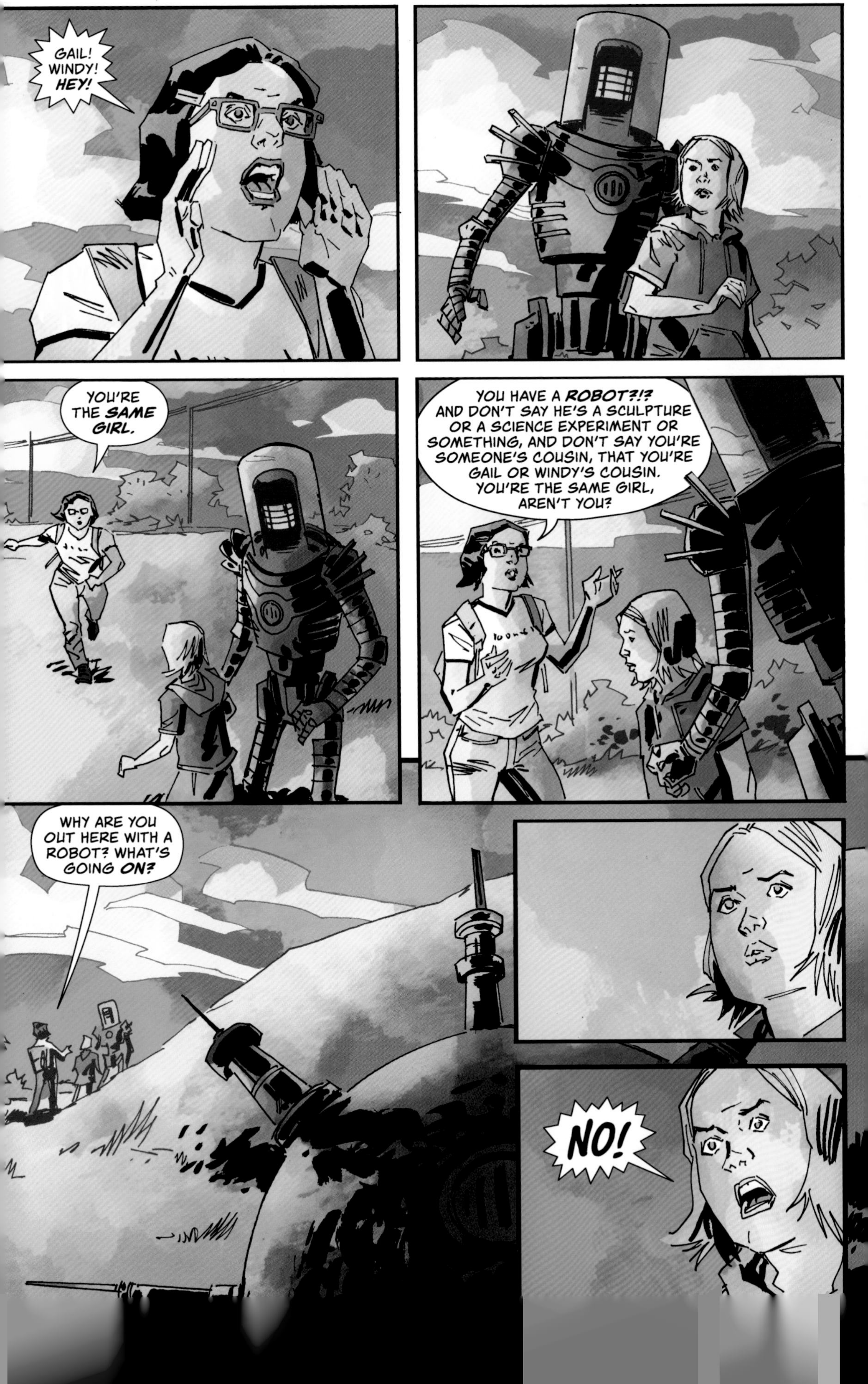
GAIL! WINDY! HEY!
YOU'RE THE SAME GIRL.
YOU HAVE A ROBOT?!? AND DON'T SAY HE'S A SCULPTURE OR A SCIENCE EXPERIMENT OR SOMETHING, AND DON'T SAY YOU'RE SOMEONE'S COUSIN, THAT YOU'RE GAIL OR WINDY'S COUSIN. YOU'RE THE SAME GIRL, AREN'T YOU?
WHY ARE YOU OUT HERE WITH A ROBOT? WHAT'S GOING ON?
NO!

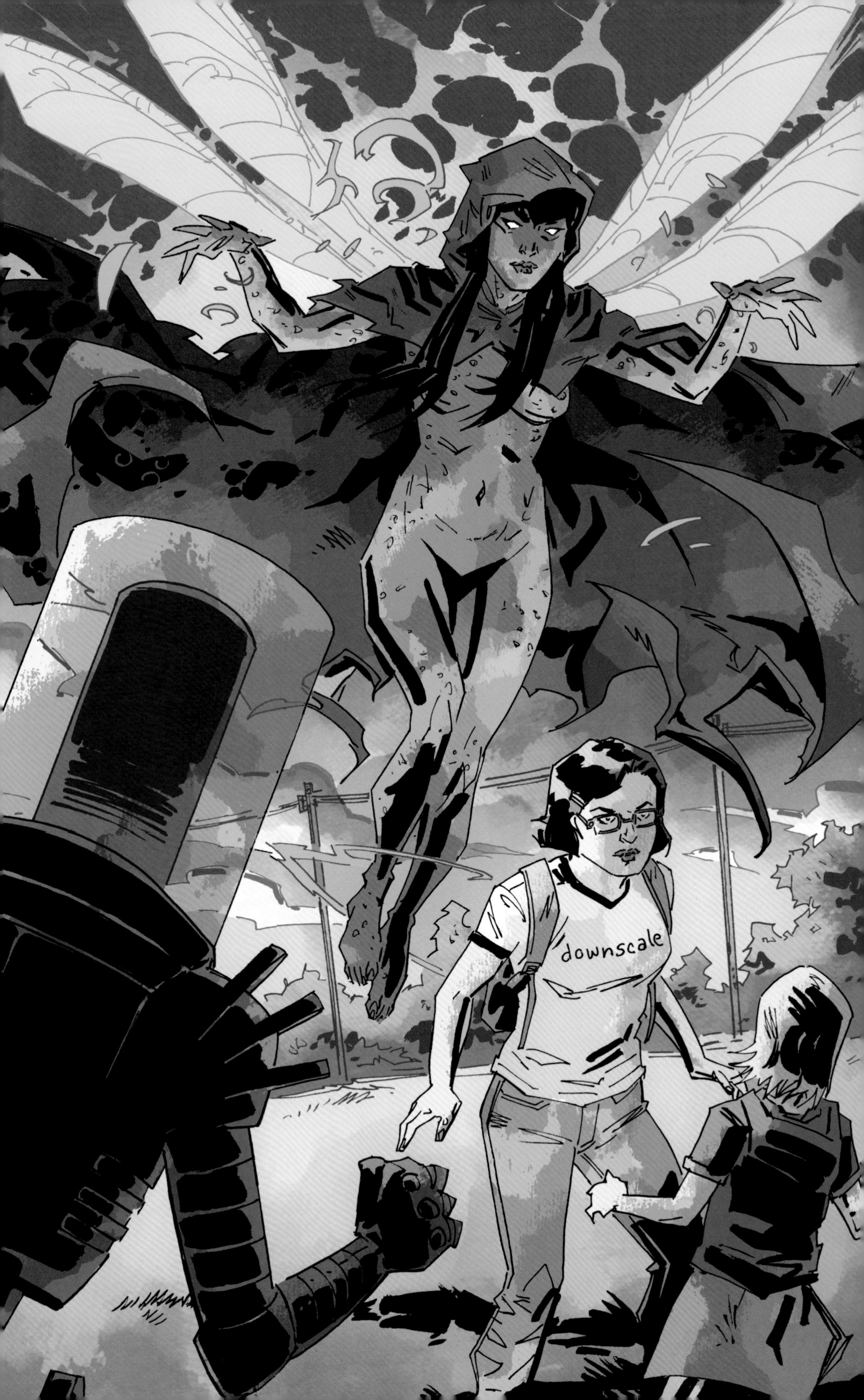
downscale

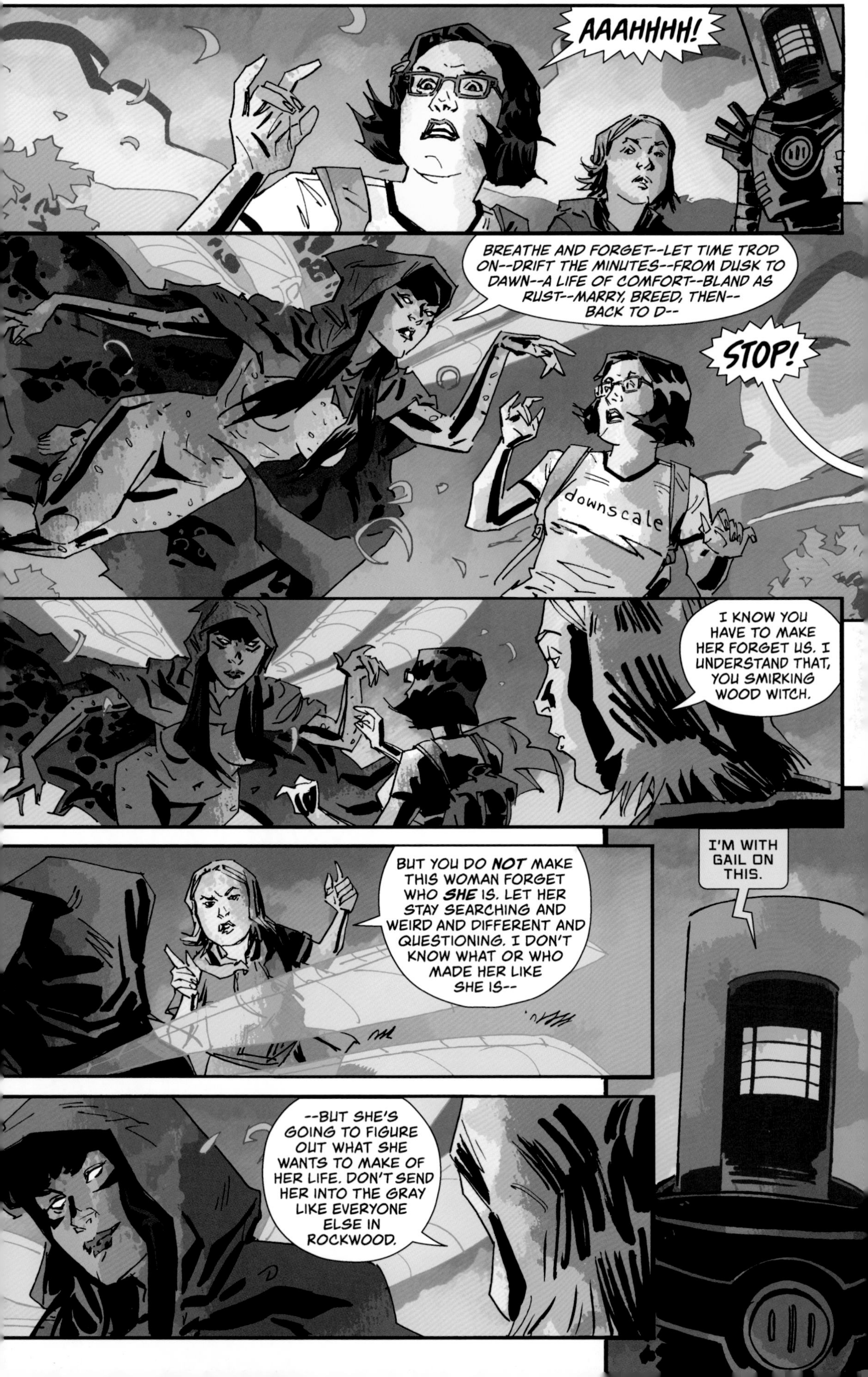
AAAHHHH!
BREATHE AND FORGET--LET TIME TROD ON--DRIFT THE MINUTES--FROM DUSK TO DAWN--A LIFE OF COMFORT--BLAND AS RUST--MARRY, BREED, THEN-- BACK TO D--
STOP!
downscale
I KNOW YOU HAVE TO MAKE HER FORGET US. I UNDERSTAND THAT, YOU SMIRKING WOOD WITCH.
BUT YOU DO NOT MAKE THIS WOMAN FORGET WHO SHE IS. LET HER STAY SEARCHING AND WEIRD AND DIFFERENT AND QUESTIONING. I DON'T KNOW WHAT OR WHO MADE HER LIKE SHE IS--
I'M WITH GAIL ON THIS.
--BUT SHE'S GOING TO FIGURE OUT WHAT SHE WANTS TO MAKE OF HER LIFE. DON'T SEND HER INTO THE GRAY LIKE EVERYONE ELSE IN ROCKWOOD.

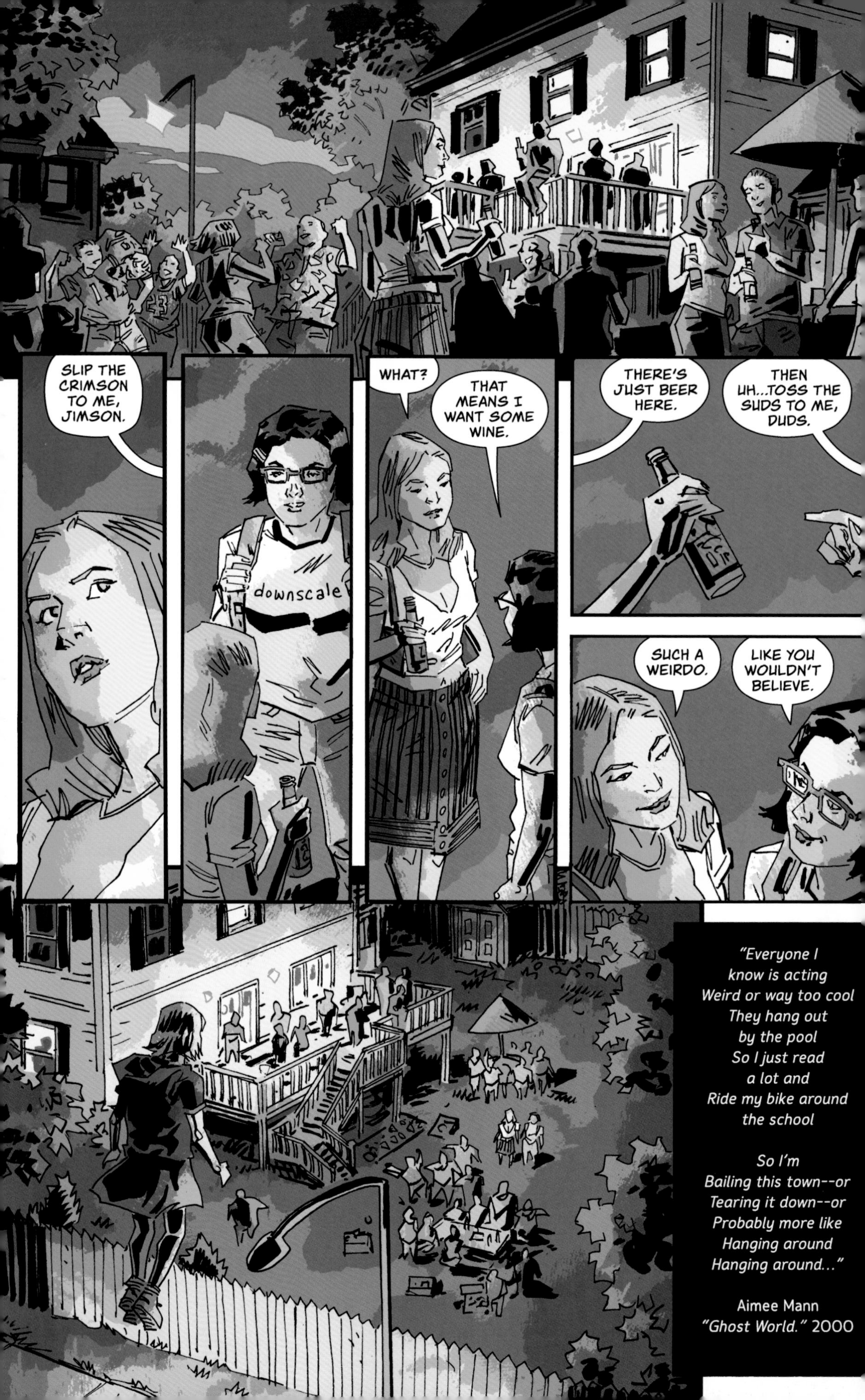
SLIP THE CRIMSON TO ME, JIMSON.
downscale
WHAT?
THAT MEANS I WANT SOME WINE.
THERE'S JUST BEER HERE.
THEN UH...TOSS THE SUDS TO ME, DUDS.
SUCH A WEIRDO.
LIKE YOU WOULDN'T BELIEVE.
"Everyone I
know is acting
Weird or way too cool
They hang out
by the pool
So I just read
a lot and
Ride my bike around
the school

So I'm
Bailing this town--or
Tearing it down--or
Probably more like
Hanging around
Hanging around..."

Aimee Mann
"Ghost World." 2000

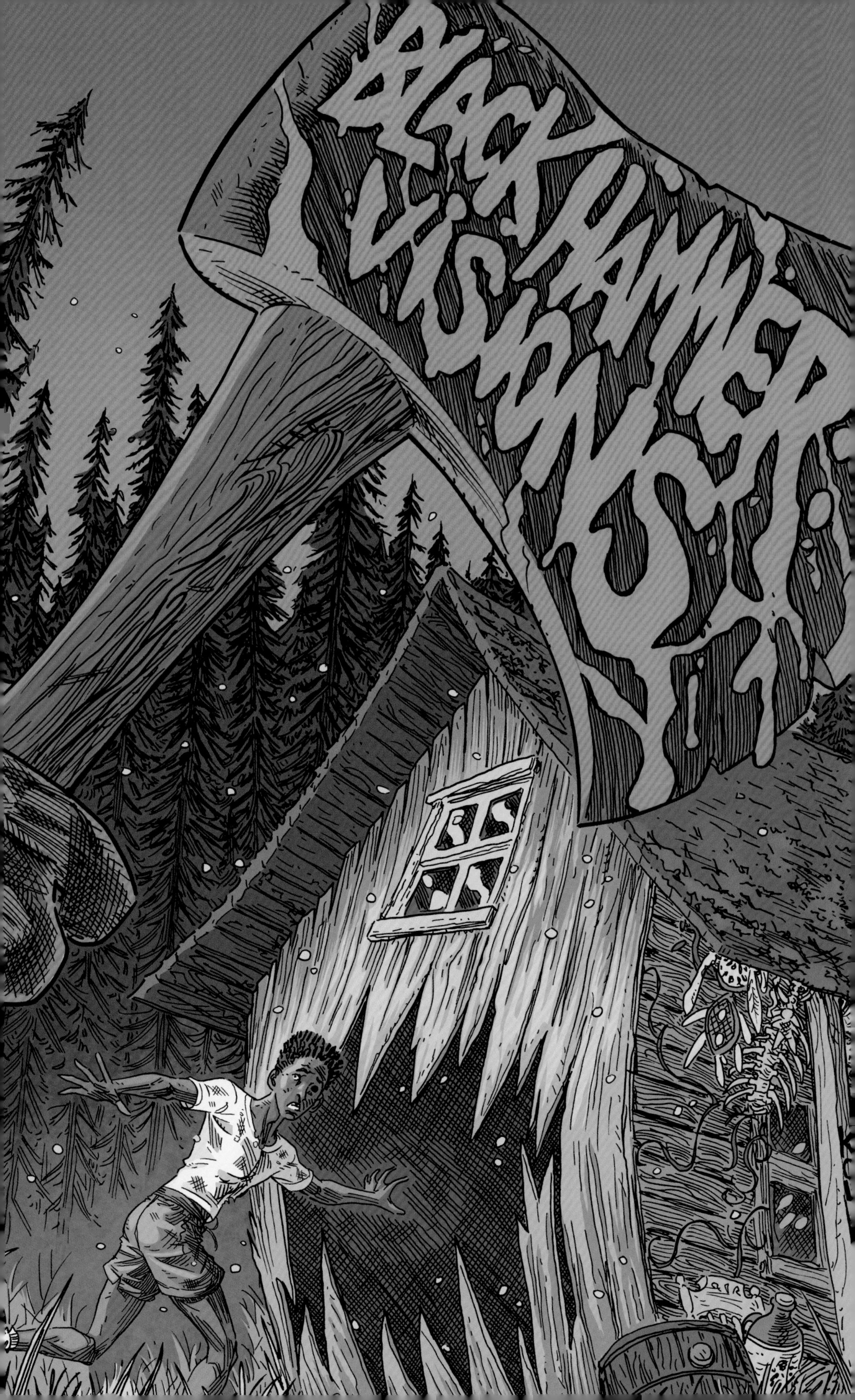

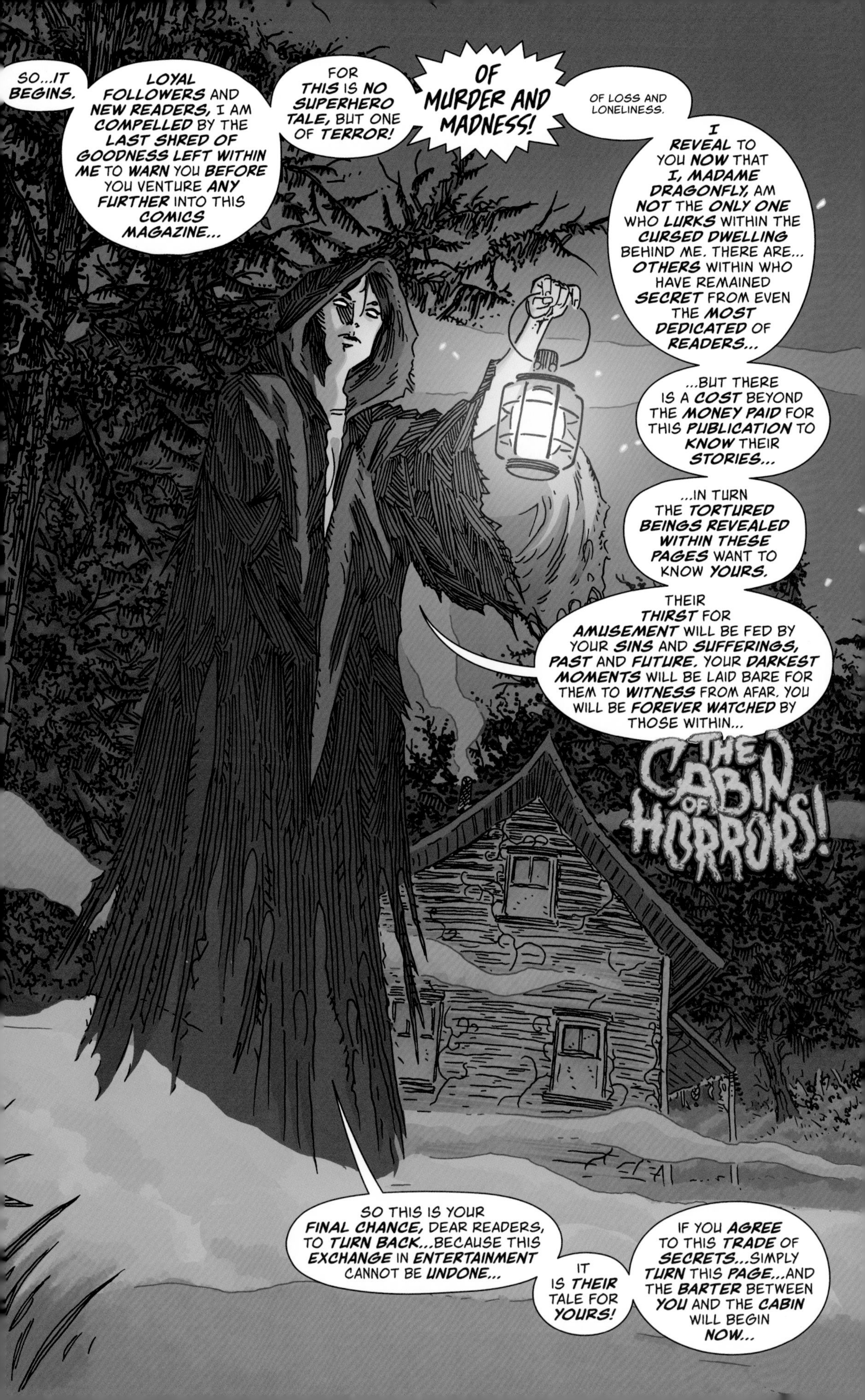
SO...IT BEGINS.
LOYAL FOLLOWERS AND NEW READERS, I AM COMPELLED BY THE LAST SHRED OF GOODNESS LEFT WITHIN ME TO WARN YOU BEFORE YOU VENTURE ANY FURTHER INTO THIS COMICS MAGAZINE...
FOR THIS IS NO SUPERHERO TALE, BUT ONE OF TERROR!
OF MURDER AND MADNESS!
OF LOSS AND LONELINESS.
I REVEAL TO YOU NOW THAT I, MADAME DRAGONFLY, AM NOT THE ONLY ONE WHO LURKS WITHIN THE CURSED DWELLING BEHIND ME. THERE ARE... OTHERS WITHIN WHO HAVE REMAINED SECRET FROM EVEN THE MOST DEDICATED OF READERS...
...BUT THERE IS A COST BEYOND THE MONEY PAID FOR THIS PUBLICATION TO KNOW THEIR STORIES...
...IN TURN THE TORTURED BEINGS REVEALED WITHIN THESE PAGES WANT TO KNOW YOURS.
THEIR THIRST FOR AMUSEMENT WILL BE FED BY YOUR SINS AND SUFFERINGS, PAST AND FUTURE. YOUR DARKEST MOMENTS WILL BE LAID BARE FOR THEM TO WITNESS FROM AFAR. YOU WILL BE FOREVER WATCHED BY THOSE WITHIN...
THE CABIN OF HORRORS!
SO THIS IS YOUR FINAL CHANCE, DEAR READERS, TO TURN BACK...BECAUSE THIS EXCHANGE IN ENTERTAINMENT CANNOT BE UNDONE...
IT IS THEIR TALE FOR YOURS!
IF YOU AGREE TO THIS TRADE OF SECRETS...SIMPLY TURN THIS PAGE...AND THE BARTER BETWEEN YOU AND THE CABIN WILL BEGIN NOW...

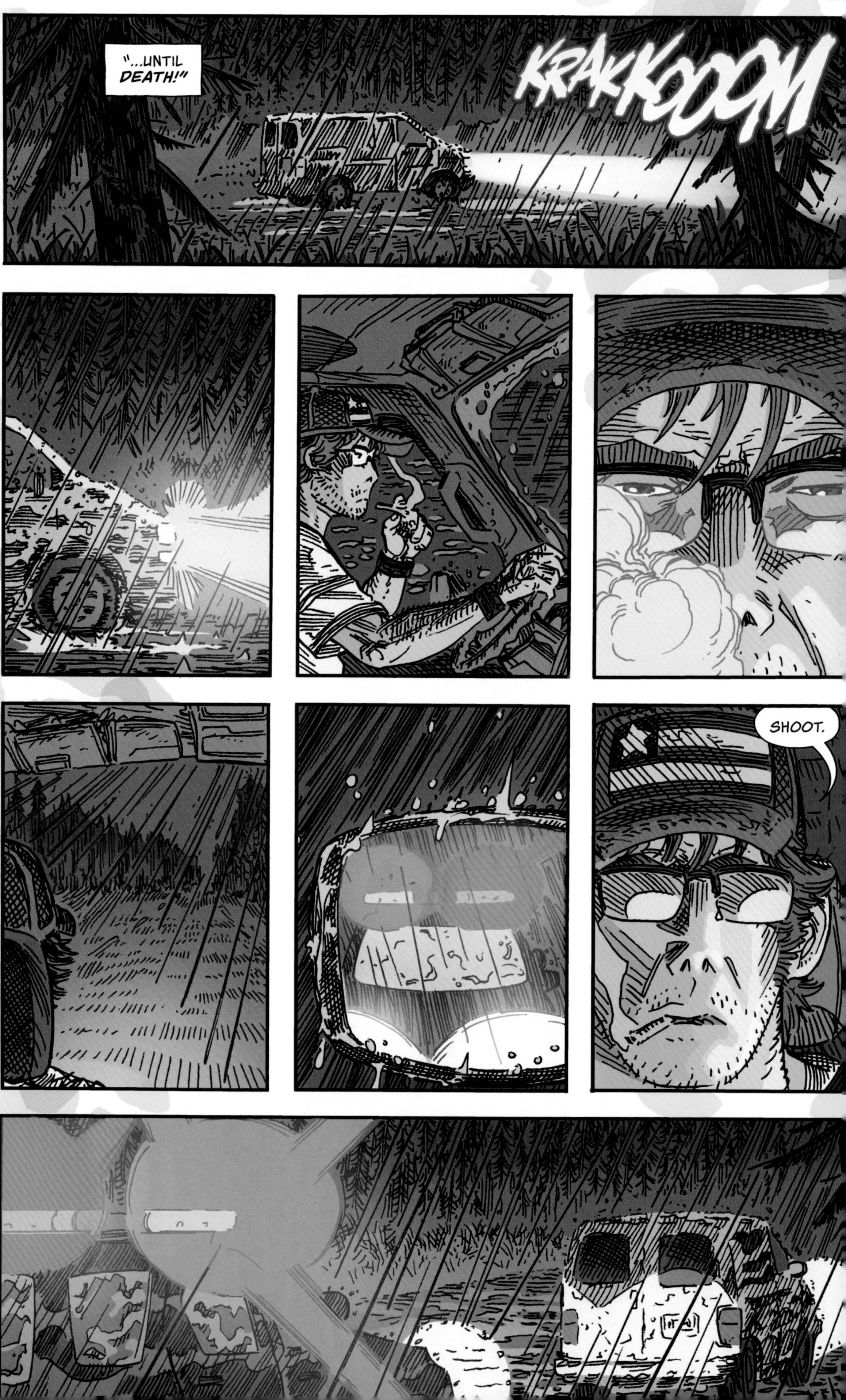
"...UNTIL DEATH!"
KRAKKOOOM
SHOOT.

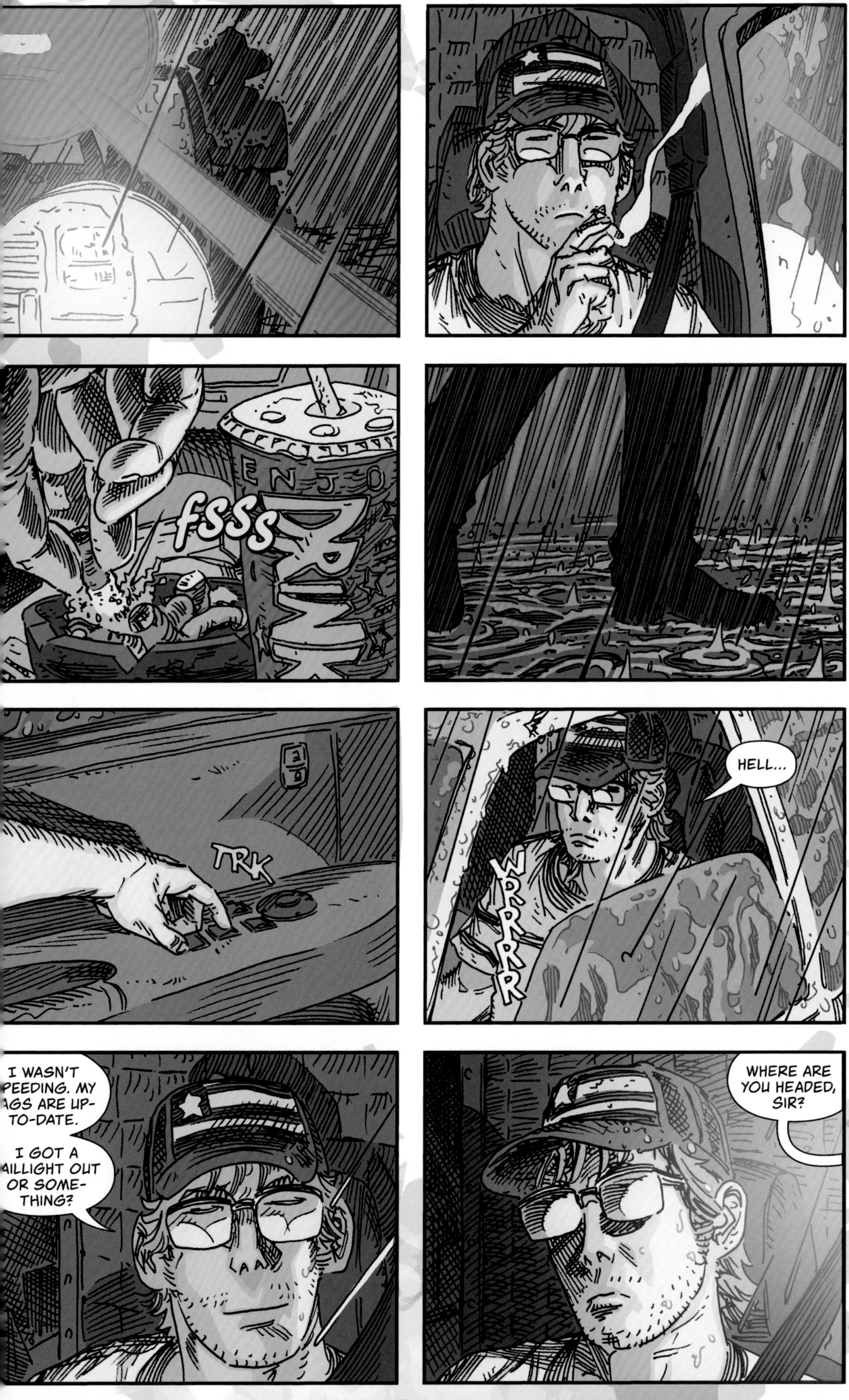
fSSS
TRK
WRRRR
HELL...
I WASN'T PEEDING. MY AGS ARE UP-TO-DATE.
I GOT A AILLIGHT OUT OR SOME-THING?
WHERE ARE YOU HEADED, SIR?

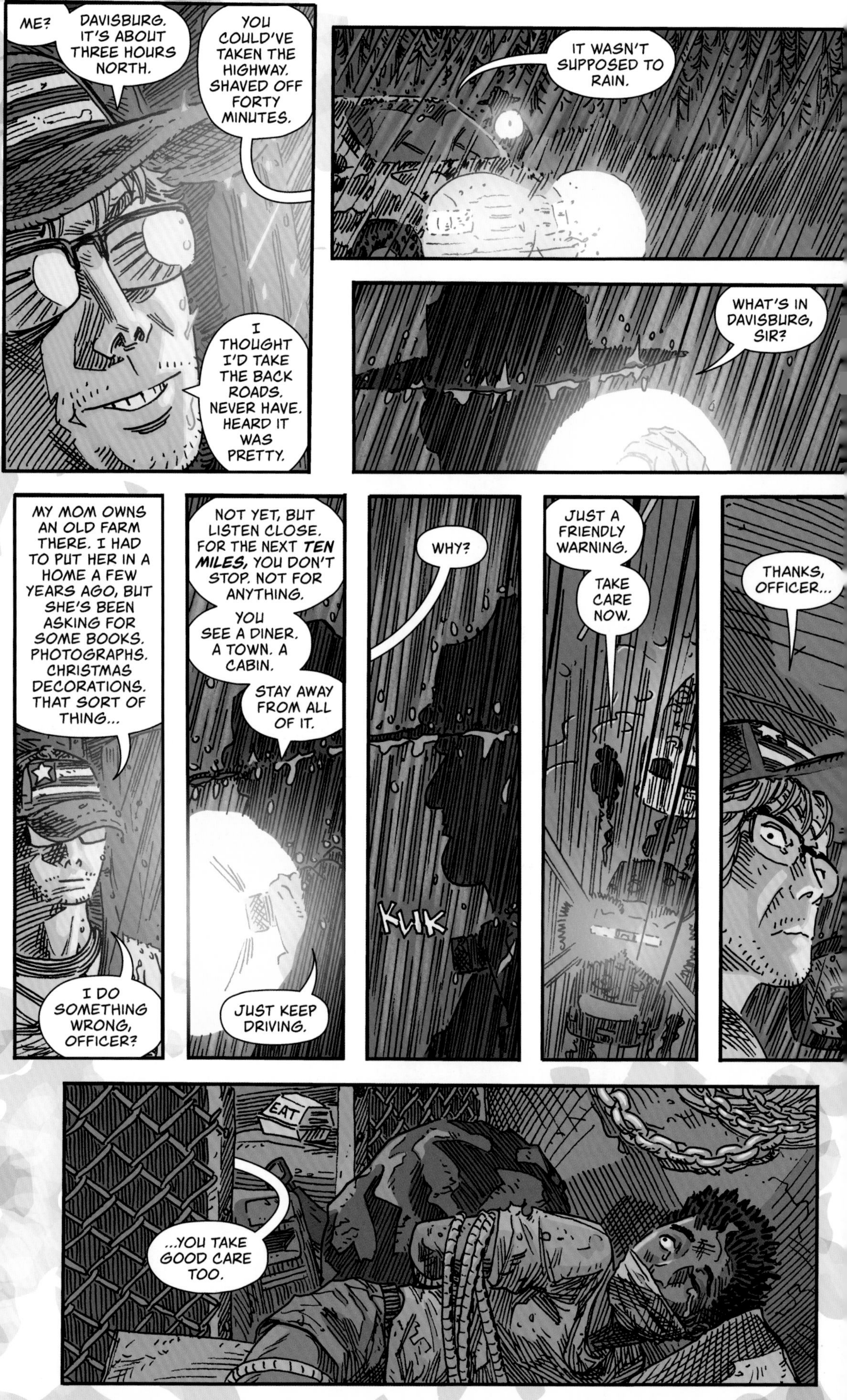
ME?
DAVISBURG. IT'S ABOUT THREE HOURS NORTH.
YOU COULD'VE TAKEN THE HIGHWAY. SHAVED OFF FORTY MINUTES.
I THOUGHT I'D TAKE THE BACK ROADS. NEVER HAVE. HEARD IT WAS PRETTY.
IT WASN'T SUPPOSED TO RAIN.
WHAT'S IN DAVISBURG, SIR?
MY MOM OWNS AN OLD FARM THERE. I HAD TO PUT HER IN A HOME A FEW YEARS AGO, BUT SHE'S BEEN ASKING FOR SOME BOOKS. PHOTOGRAPHS. CHRISTMAS DECORATIONS. THAT SORT OF THING...
I DO SOMETHING WRONG, OFFICER?
NOT YET, BUT LISTEN CLOSE. FOR THE NEXT TEN MILES, YOU DON'T STOP. NOT FOR ANYTHING.
YOU SEE A DINER. A TOWN. A CABIN.
STAY AWAY FROM ALL OF IT.
JUST KEEP DRIVING.
WHY?
KLIK
JUST A FRIENDLY WARNING.
TAKE CARE NOW.
THANKS, OFFICER...
EAT
...YOU TAKE GOOD CARE TOO.

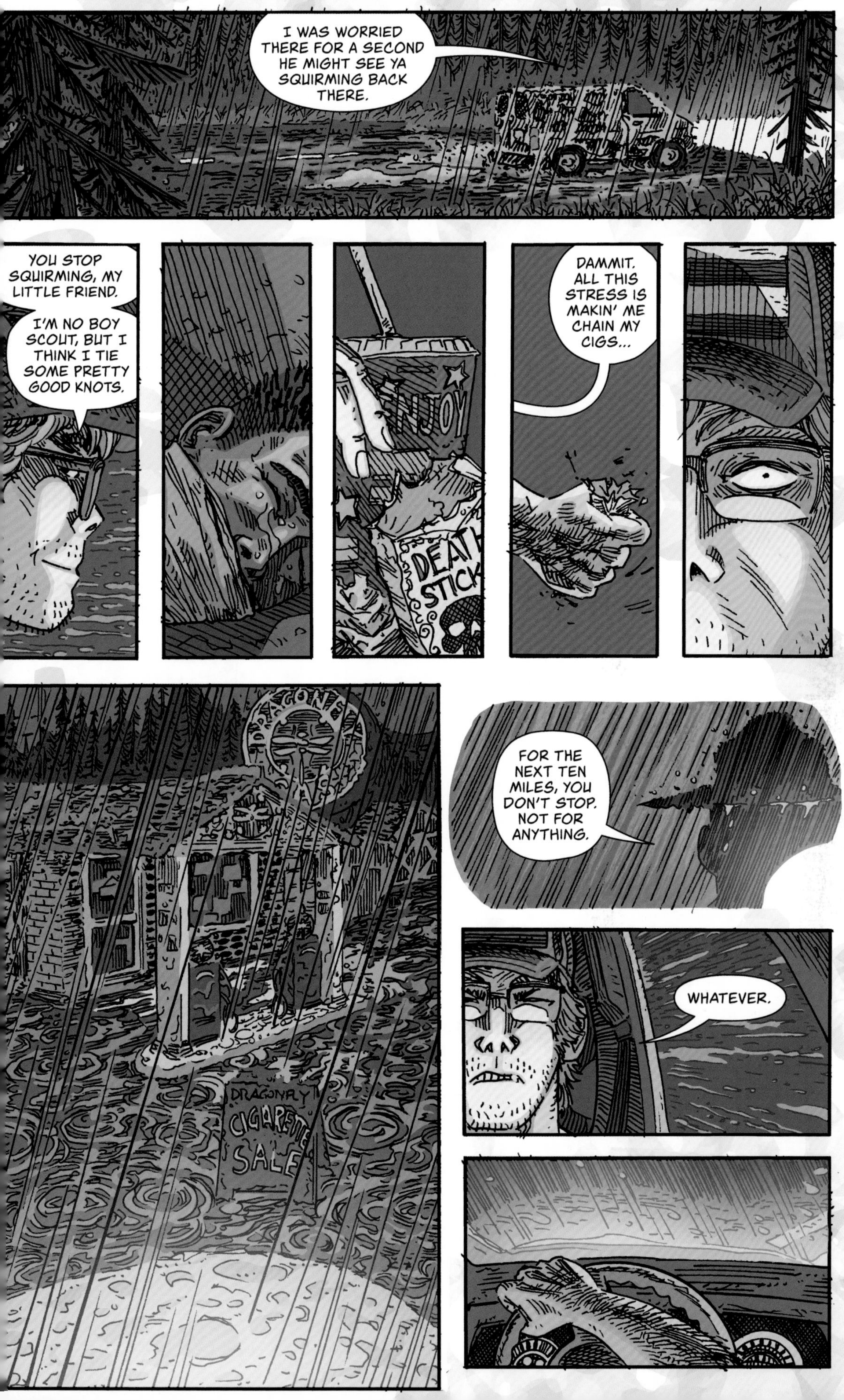

I WAS WORRIED THERE FOR A SECOND HE MIGHT SEE YA SQUIRMING BACK THERE.
YOU STOP SQUIRMING, MY LITTLE FRIEND.
I'M NO BOY SCOUT, BUT I THINK I TIE SOME PRETTY GOOD KNOTS.
ENJOY
DEATH STICK
DAMMIT. ALL THIS STRESS IS MAKIN' ME CHAIN MY CIGS...
DRAGONFLY
CIGARETTE SALE
FOR THE NEXT TEN MILES, YOU DON'T STOP. NOT FOR ANYTHING.
WHATEVER.

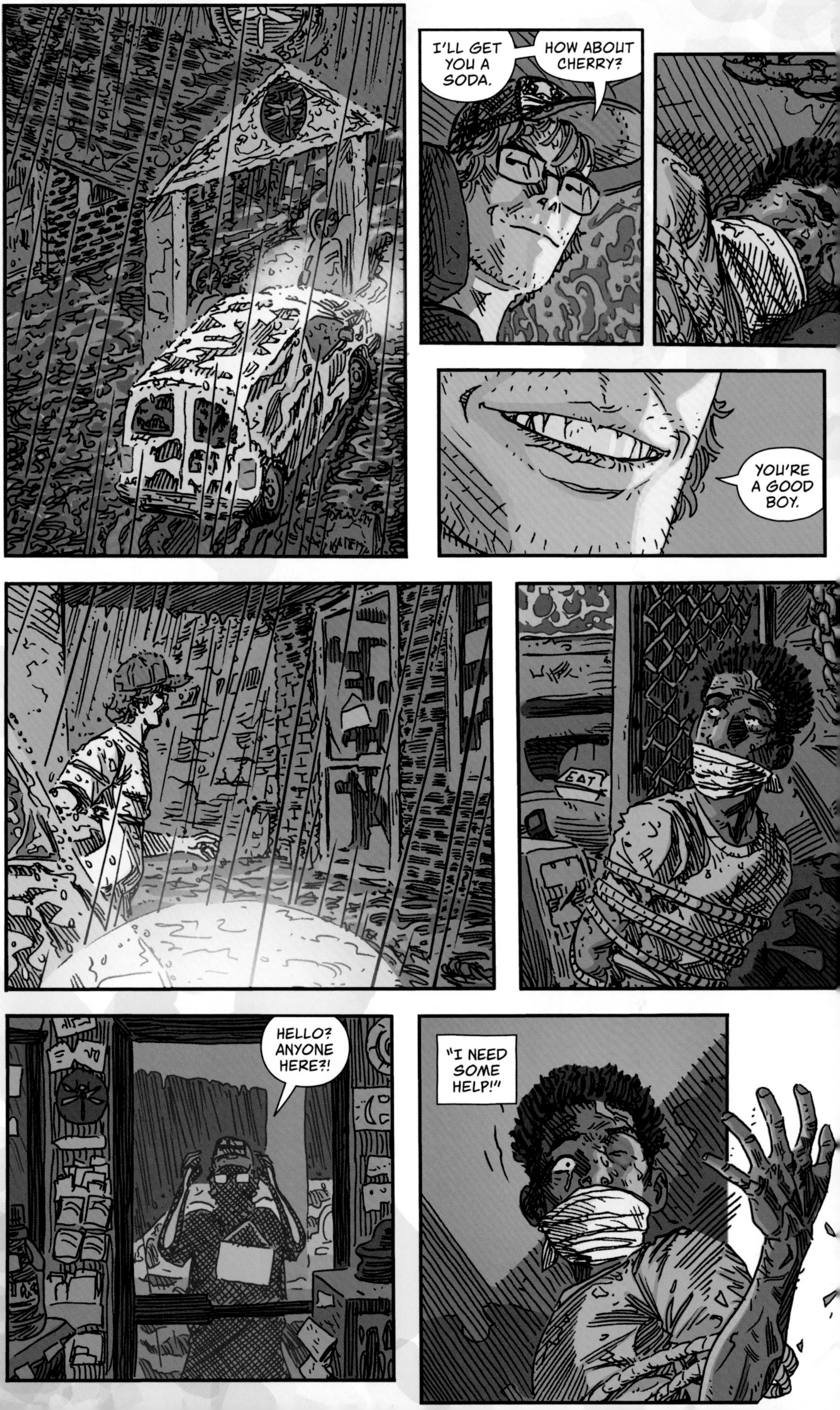
I'LL GET YOU A SODA.
HOW ABOUT CHERRY?
YOU'RE A GOOD BOY.
EAT
HELLO? ANYONE HERE?!
"I NEED SOME HELP!"

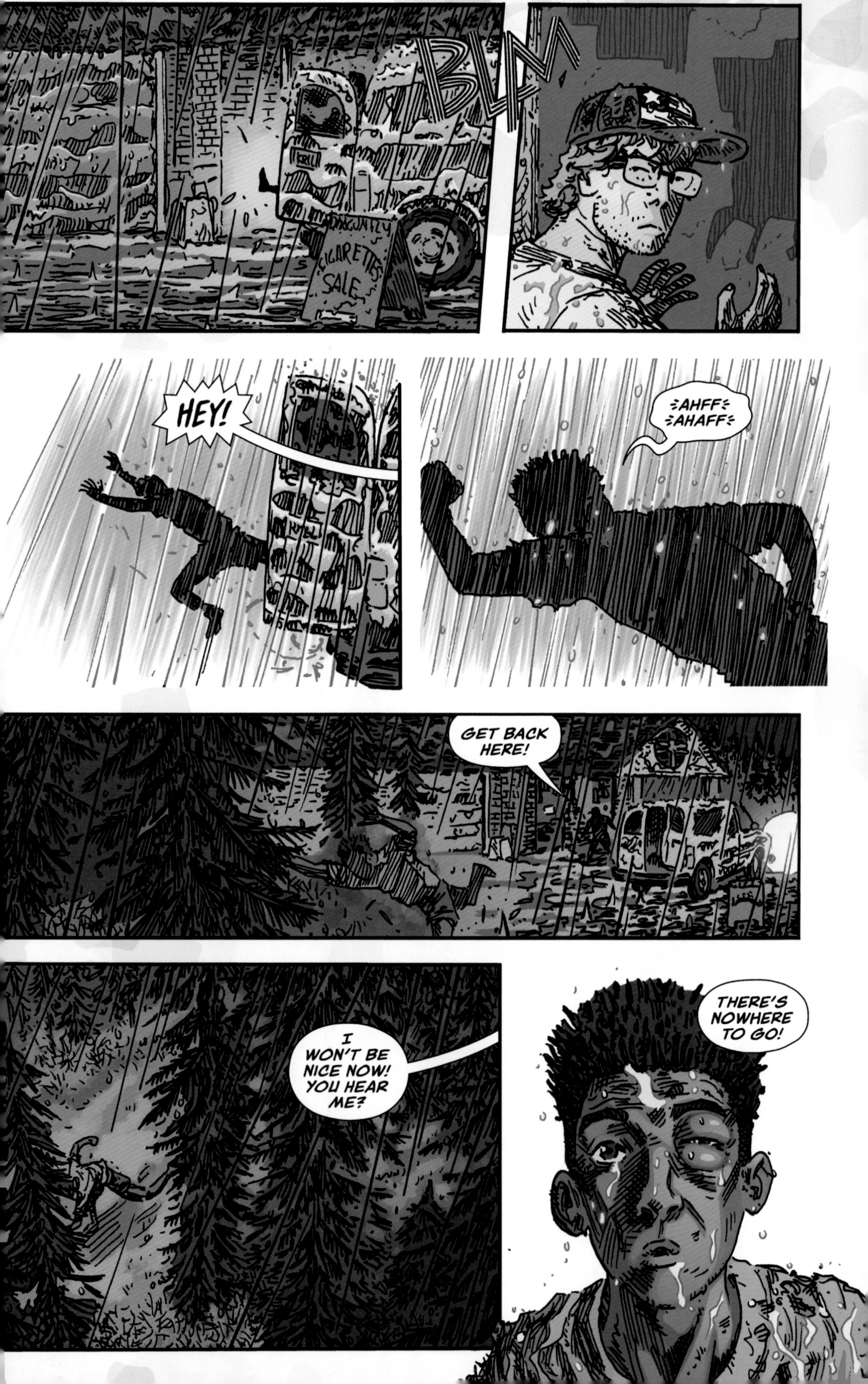
BLAM
CIGARETTES SALE
HEY!
AHFF AHAFF
GET BACK HERE!
I WON'T BE NICE NOW! YOU HEAR ME?
THERE'S NOWHERE TO GO!

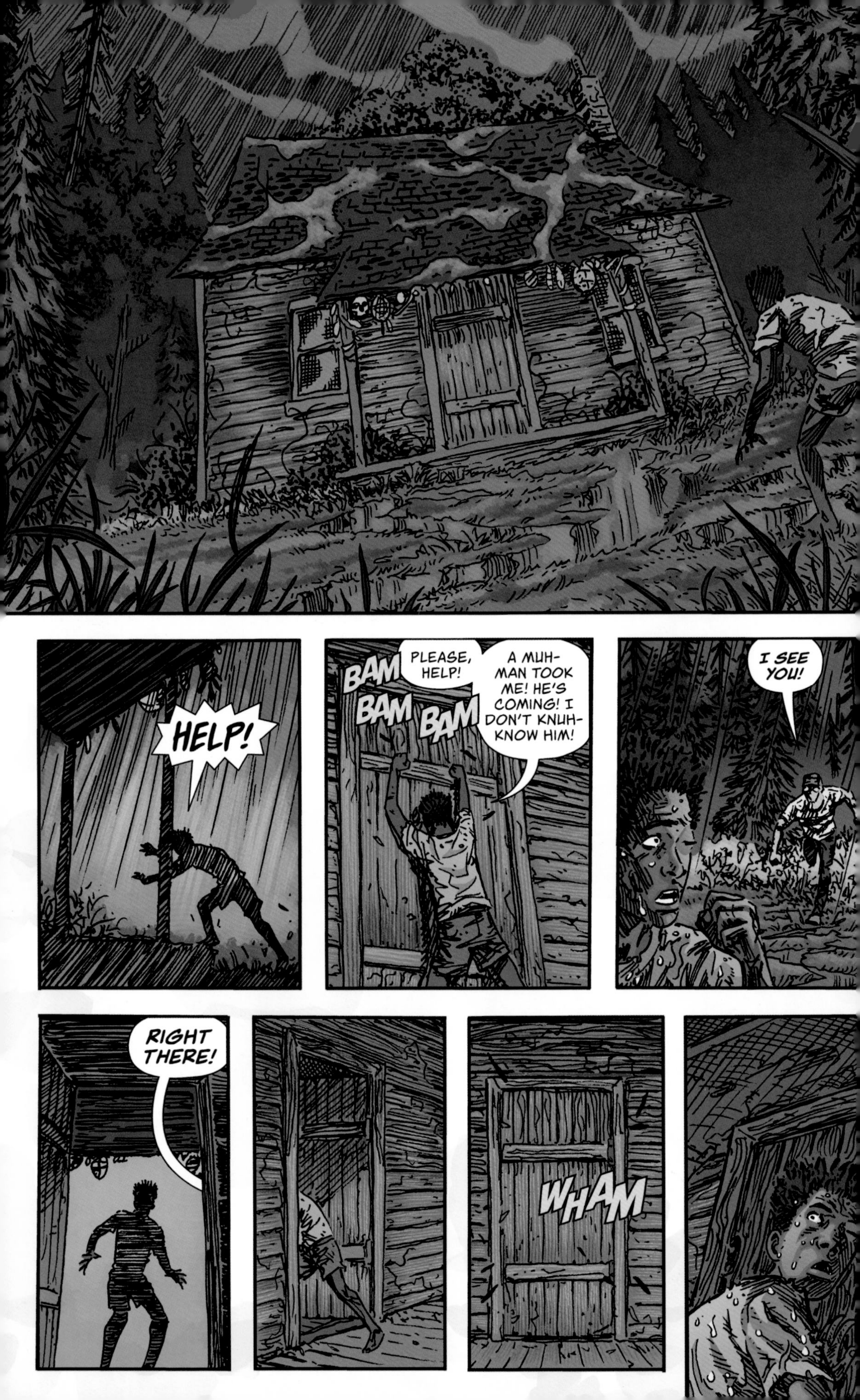
HELP!
BAM
BAM
BAM
PLEASE, HELP!
A MUH-MAN TOOK ME! HE'S COMING! I DON'T KNUH-KNOW HIM!
I SEE YOU!
RIGHT THERE!
WHAM

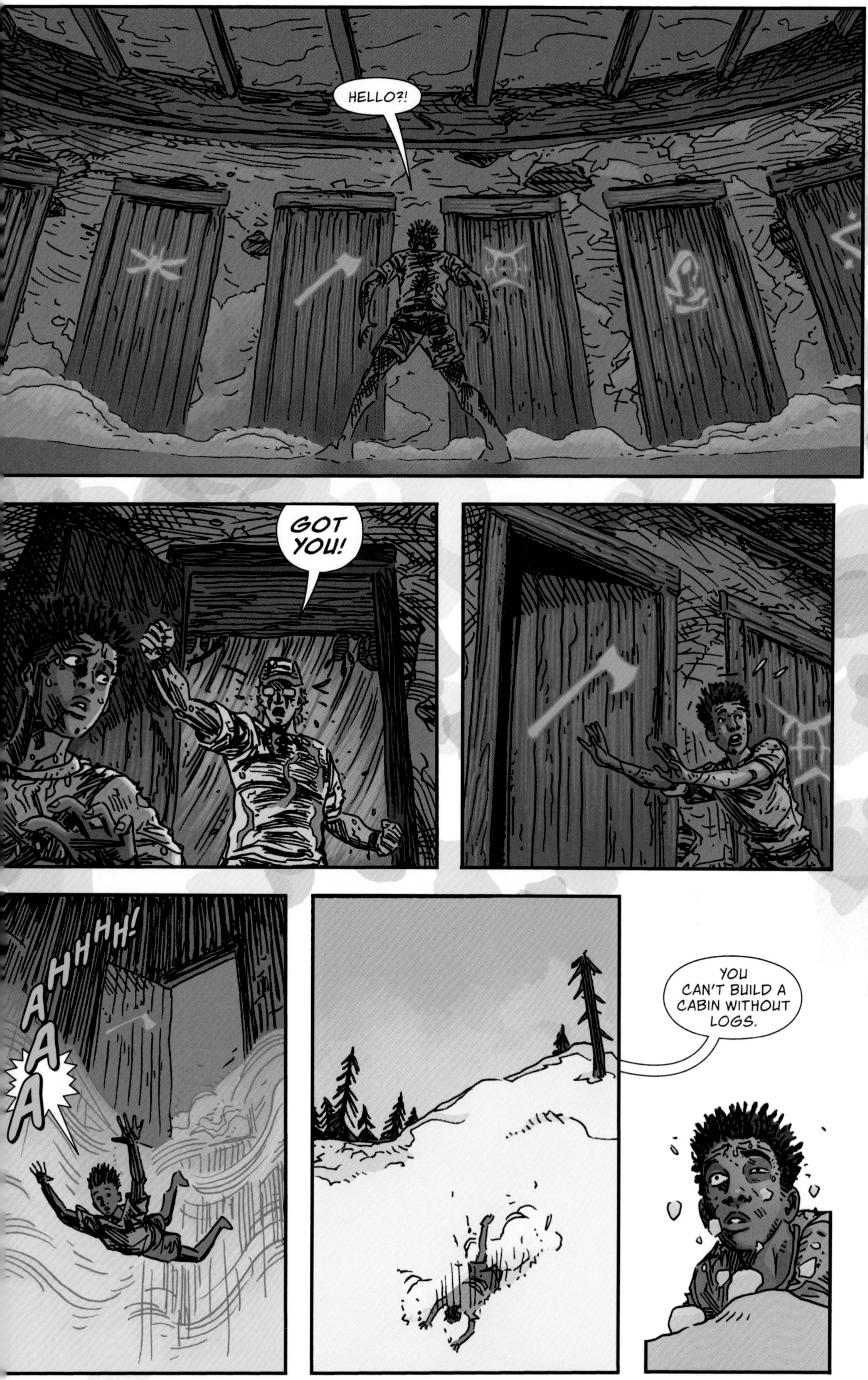
HELLO?!
GOT YOU!
AAAAHHHHH!
YOU CAN'T BUILD A CABIN WITHOUT LOGS.

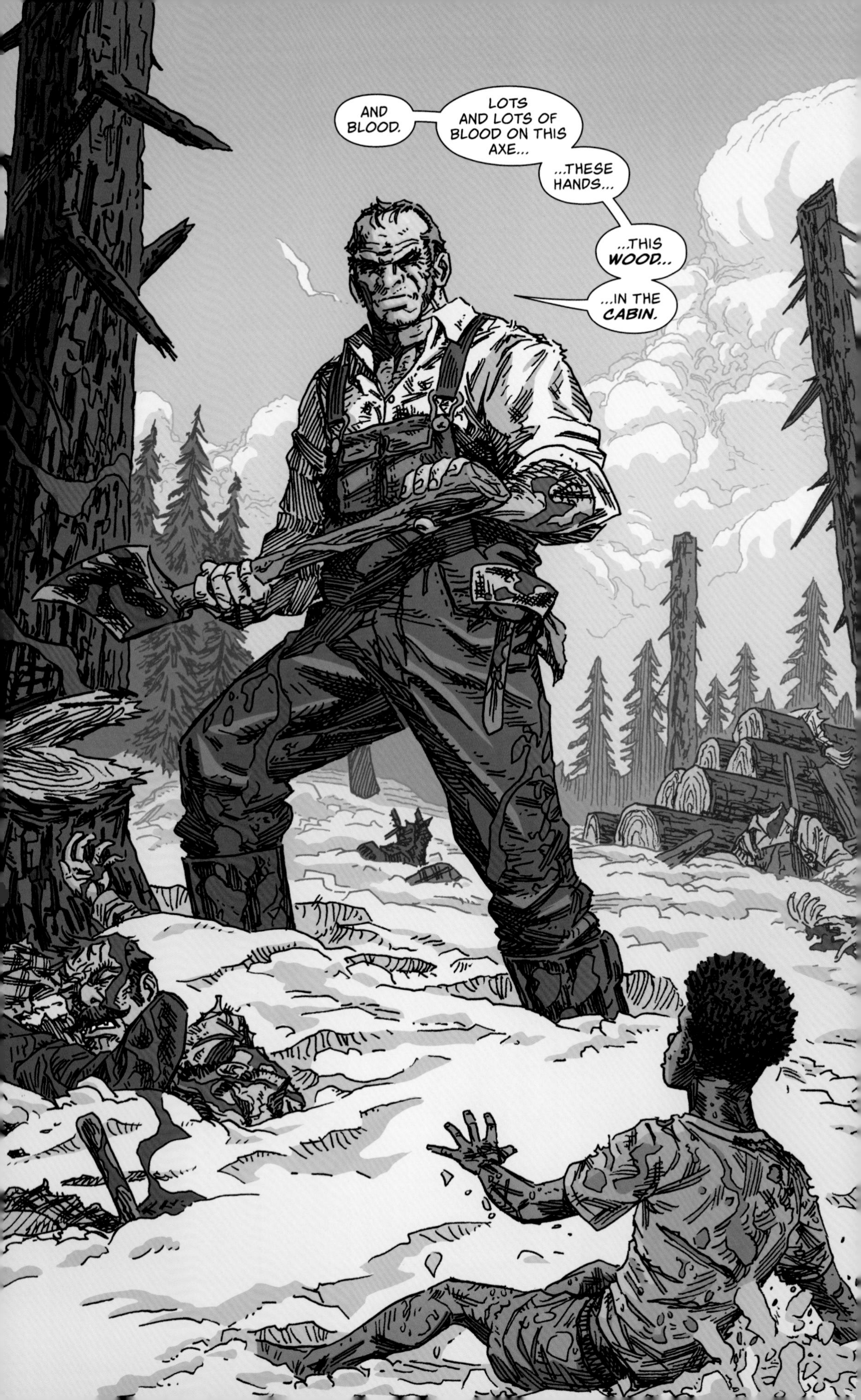

AND BLOOD.
LOTS AND LOTS OF BLOOD ON THIS AXE...
...THESE HANDS...
...THIS WOOD...
...IN THE CABIN.

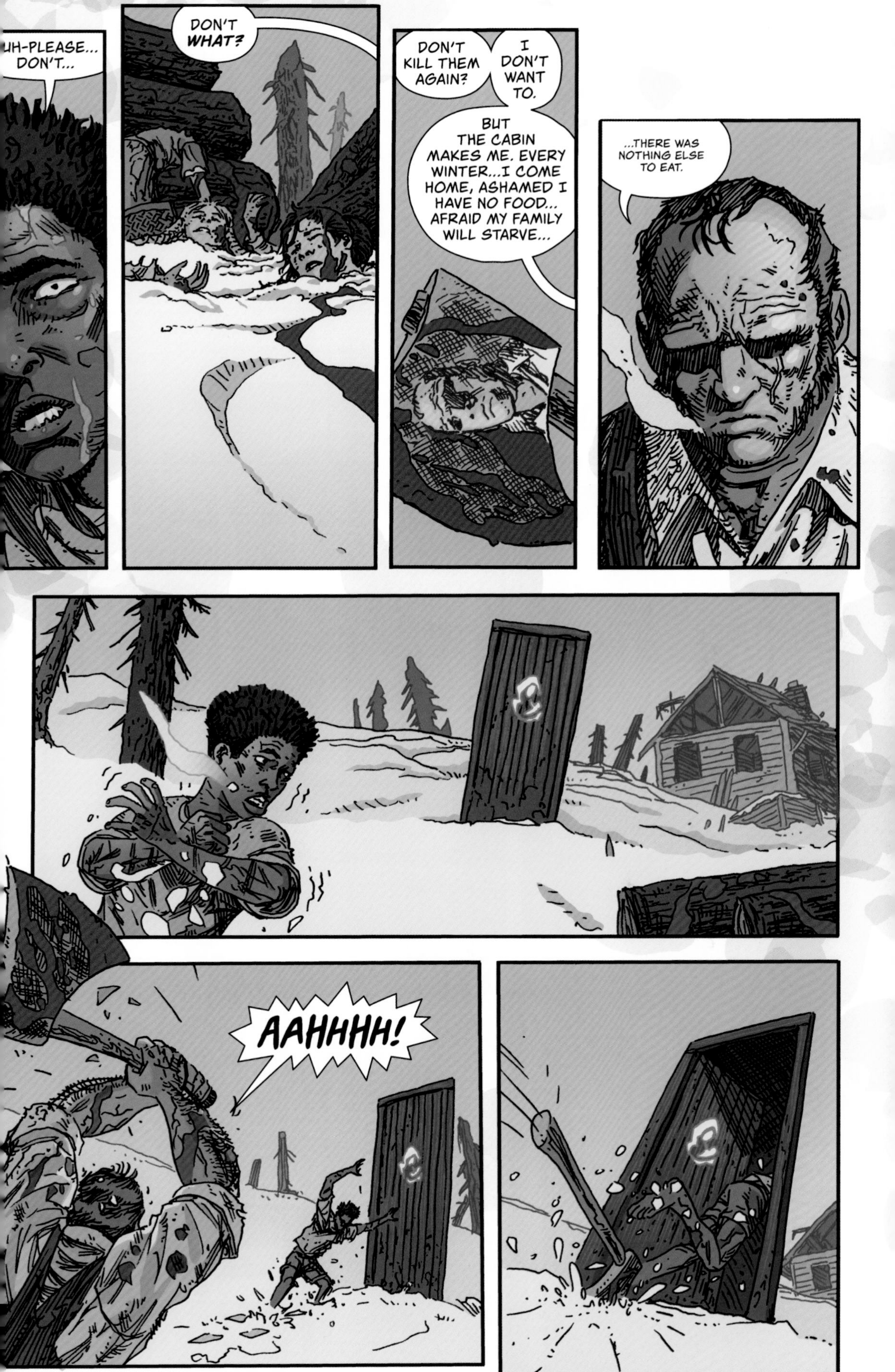
UH-PLEASE... DON'T...
DON'T *WHAT?*
DON'T KILL THEM AGAIN?
I DON'T WANT TO.
BUT THE CABIN MAKES ME. EVERY WINTER...I COME HOME, ASHAMED I HAVE NO FOOD... AFRAID MY FAMILY WILL STARVE...
...THERE WAS NOTHING ELSE TO EAT.
AAHHHH!

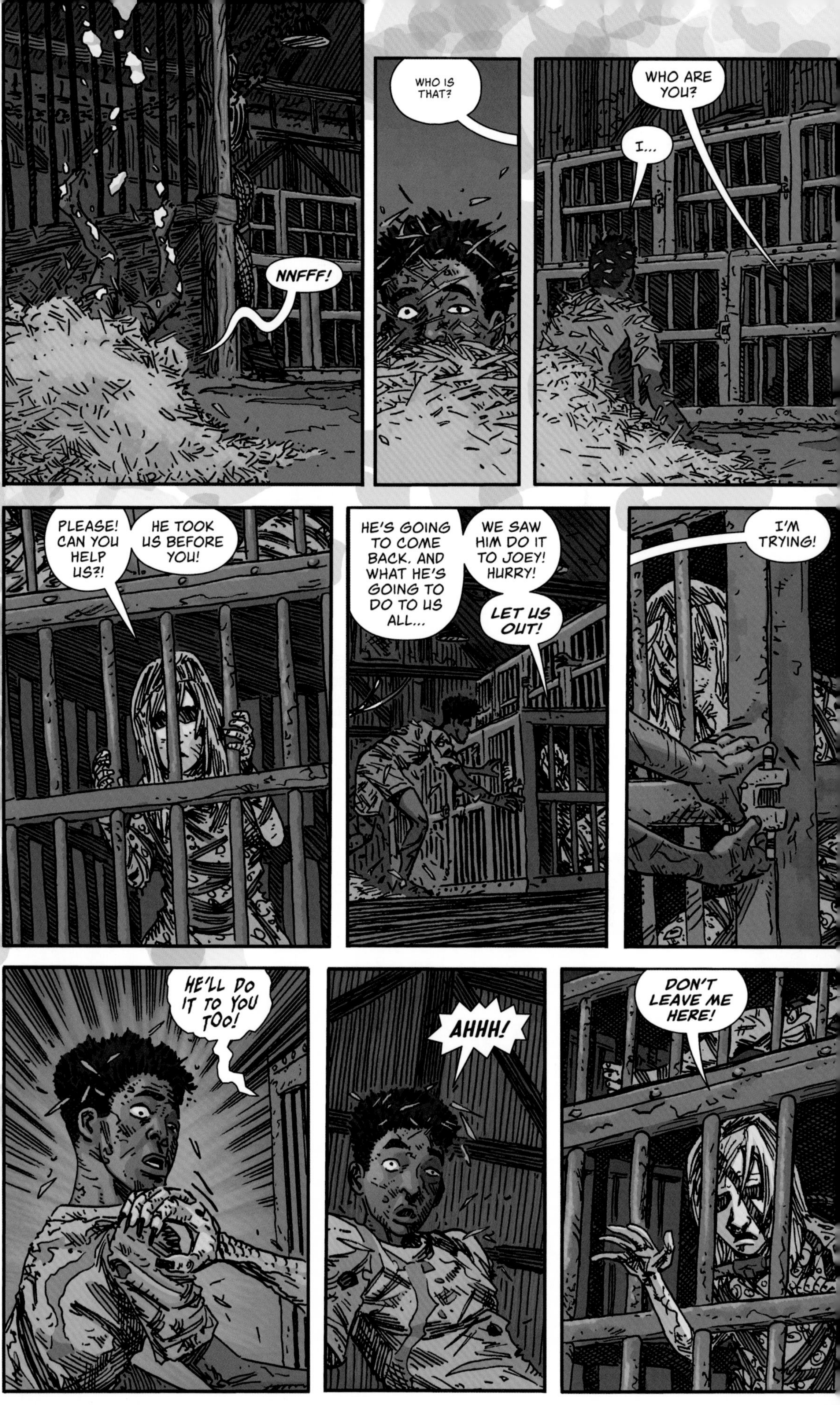
NNFFF!
WHO IS THAT?
WHO ARE YOU?
I...
PLEASE! CAN YOU HELP US?!
HE TOOK US BEFORE YOU!
HE'S GOING TO COME BACK. AND WHAT HE'S GOING TO DO TO US ALL...
WE SAW HIM DO IT TO JOEY! HURRY!
LET US OUT!
I'M TRYING!
HE'LL DO IT TO YOU TOO!
AHHH!
DON'T LEAVE ME HERE!

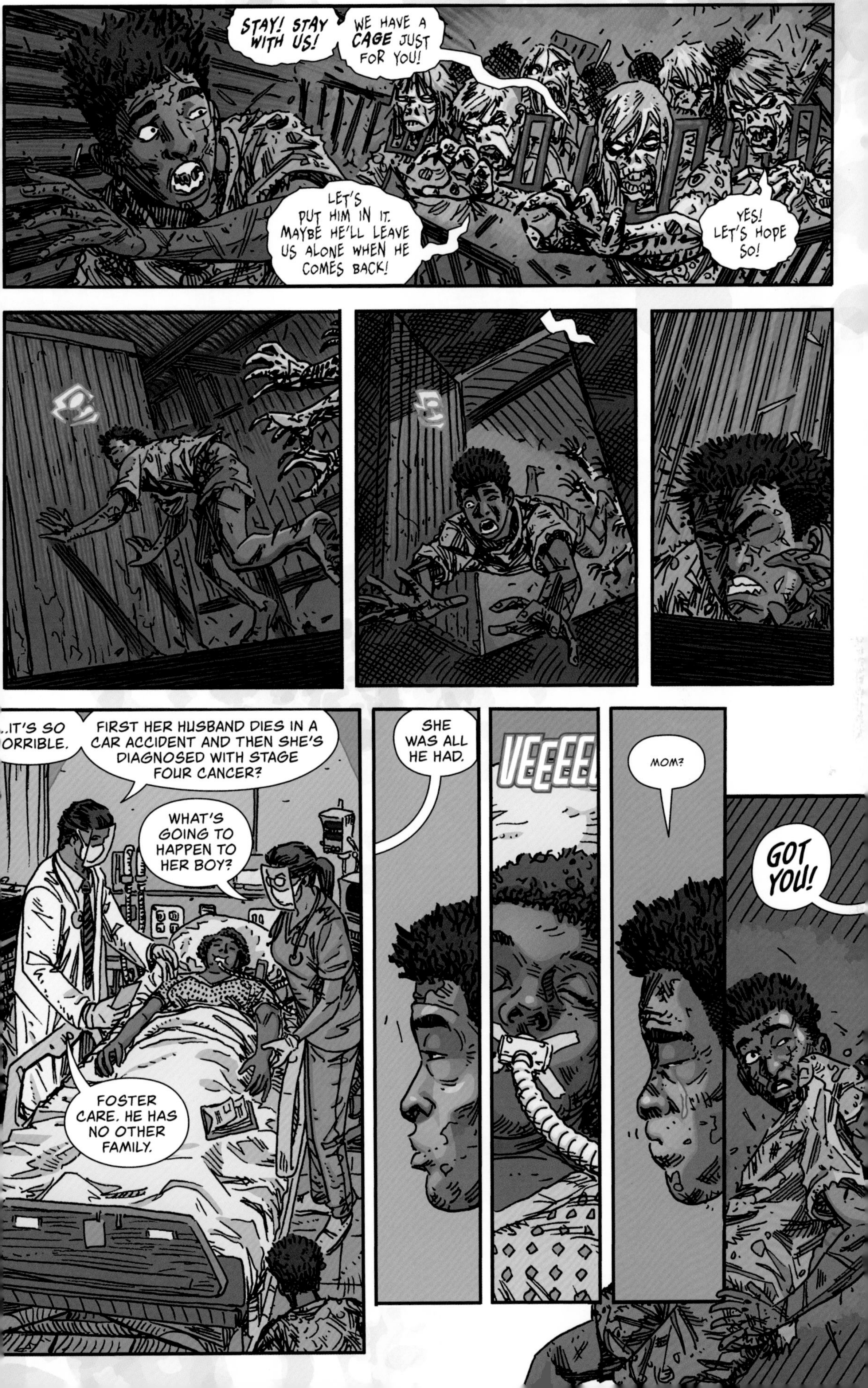
STAY! STAY WITH US!
WE HAVE A CAGE JUST FOR YOU!
LET'S PUT HIM IN IT. MAYBE HE'LL LEAVE US ALONE WHEN HE COMES BACK!
YES! LET'S HOPE SO!
..IT'S SO ORRIBLE.
FIRST HER HUSBAND DIES IN A CAR ACCIDENT AND THEN SHE'S DIAGNOSED WITH STAGE FOUR CANCER?
WHAT'S GOING TO HAPPEN TO HER BOY?
FOSTER CARE. HE HAS NO OTHER FAMILY.
SHE WAS ALL HE HAD.
VEEEE
MOM?
GOT YOU!

I TOLD YOU, YOU COULDN'T GET AWAY!

AND NOW...

...I'M NOT GOING TO BOTHER TAKING YOU TO THE FARM.

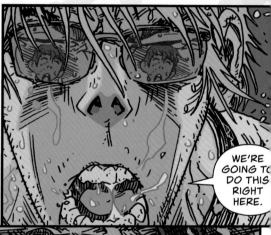

WE'RE GOING TO DO THIS RIGHT HERE.

NO.

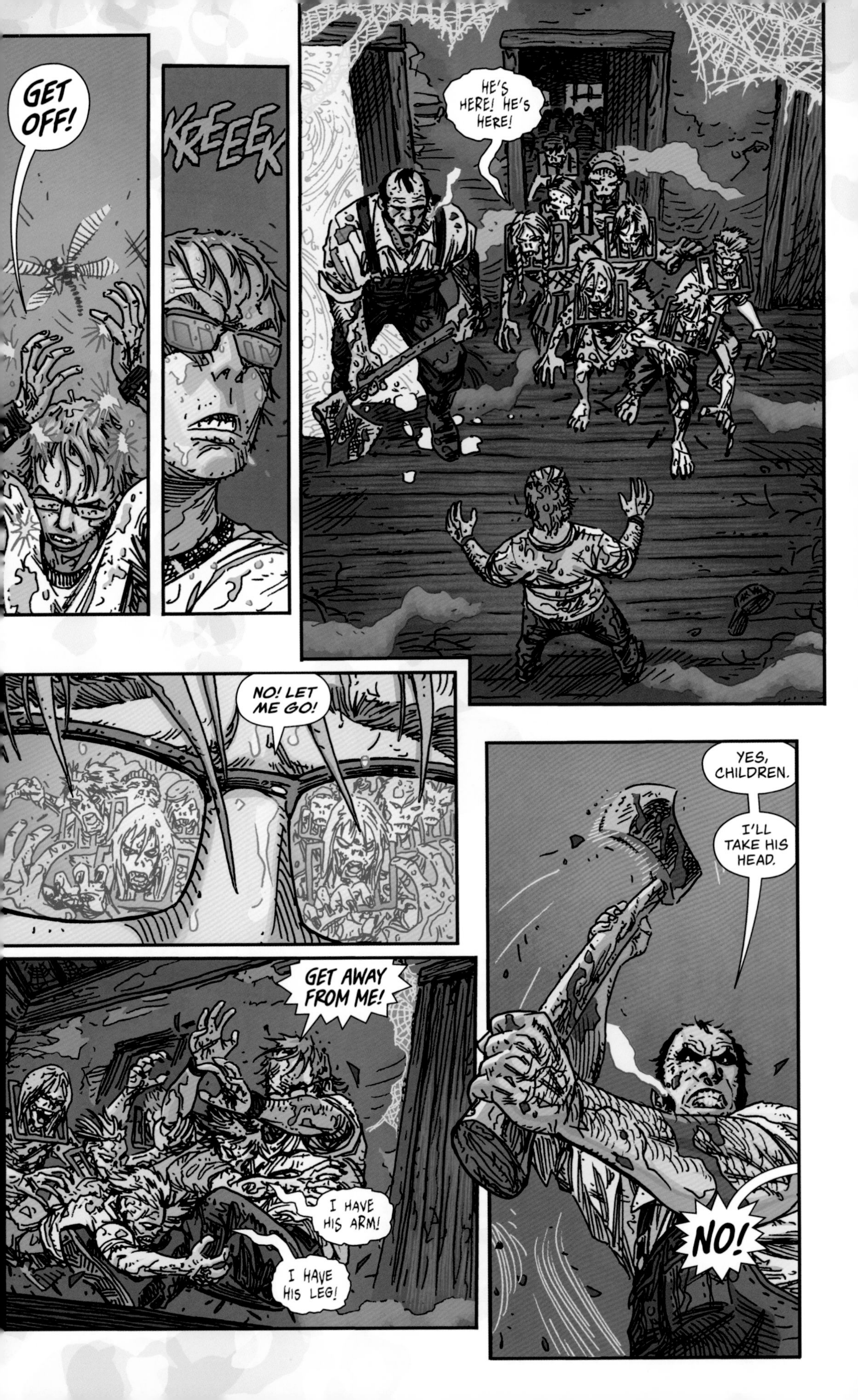
GET OFF!
KREEEK
HE'S HERE! HE'S HERE!
NO! LET ME GO!
YES, CHILDREN.
I'LL TAKE HIS HEAD.
GET AWAY FROM ME!
I HAVE HIS ARM!
I HAVE HIS LEG!
NO!

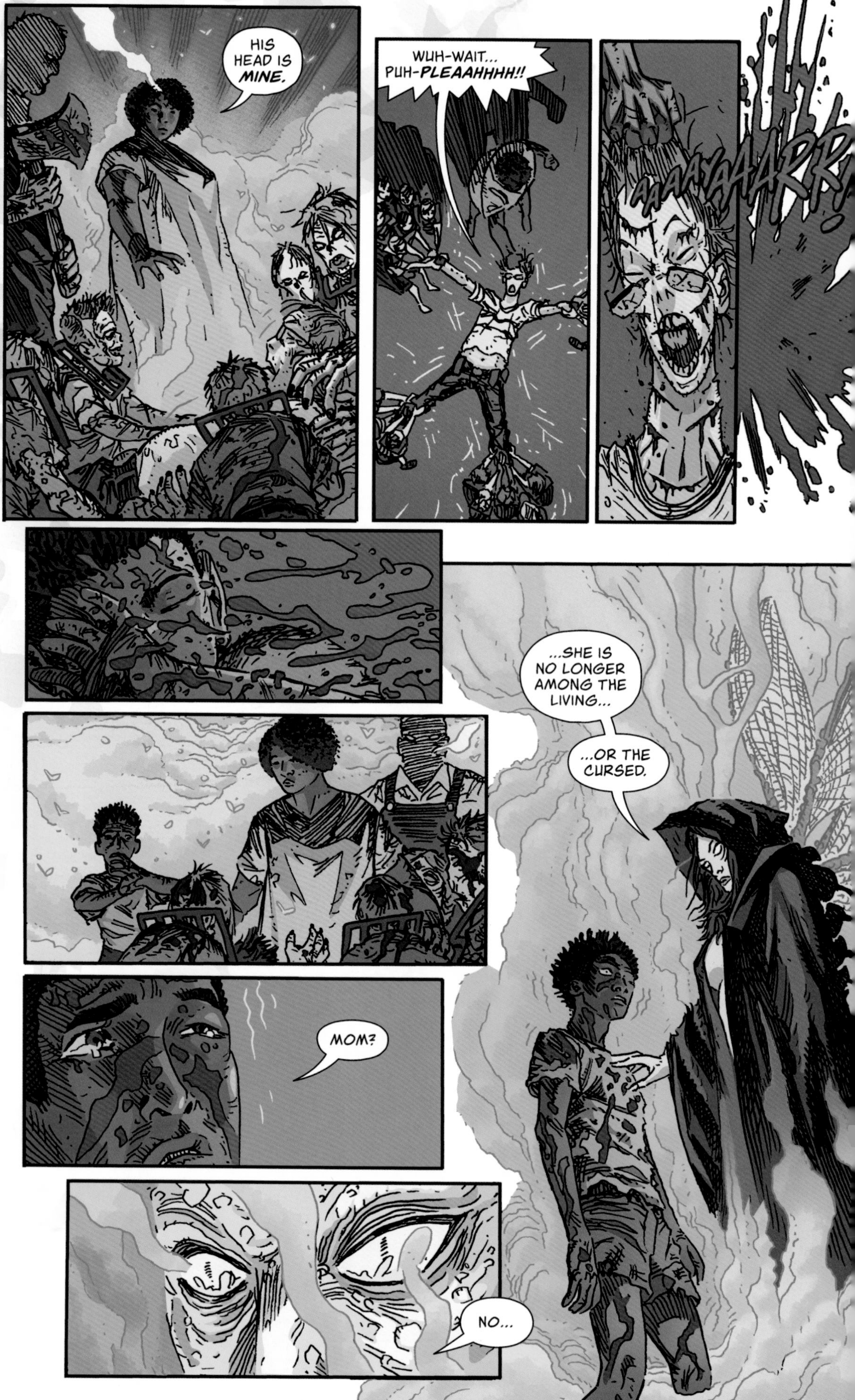
HIS HEAD IS MINE.
WUH-WAIT... PUH-PLEAAHHHH!!
AAAAYAAARR!
...SHE IS NO LONGER AMONG THE LIVING...
...OR THE CURSED.
MOM?
NO...

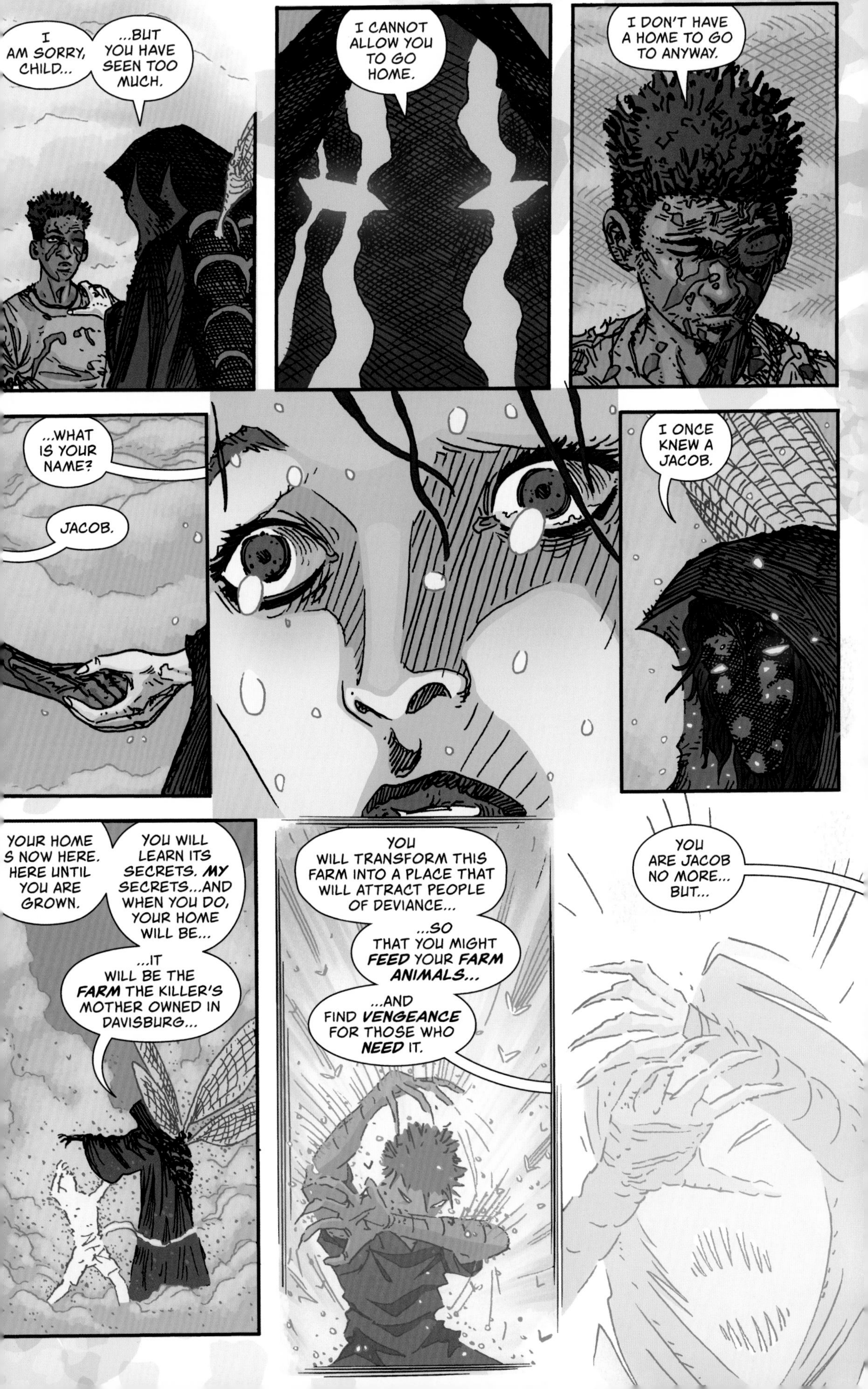
I AM SORRY, CHILD...
...BUT YOU HAVE SEEN TOO MUCH.
I CANNOT ALLOW YOU TO GO HOME.
I DON'T HAVE A HOME TO GO TO ANYWAY.
...WHAT IS YOUR NAME?
JACOB.
I ONCE KNEW A JACOB.
YOUR HOME S NOW HERE. HERE UNTIL YOU ARE GROWN.
YOU WILL LEARN ITS SECRETS. MY SECRETS...AND WHEN YOU DO, YOUR HOME WILL BE...
...IT WILL BE THE FARM THE KILLER'S MOTHER OWNED IN DAVISBURG...
YOU WILL TRANSFORM THIS FARM INTO A PLACE THAT WILL ATTRACT PEOPLE OF DEVIANCE...
...SO THAT YOU MIGHT FEED YOUR FARM ANIMALS...
...AND FIND VENGEANCE FOR THOSE WHO NEED IT.
YOU ARE JACOB NO MORE... BUT...

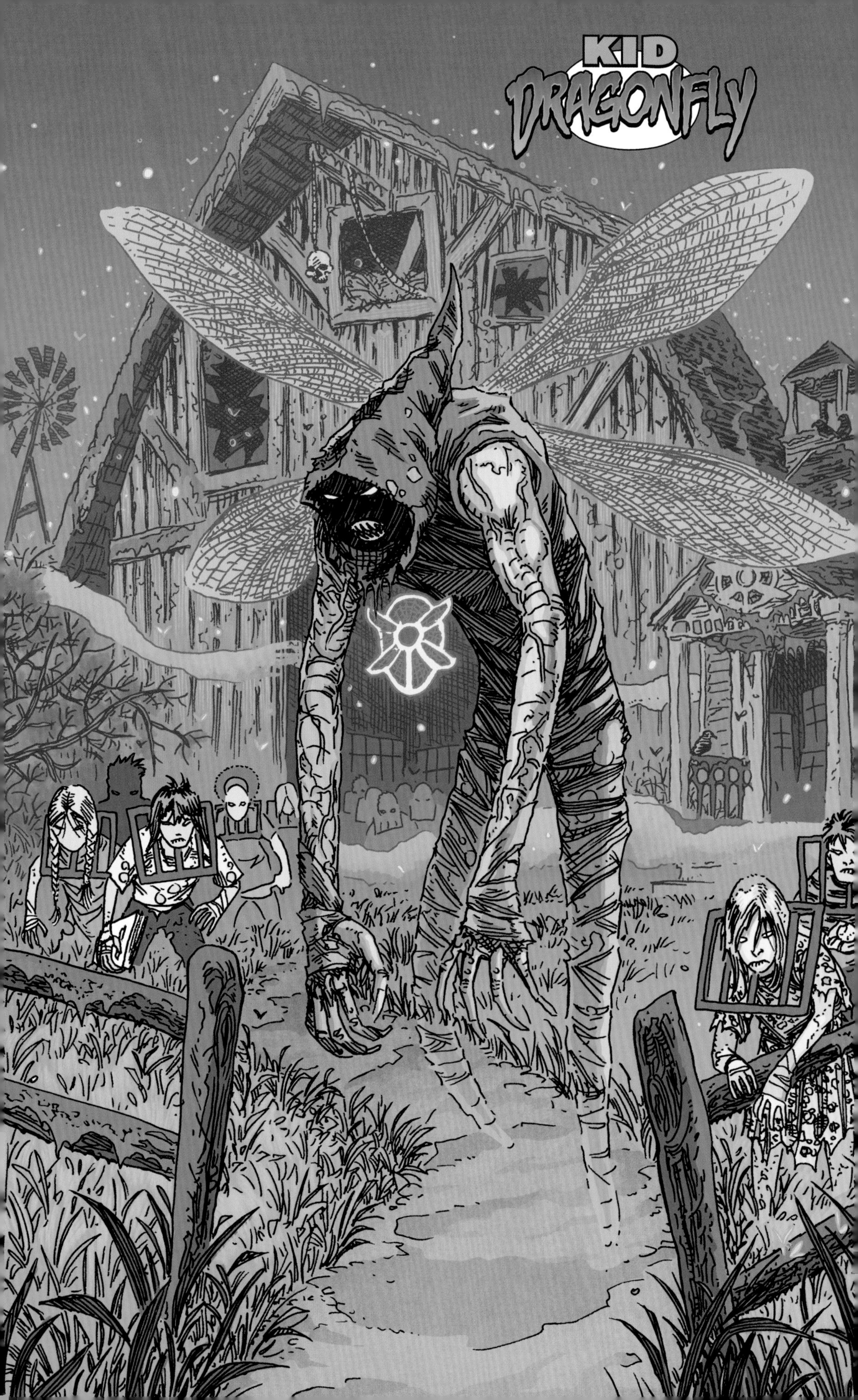
KID
DRAGONFLY

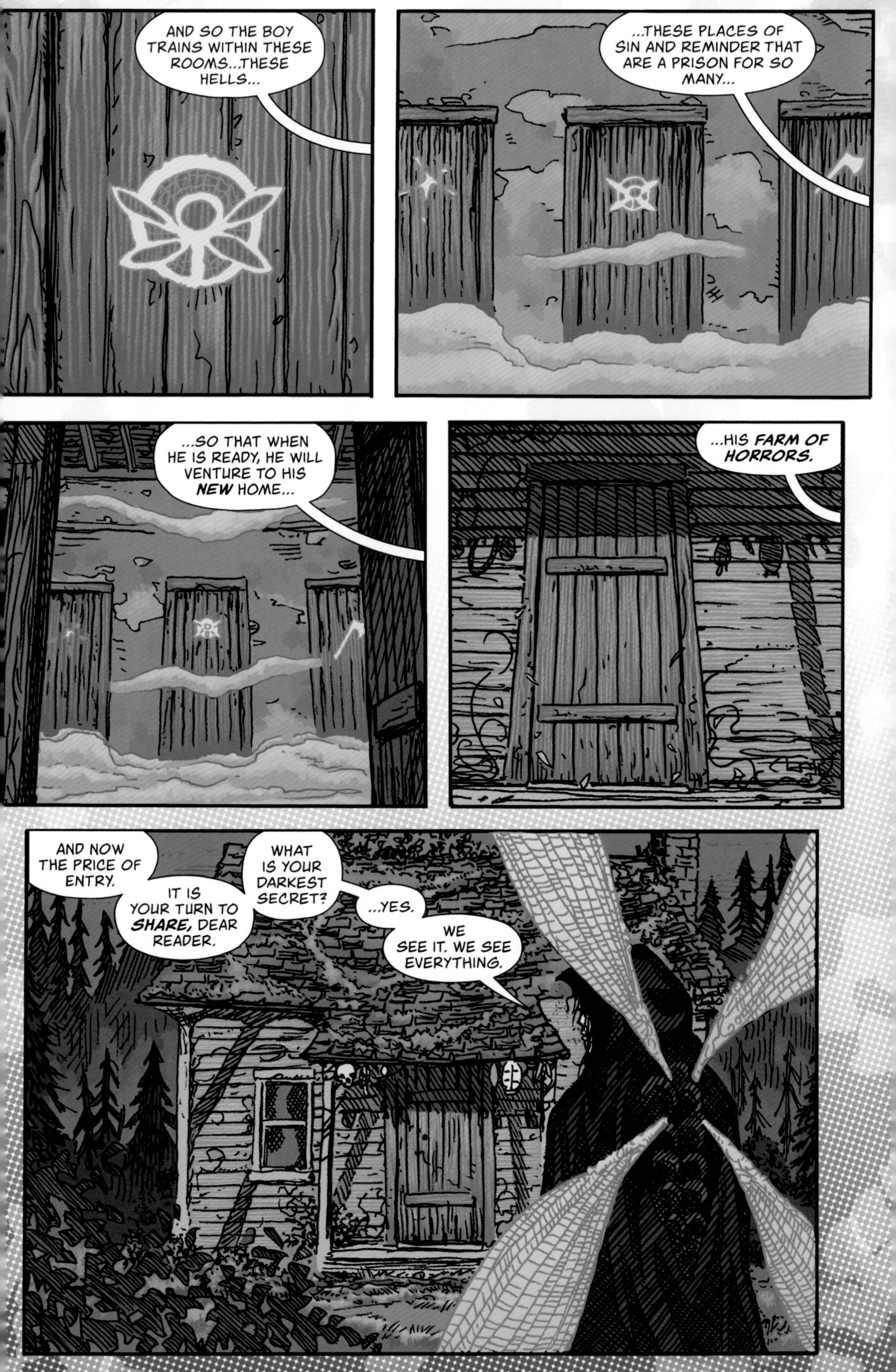
AND SO THE BOY TRAINS WITHIN THESE ROOMS...THESE HELLS...
...THESE PLACES OF SIN AND REMINDER THAT ARE A PRISON FOR SO MANY...
...SO THAT WHEN HE IS READY, HE WILL VENTURE TO HIS NEW HOME...
...HIS FARM OF HORRORS.
AND NOW THE PRICE OF ENTRY.
IT IS YOUR TURN TO SHARE, DEAR READER.
WHAT IS YOUR DARKEST SECRET?
...YES.
WE SEE IT. WE SEE EVERYTHING.

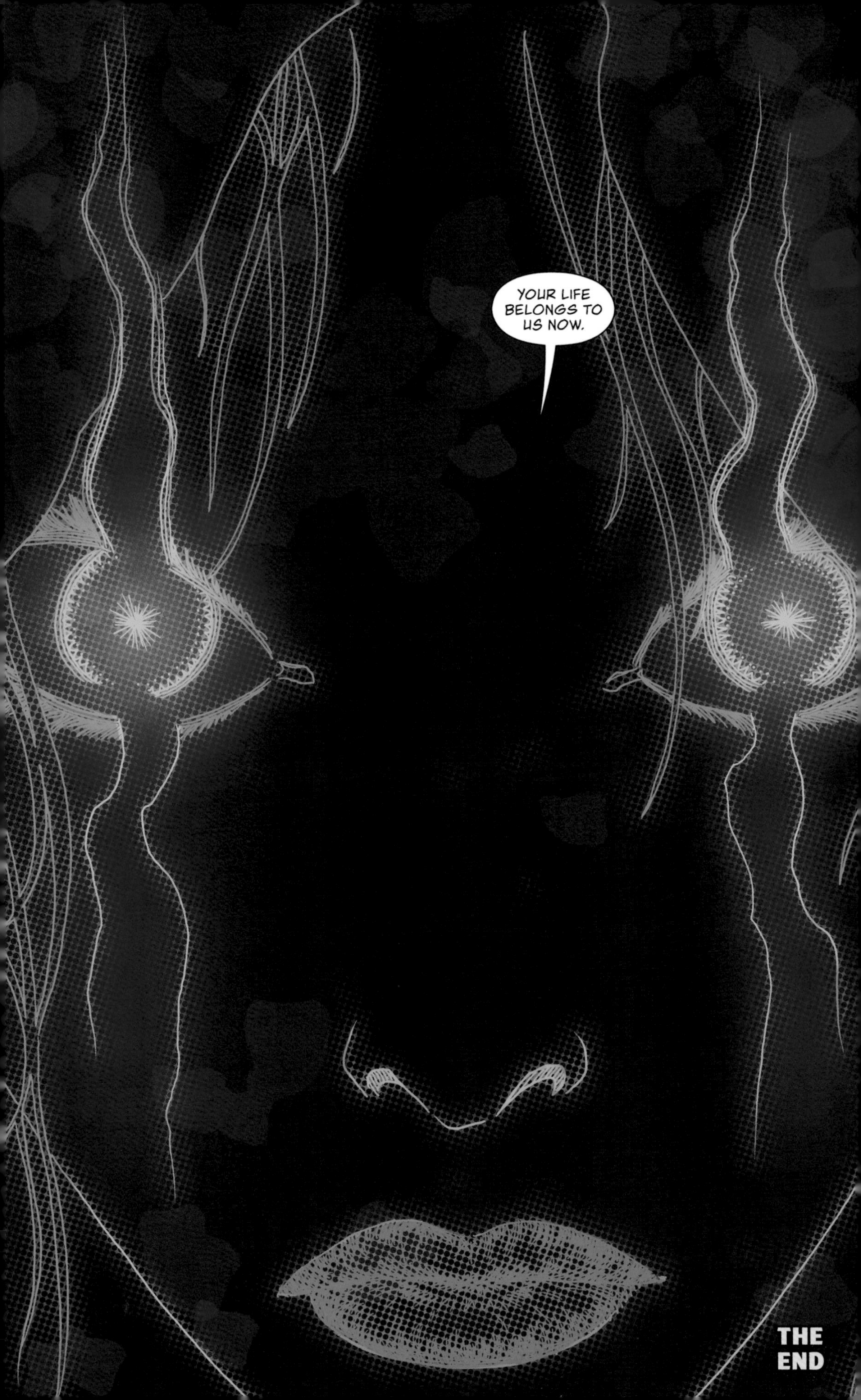
YOUR LIFE BELONGS TO US NOW.
THE END

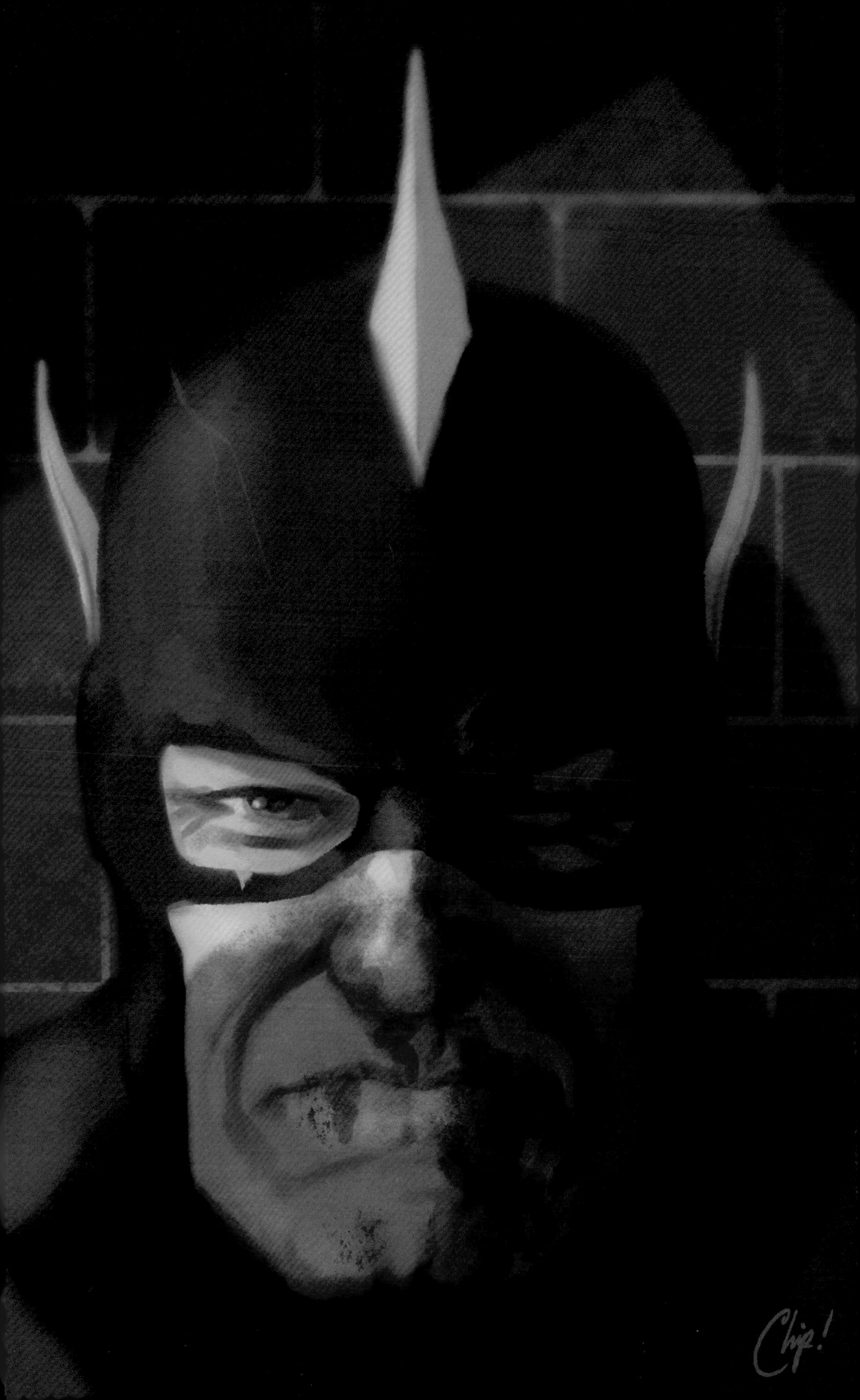
Chip!

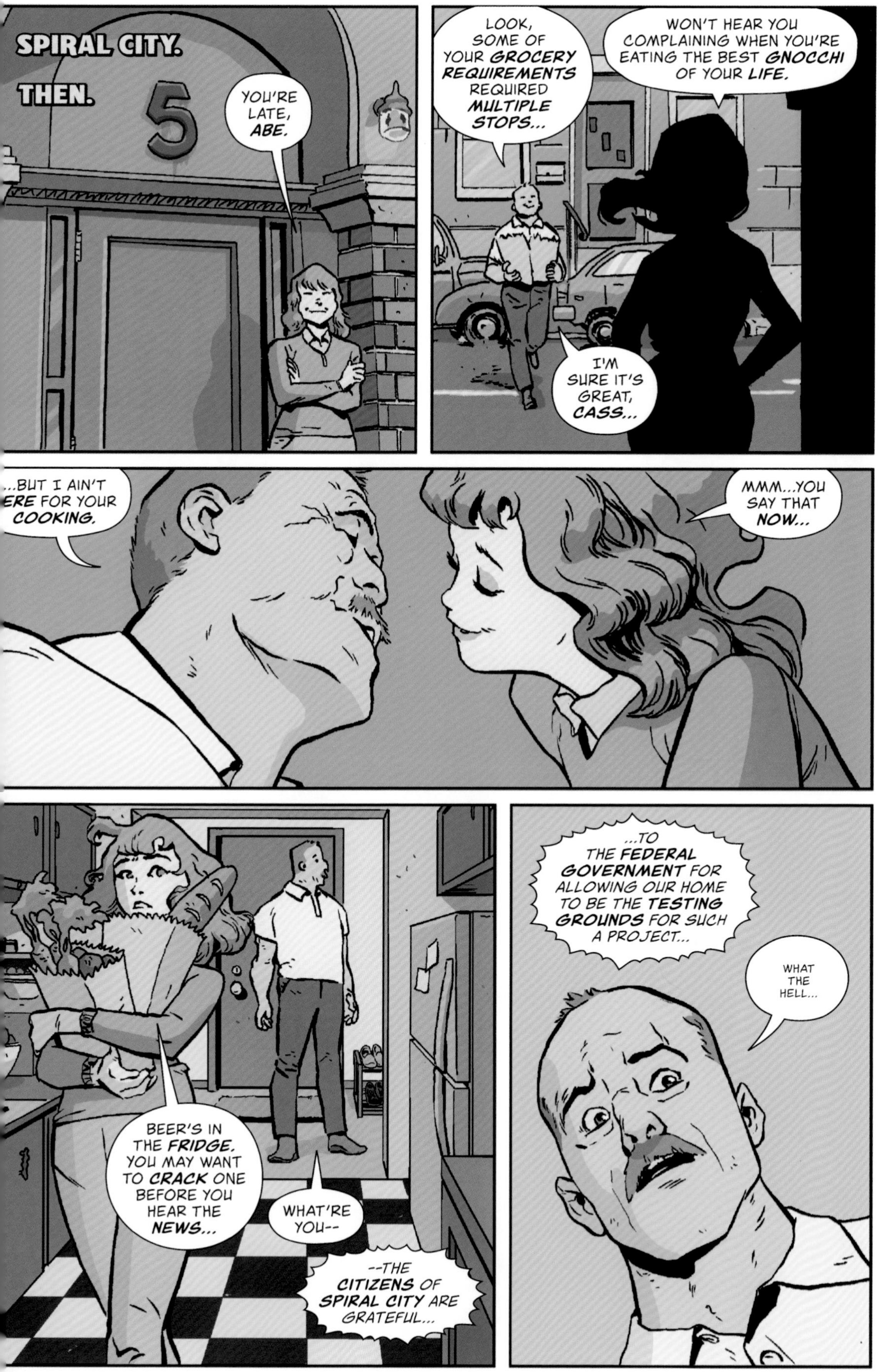
SPIRAL CITY.
THEN.
5
YOU'RE LATE, ABE.
LOOK, SOME OF YOUR GROCERY REQUIREMENTS REQUIRED MULTIPLE STOPS...
WON'T HEAR YOU COMPLAINING WHEN YOU'RE EATING THE BEST GNOCCHI OF YOUR LIFE.
I'M SURE IT'S GREAT, CASS...
...BUT I AIN'T ERE FOR YOUR COOKING.
MMM...YOU SAY THAT NOW...
BEER'S IN THE FRIDGE. YOU MAY WANT TO CRACK ONE BEFORE YOU HEAR THE NEWS...
WHAT'RE YOU--
--THE CITIZENS OF SPIRAL CITY ARE GRATEFUL...
...TO THE FEDERAL GOVERNMENT FOR ALLOWING OUR HOME TO BE THE TESTING GROUNDS FOR SUCH A PROJECT...
WHAT THE HELL...

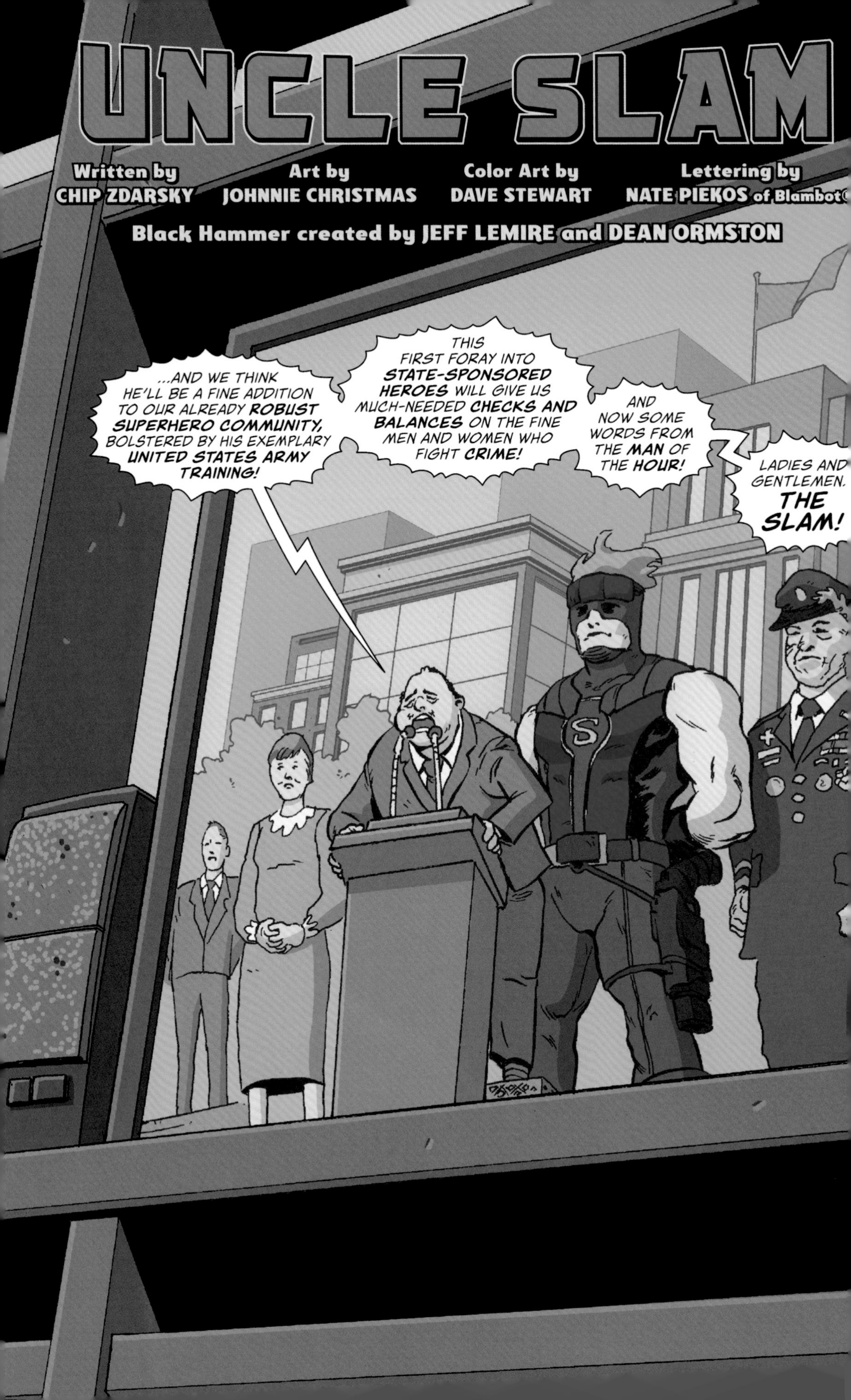
UNCLE SLAM
Written by CHIP ZDARSKY
Art by JOHNNIE CHRISTMAS
Color Art by DAVE STEWART
Lettering by NATE PIEKOS of Blambot®
Black Hammer created by JEFF LEMIRE and DEAN ORMSTON
...AND WE THINK HE'LL BE A FINE ADDITION TO OUR ALREADY ROBUST SUPERHERO COMMUNITY, BOLSTERED BY HIS EXEMPLARY UNITED STATES ARMY TRAINING!
THIS FIRST FORAY INTO STATE-SPONSORED HEROES WILL GIVE US MUCH-NEEDED CHECKS AND BALANCES ON THE FINE MEN AND WOMEN WHO FIGHT CRIME!
AND NOW SOME WORDS FROM THE MAN OF THE HOUR!
LADIES AND GENTLEMEN. THE SLAM!

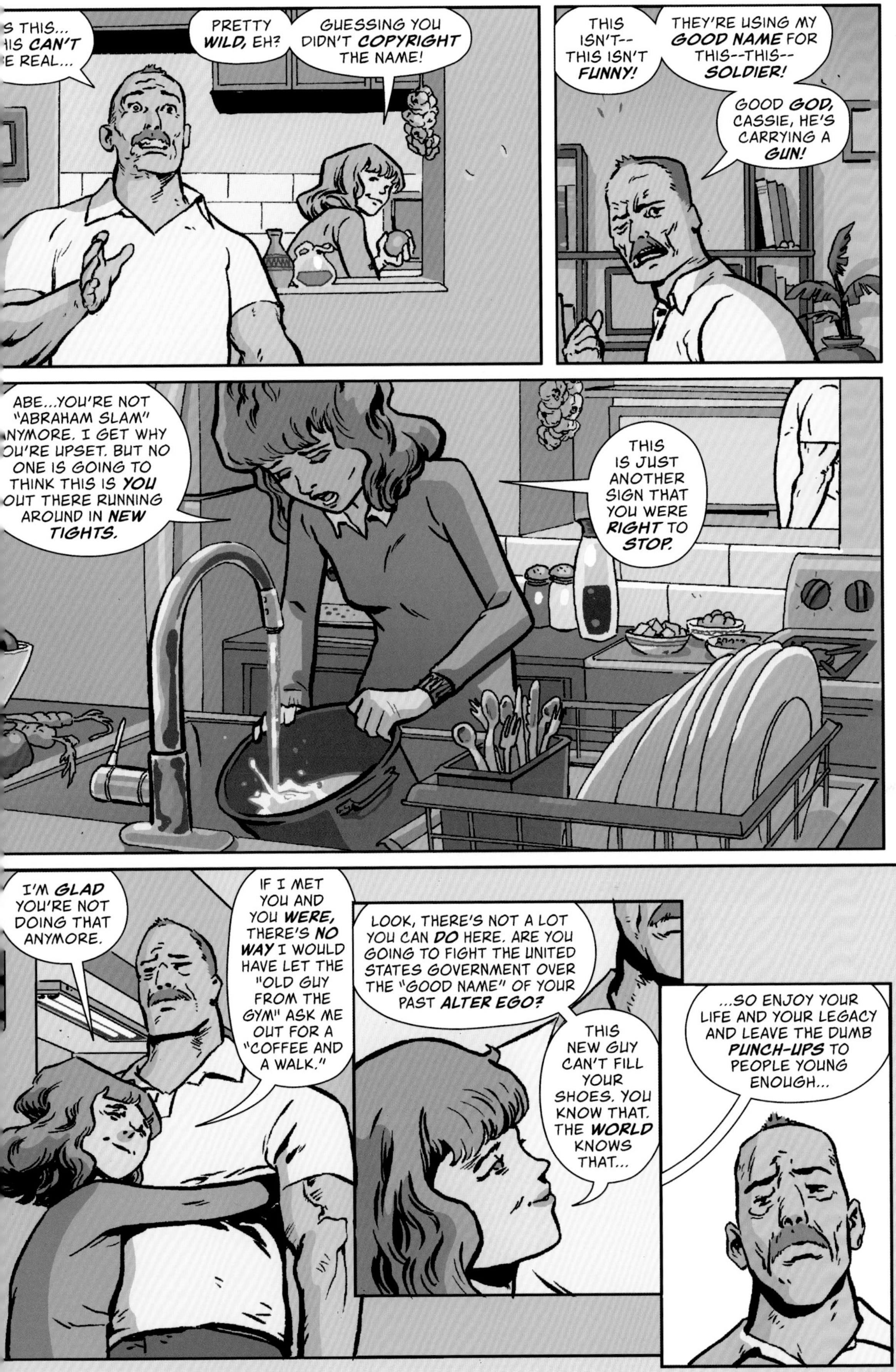

S THIS... HIS CAN'T E REAL...
PRETTY WILD, EH?
GUESSING YOU DIDN'T COPYRIGHT THE NAME!
THIS ISN'T-- THIS ISN'T FUNNY!
THEY'RE USING MY GOOD NAME FOR THIS--THIS-- SOLDIER!
GOOD GOD, CASSIE, HE'S CARRYING A GUN!
ABE...YOU'RE NOT "ABRAHAM SLAM" NYMORE. I GET WHY OU'RE UPSET. BUT NO ONE IS GOING TO THINK THIS IS YOU OUT THERE RUNNING AROUND IN NEW TIGHTS.
THIS IS JUST ANOTHER SIGN THAT YOU WERE RIGHT TO STOP.
I'M GLAD YOU'RE NOT DOING THAT ANYMORE.
IF I MET YOU AND YOU WERE, THERE'S NO WAY I WOULD HAVE LET THE "OLD GUY FROM THE GYM" ASK ME OUT FOR A "COFFEE AND A WALK."
LOOK, THERE'S NOT A LOT YOU CAN DO HERE. ARE YOU GOING TO FIGHT THE UNITED STATES GOVERNMENT OVER THE "GOOD NAME" OF YOUR PAST ALTER EGO?
THIS NEW GUY CAN'T FILL YOUR SHOES. YOU KNOW THAT. THE WORLD KNOWS THAT...
...SO ENJOY YOUR LIFE AND YOUR LEGACY AND LEAVE THE DUMB PUNCH-UPS TO PEOPLE YOUNG ENOUGH...

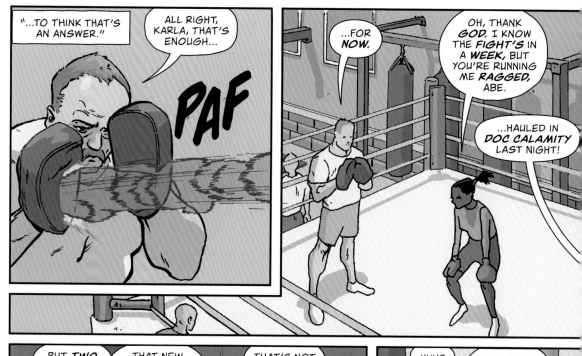

"...TO THINK THAT'S AN ANSWER."

ALL RIGHT, KARLA, THAT'S ENOUGH...

PAF

...FOR NOW.

OH, THANK GOD. I KNOW THE FIGHT'S IN A WEEK, BUT YOU'RE RUNNING ME RAGGED, ABE.

...HAULED IN DOC CALAMITY LAST NIGHT!

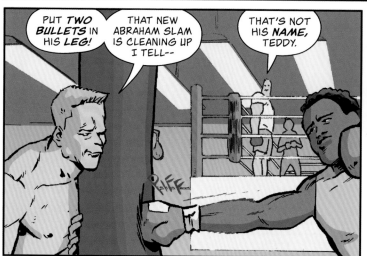

PUT TWO BULLETS IN HIS LEG! THAT NEW ABRAHAM SLAM IS CLEANING UP I TELL--

THAT'S NOT HIS NAME, TEDDY.

HUH?

HE'S "THE SLAM." HE'S NOTHING LIKE "ABRAHAM SLAM," SON.

YEAH, I GUESS SO...

...THIS GUY ISN'T A MILLION YEARS OLD.

HAHAHA!

HAHAHA--

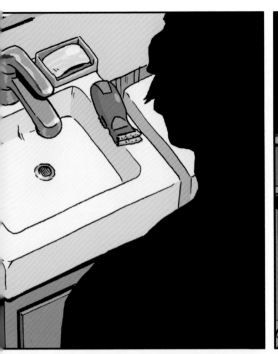

IT'S NOT RIGHT.

SHOOTING PEOPLE. WHAT HE'S DOING...IT'S NOT RIGHT.

AND IF IT'S **NOT** RIGHT...

...THEN I NEED TO STOP IT.

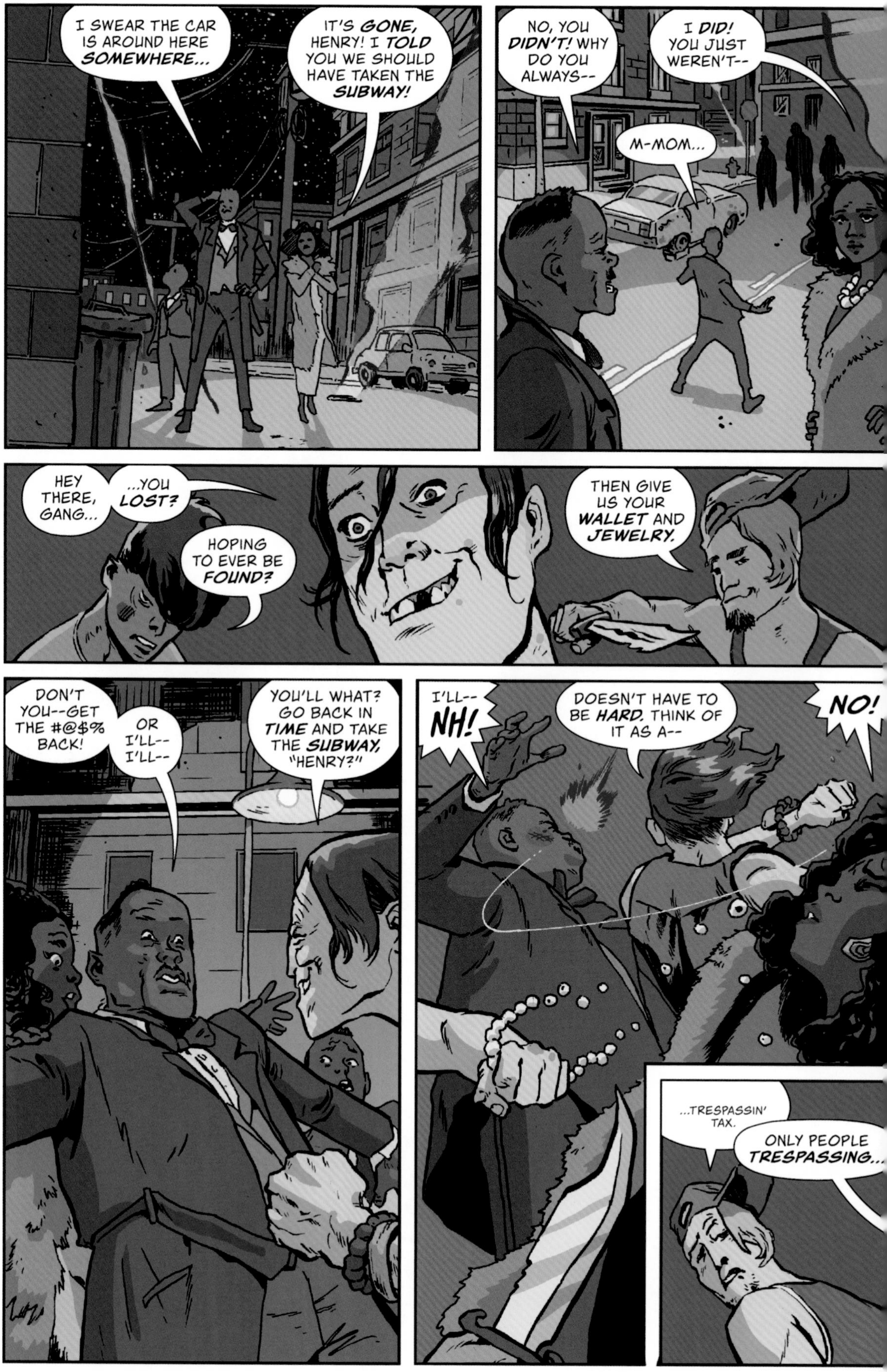
I SWEAR THE CAR IS AROUND HERE SOMEWHERE...
IT'S GONE, HENRY! I TOLD YOU WE SHOULD HAVE TAKEN THE SUBWAY!
NO, YOU DIDN'T! WHY DO YOU ALWAYS--
I DID! YOU JUST WEREN'T--
M-MOM...
HEY THERE, GANG...
...YOU LOST?
HOPING TO EVER BE FOUND?
THEN GIVE US YOUR WALLET AND JEWELRY.
DON'T YOU--GET THE #@$% BACK!
OR I'LL-- I'LL--
YOU'LL WHAT? GO BACK IN TIME AND TAKE THE SUBWAY, "HENRY?"
I'LL--
NH!
DOESN'T HAVE TO BE HARD. THINK OF IT AS A--
NO!
...TRESPASSIN' TAX.
ONLY PEOPLE TRESPASSING...

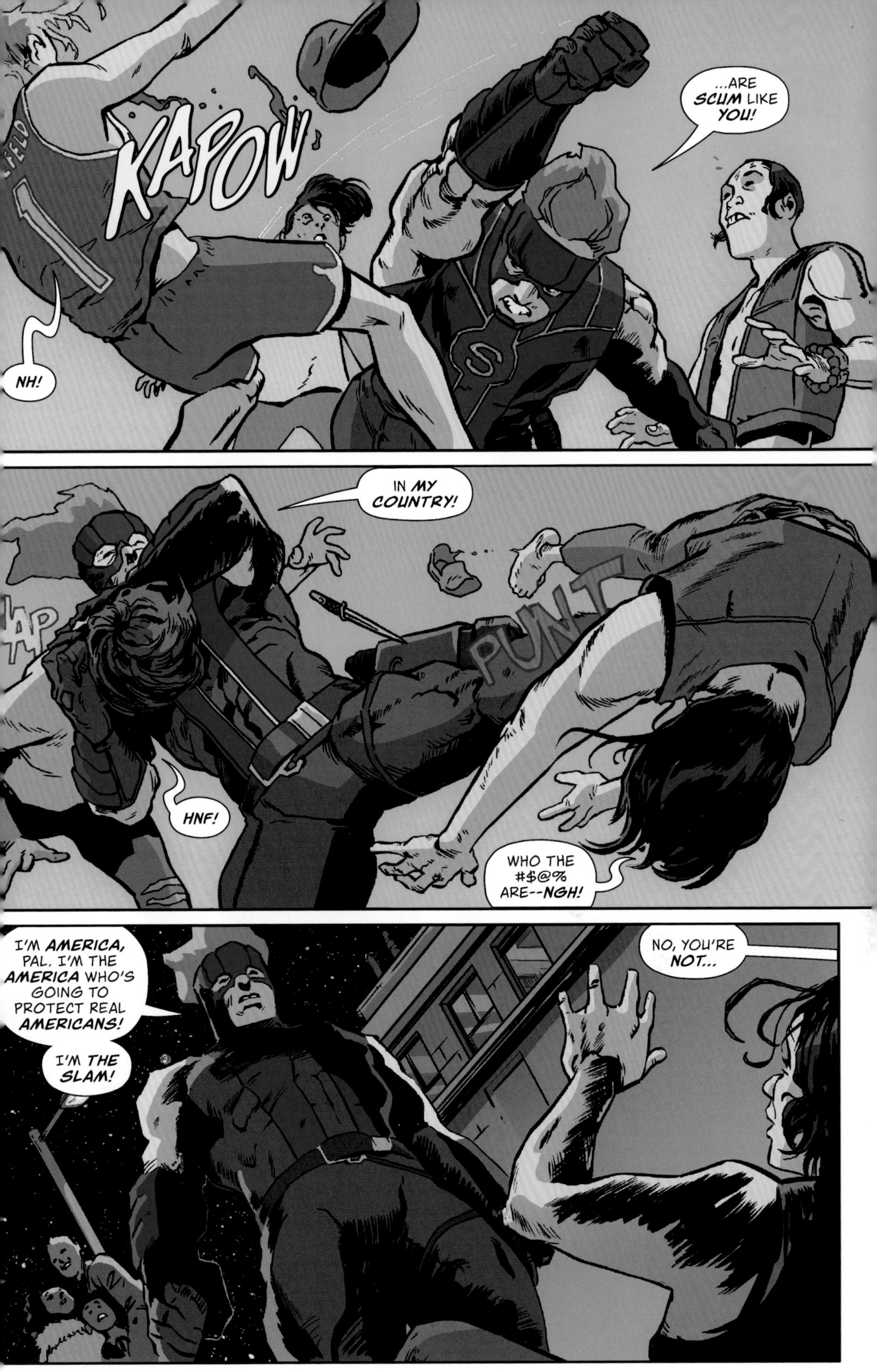
KAPOW
...ARE SCUM LIKE YOU!
NH!
IN MY COUNTRY!
PUNT
HNF!
WHO THE #$@% ARE--NGH!
I'M AMERICA, PAL. I'M THE AMERICA WHO'S GOING TO PROTECT REAL AMERICANS!
I'M THE SLAM!
NO, YOU'RE NOT...

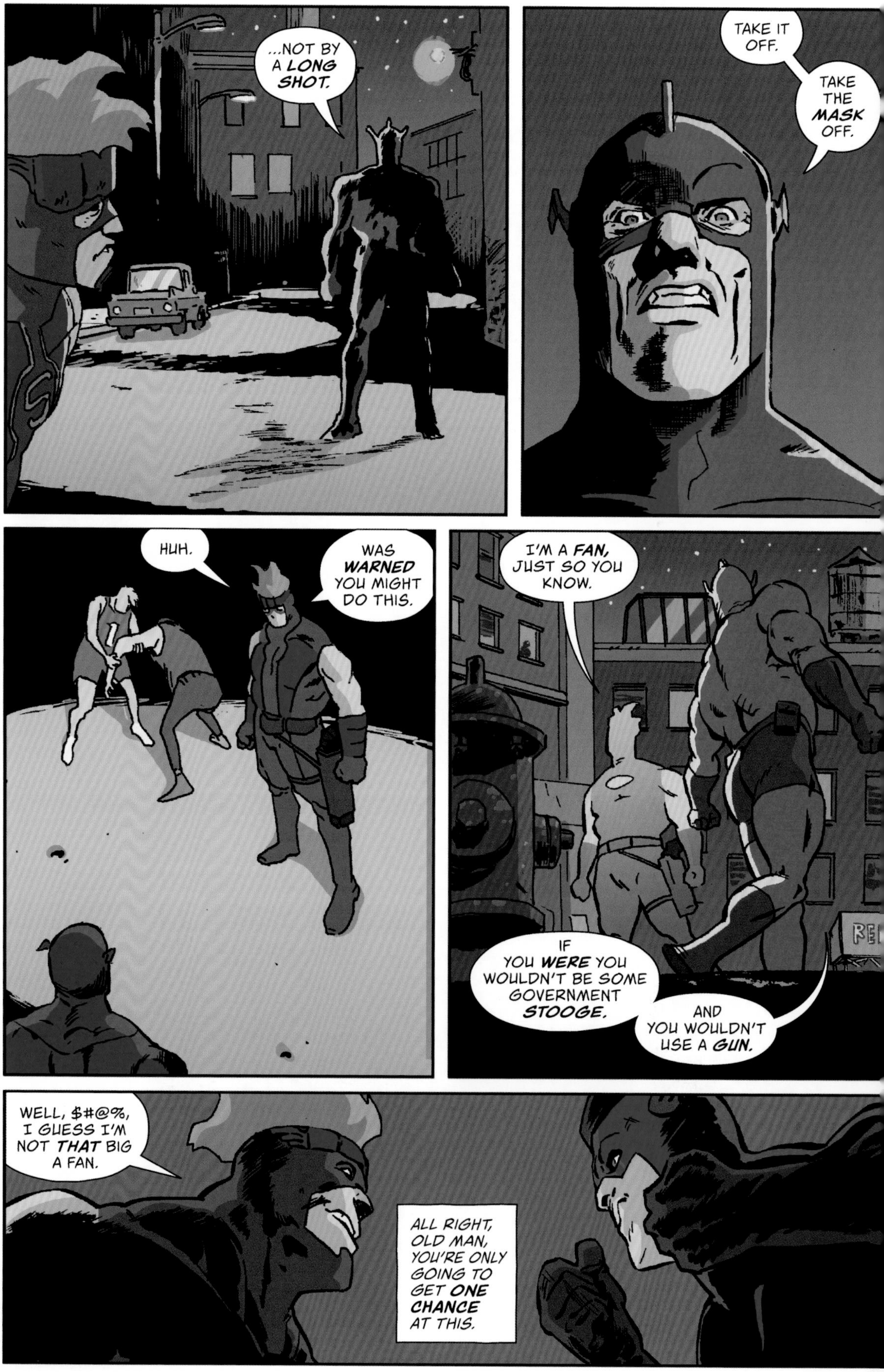

...NOT BY A LONG SHOT.
TAKE IT OFF.
TAKE THE MASK OFF.
HUH.
WAS WARNED YOU MIGHT DO THIS.
I'M A FAN, JUST SO YOU KNOW.
IF YOU WERE YOU WOULDN'T BE SOME GOVERNMENT STOOGE.
AND YOU WOULDN'T USE A GUN.
WELL, $#@%, I GUESS I'M NOT THAT BIG A FAN.
ALL RIGHT, OLD MAN, YOU'RE ONLY GOING TO GET ONE CHANCE AT THIS.

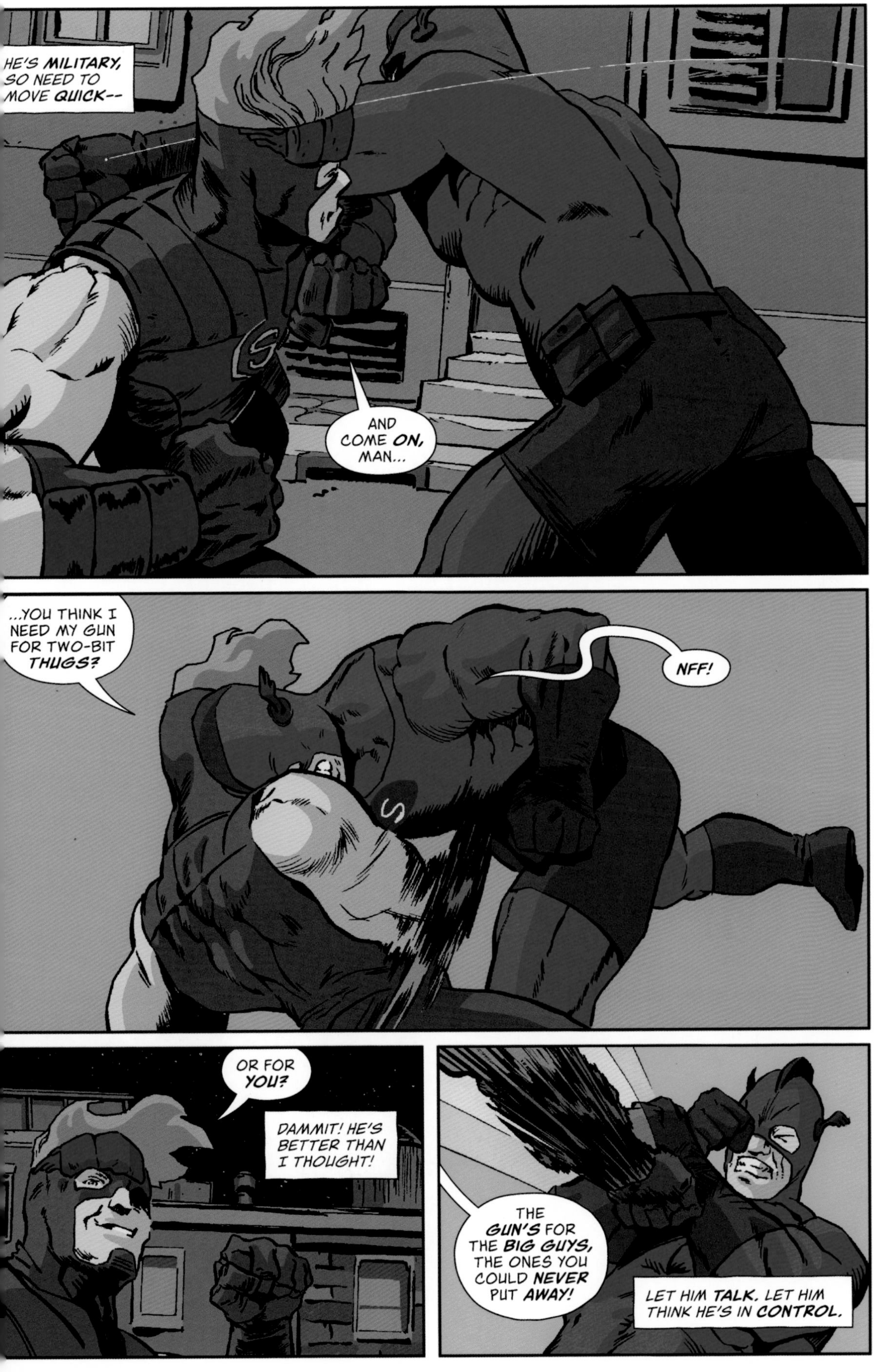
HE'S MILITARY, SO NEED TO MOVE QUICK--
AND COME ON, MAN...
...YOU THINK I NEED MY GUN FOR TWO-BIT THUGS?
NFF!
OR FOR YOU?
DAMMIT! HE'S BETTER THAN I THOUGHT!
THE GUN'S FOR THE BIG GUYS, THE ONES YOU COULD NEVER PUT AWAY!
LET HIM TALK. LET HIM THINK HE'S IN CONTROL.

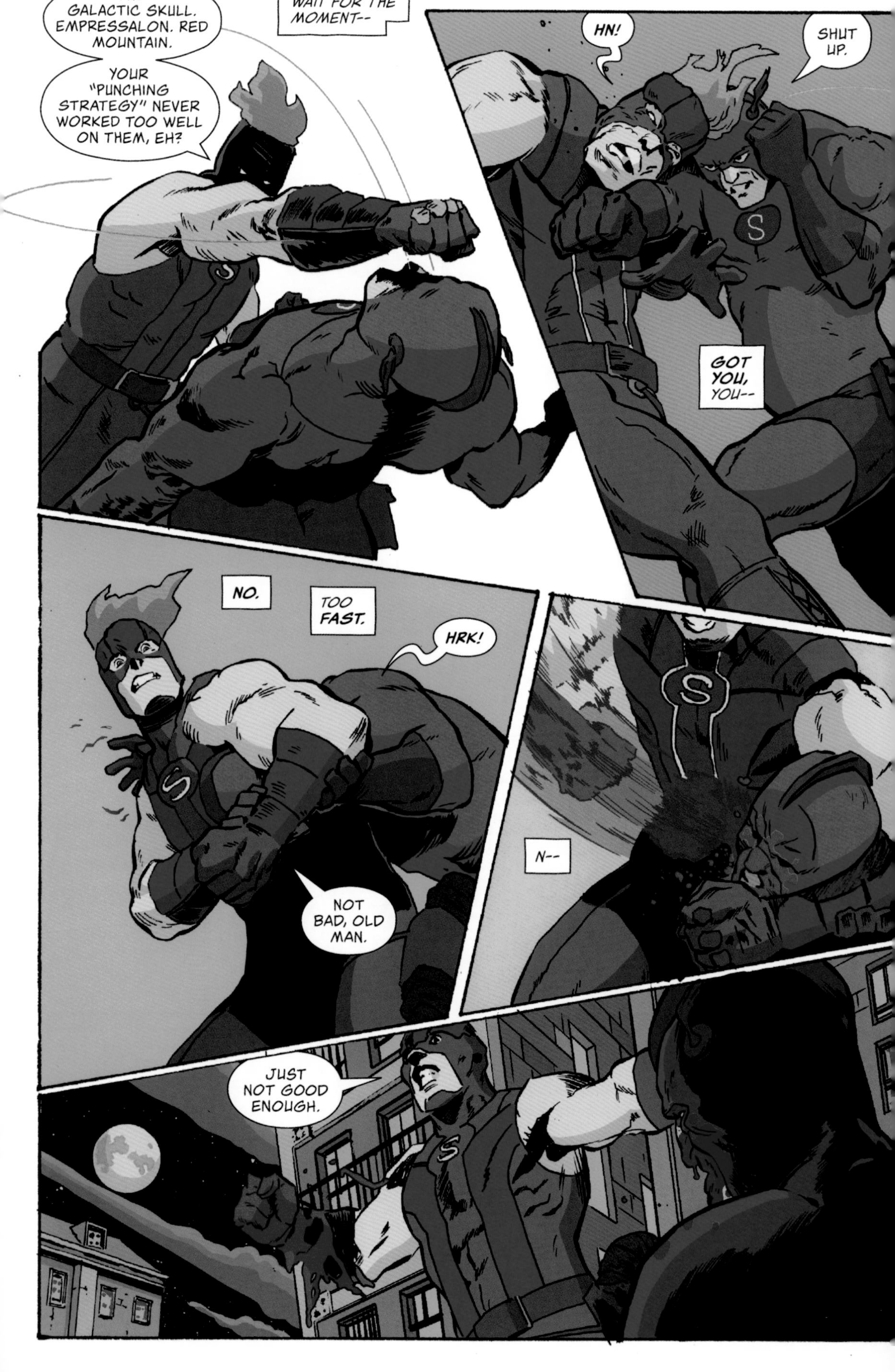
THE GALACTIC SKULL. EMPRESSALON. RED MOUNTAIN.
YOUR "PUNCHING STRATEGY" NEVER WORKED TOO WELL ON THEM, EH?
WAIT FOR THE MOMENT--
HN!
SHUT UP.
GOT YOU, YOU--
NO.
TOO FAST.
HRK!
NOT BAD, OLD MAN.
N--
JUST NOT GOOD ENOUGH.

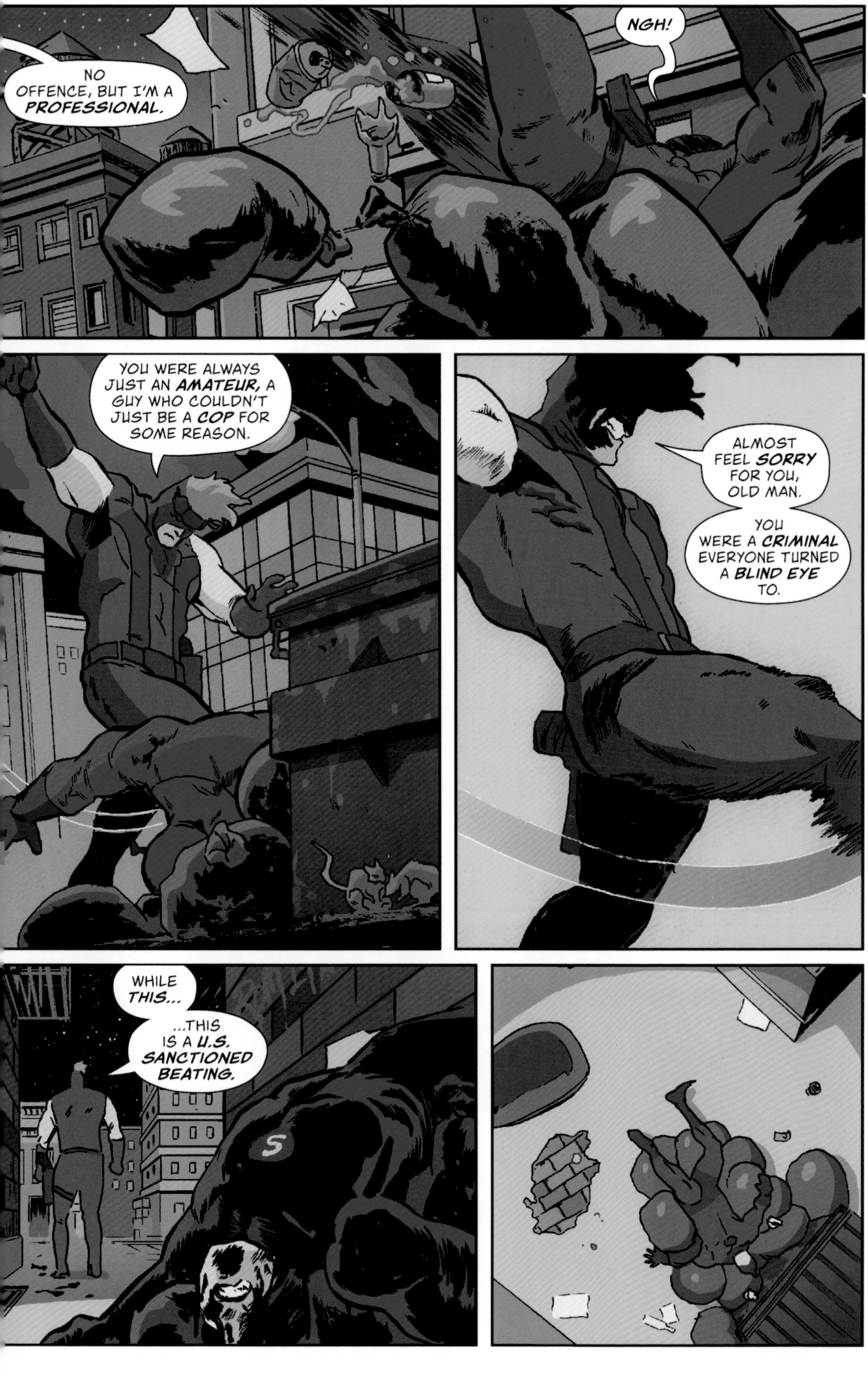
NO OFFENCE, BUT I'M A PROFESSIONAL.
NGH!
YOU WERE ALWAYS JUST AN AMATEUR, A GUY WHO COULDN'T JUST BE A COP FOR SOME REASON.
ALMOST FEEL SORRY FOR YOU, OLD MAN.
YOU WERE A CRIMINAL EVERYONE TURNED A BLIND EYE TO.
WHILE THIS...
...THIS IS A U.S. SANCTIONED BEATING.

--MINIMUM SIX WEEKS UNTIL HIS RIBS HEAL. MORE THAN LIKELY *SEVEN.*

HE'S LUCKY THEY DIDN'T PUNCTURE A *LUNG.*

YEAH. LUCKY.

I'LL, UH, GIVE YOU SOME TIME BEFORE I SEND THE NURSE IN.

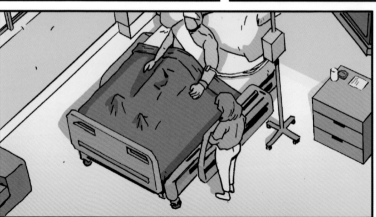

CASSIE, I...

YOU *WHAT,* ABE?

I HAD TO *BEG* THE DOCTORS AND COPS TO NOT REVEAL THAT IT WAS *YOU* IN THOSE *TIGHTS.* THOSE COLORFUL, CHILDREN'S CLOTHES.

A GROWN-ASS MAN.

ALL MY FRIENDS WERE *STUNNED* WHEN WE STARTED DATING. TWENTY YEARS DIFFERENCE. WHAT DID I SEE IN YOU, THEY'D ASK.

BUT IT WAS NICE. YOU WEREN'T *LOST.* YOU WEREN'T TRYING TO *PROVE* YOURSELF LIKE TH YOUNG GUYS I USED TO DATE. YOU WERE *QUIETL CONFIDENT.* I THOUGHT YOU WERE A *GROWN-UP...*

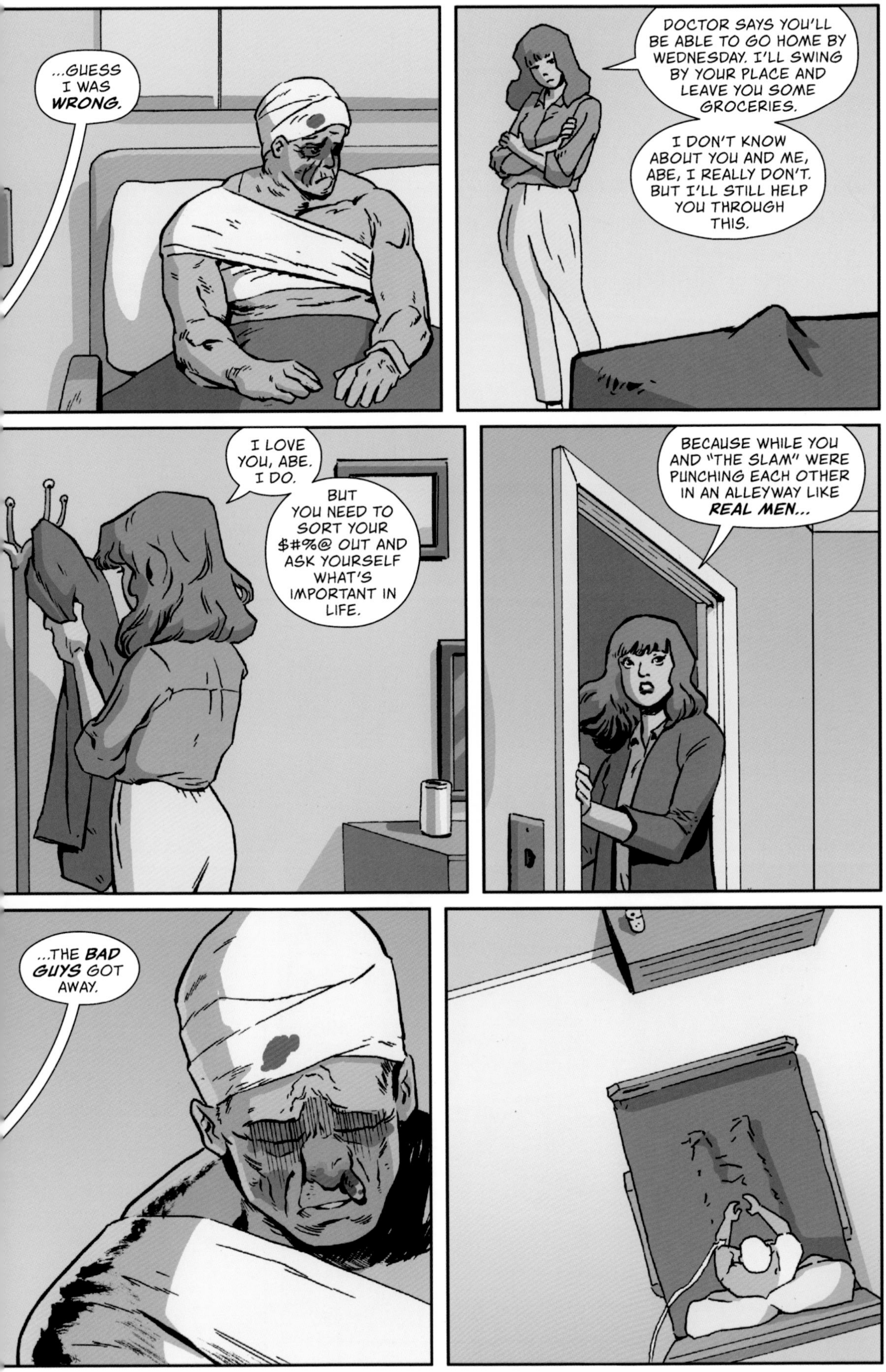
...GUESS I WAS **WRONG.**
DOCTOR SAYS YOU'LL BE ABLE TO GO HOME BY WEDNESDAY. I'LL SWING BY YOUR PLACE AND LEAVE YOU SOME GROCERIES.
I DON'T KNOW ABOUT YOU AND ME, ABE, I REALLY DON'T. BUT I'LL STILL HELP YOU THROUGH THIS.
I LOVE YOU, ABE. I DO.
BUT YOU NEED TO SORT YOUR $#%@ OUT AND ASK YOURSELF WHAT'S IMPORTANT IN LIFE.
BECAUSE WHILE YOU AND "THE SLAM" WERE PUNCHING EACH OTHER IN AN ALLEYWAY LIKE ***REAL MEN...***
...THE ***BAD GUYS*** GOT AWAY.

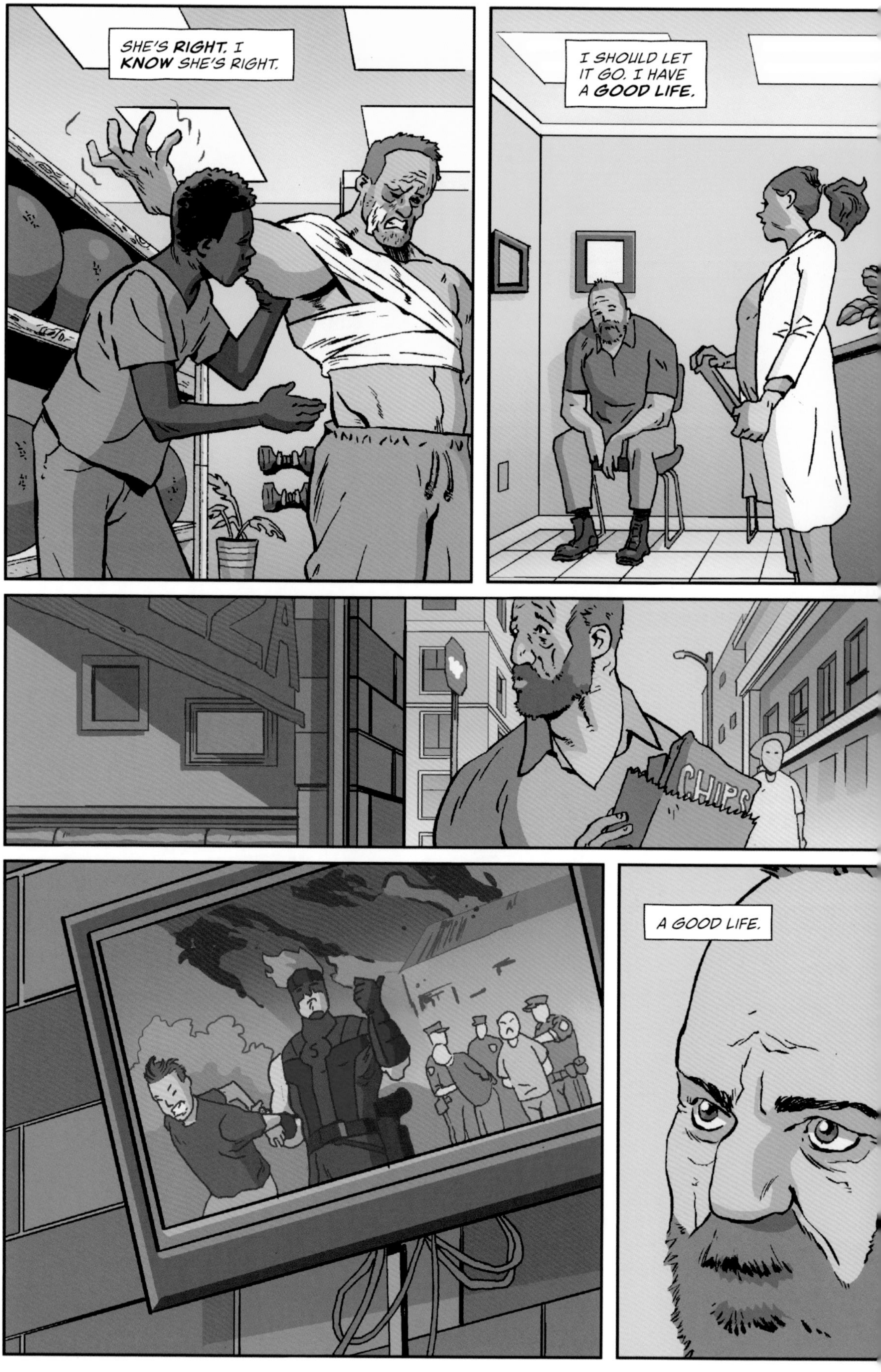
SHE'S **RIGHT.** I **KNOW** SHE'S RIGHT.
I SHOULD LET IT GO. I HAVE A **GOOD LIFE.**
CHIPS
A GOOD LIFE.

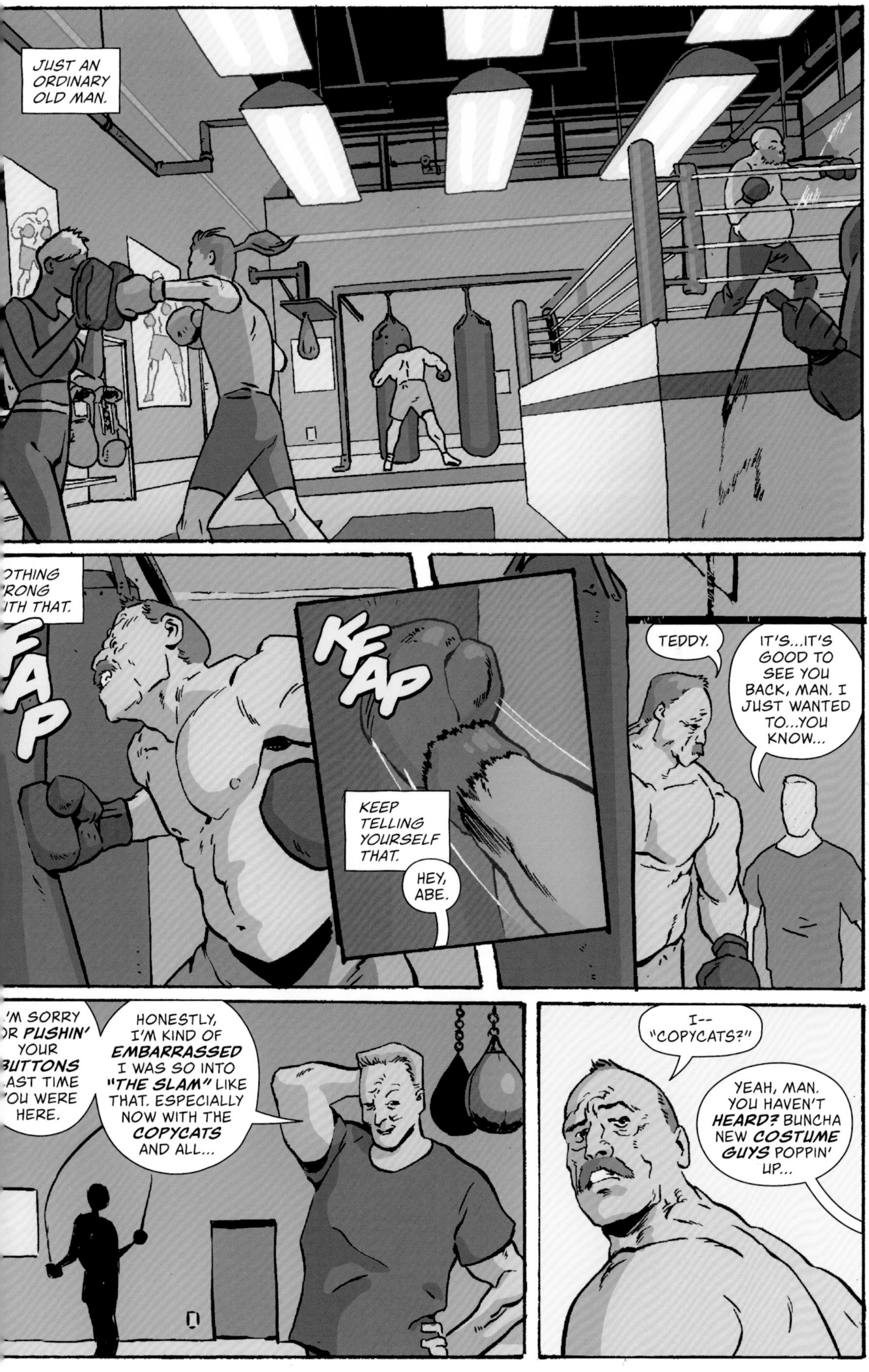

JUST AN ORDINARY OLD MAN.
OTHING RONG ITH THAT.
FAP
KFAP
KEEP TELLING YOURSELF THAT.
HEY, ABE.
TEDDY.
IT'S...IT'S GOOD TO SEE YOU BACK, MAN. I JUST WANTED TO...YOU KNOW...
'M SORRY OR PUSHIN' YOUR BUTTONS AST TIME OU WERE HERE.
HONESTLY, I'M KIND OF EMBARRASSED I WAS SO INTO "THE SLAM" LIKE THAT. ESPECIALLY NOW WITH THE COPYCATS AND ALL...
I-- "COPYCATS?"
YEAH, MAN. YOU HAVEN'T HEARD? BUNCHA NEW COSTUME GUYS POPPIN' UP...

"...PACKIN' *HEAT.*"

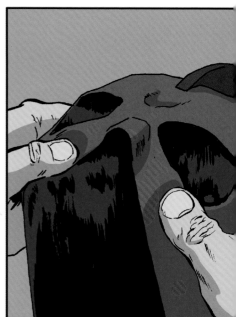

IT'S A GOOD LIFE.

BUT *DAMMIT,* HOW CAN I SIT HERE AND *HAVE* A GOOD LIFE WHEN THERE'S--

brnng
brnng

brnng
brnng

WH-- CASSIE?

HOW *ARE* YOU? I DIDN'T EXPECT--

SLOW DOWN, I CAN'T...

...WHAT?

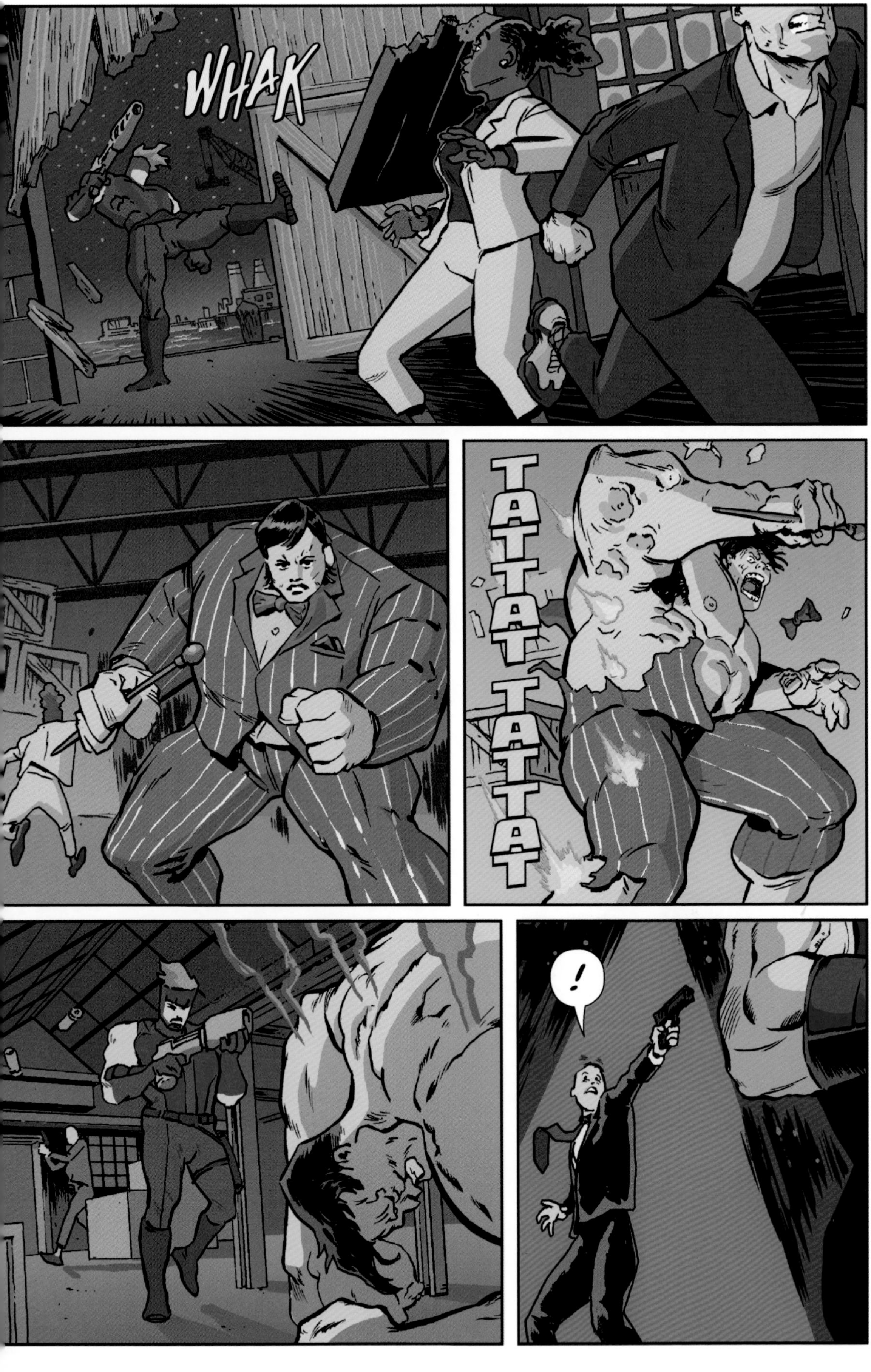
WHAK
TATTAT TATTAT
!

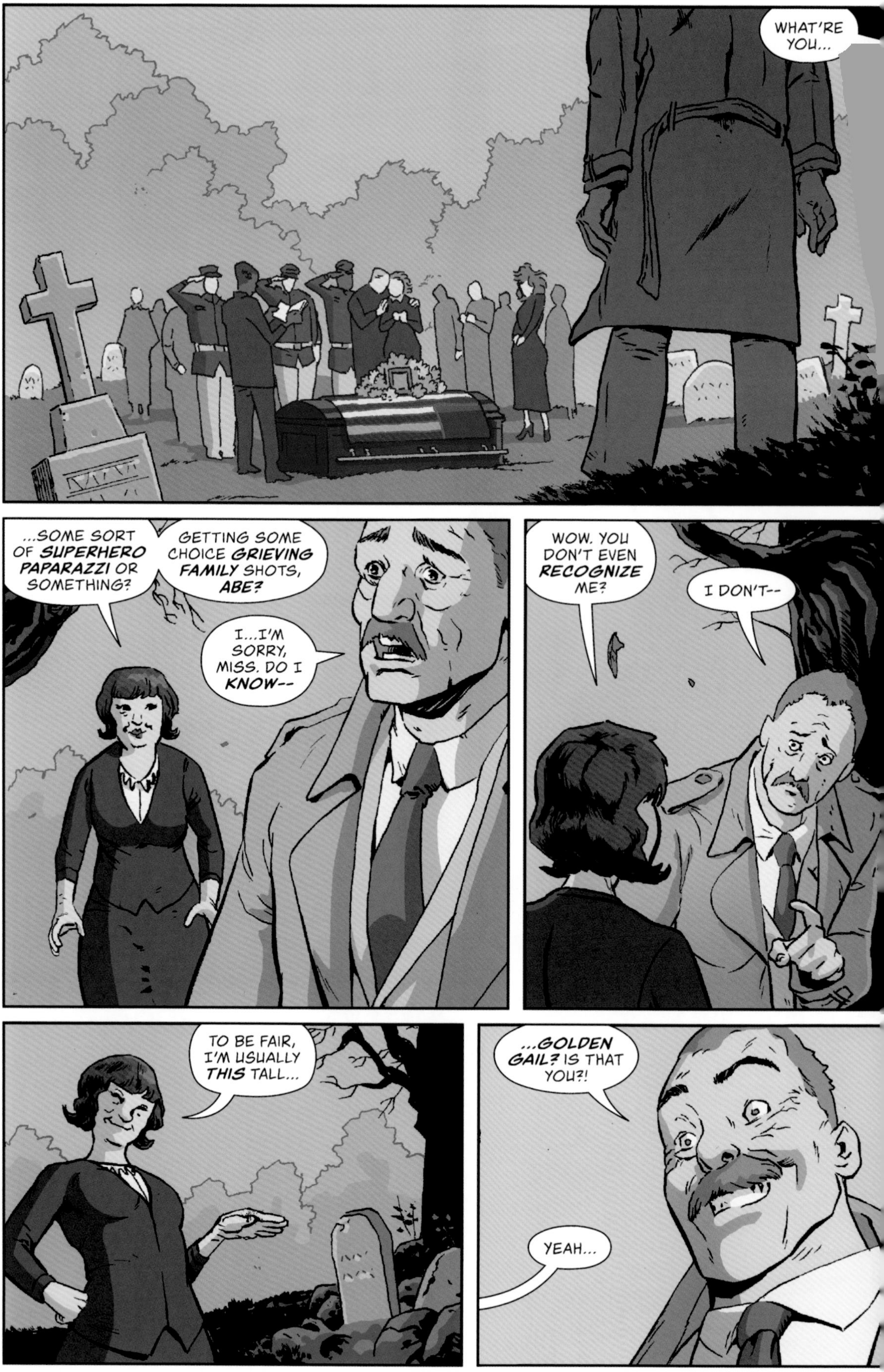
WHAT'RE YOU...
...SOME SORT OF SUPERHERO PAPARAZZI OR SOMETHING?
GETTING SOME CHOICE GRIEVING FAMILY SHOTS, ABE?
I...I'M SORRY, MISS. DO I KNOW--
WOW. YOU DON'T EVEN RECOGNIZE ME?
I DON'T--
TO BE FAIR, I'M USUALLY THIS TALL...
...GOLDEN GAIL? IS THAT YOU?!
YEAH...

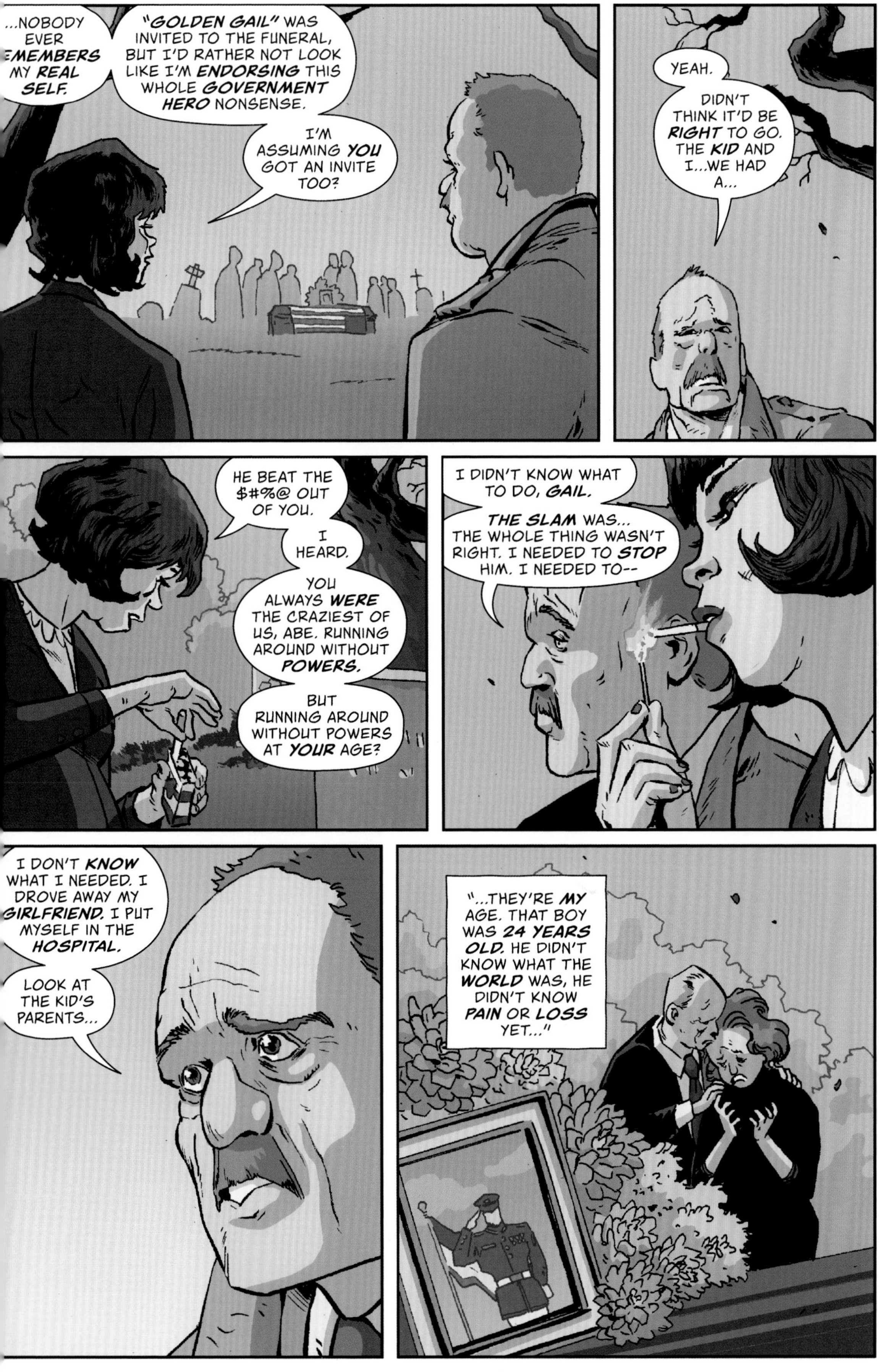
...NOBODY EVER REMEMBERS MY REAL SELF.
"GOLDEN GAIL" WAS INVITED TO THE FUNERAL, BUT I'D RATHER NOT LOOK LIKE I'M ENDORSING THIS WHOLE GOVERNMENT HERO NONSENSE.
I'M ASSUMING YOU GOT AN INVITE TOO?
YEAH.
DIDN'T THINK IT'D BE RIGHT TO GO. THE KID AND I...WE HAD A...
HE BEAT THE $#%@ OUT OF YOU.
I HEARD.
YOU ALWAYS WERE THE CRAZIEST OF US, ABE. RUNNING AROUND WITHOUT POWERS.
BUT RUNNING AROUND WITHOUT POWERS AT YOUR AGE?
I DIDN'T KNOW WHAT TO DO, GAIL.
THE SLAM WAS... THE WHOLE THING WASN'T RIGHT. I NEEDED TO STOP HIM. I NEEDED TO--
I DON'T KNOW WHAT I NEEDED. I DROVE AWAY MY GIRLFRIEND. I PUT MYSELF IN THE HOSPITAL.
LOOK AT THE KID'S PARENTS...
"...THEY'RE MY AGE. THAT BOY WAS 24 YEARS OLD. HE DIDN'T KNOW WHAT THE WORLD WAS, HE DIDN'T KNOW PAIN OR LOSS YET..."

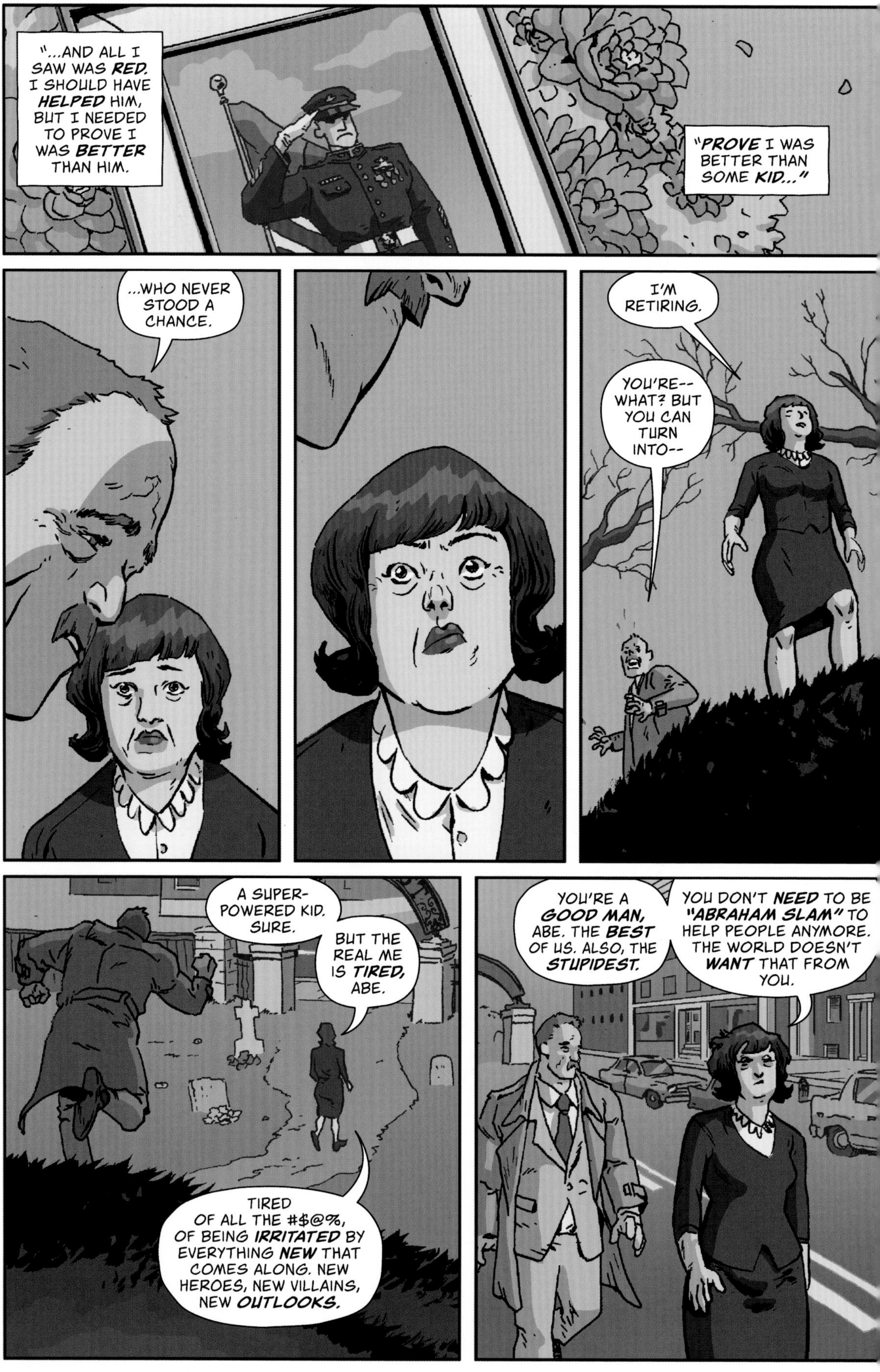
"...AND ALL I SAW WAS RED. I SHOULD HAVE HELPED HIM, BUT I NEEDED TO PROVE I WAS BETTER THAN HIM.
"PROVE I WAS BETTER THAN SOME KID..."
...WHO NEVER STOOD A CHANCE.
I'M RETIRING.
YOU'RE--WHAT? BUT YOU CAN TURN INTO--
A SUPER-POWERED KID, SURE.
BUT THE REAL ME IS TIRED, ABE.
TIRED OF ALL THE #$@%, OF BEING IRRITATED BY EVERYTHING NEW THAT COMES ALONG. NEW HEROES, NEW VILLAINS, NEW OUTLOOKS.
YOU'RE A GOOD MAN, ABE. THE BEST OF US. ALSO, THE STUPIDEST.
YOU DON'T NEED TO BE "ABRAHAM SLAM" TO HELP PEOPLE ANYMORE. THE WORLD DOESN'T WANT THAT FROM YOU.

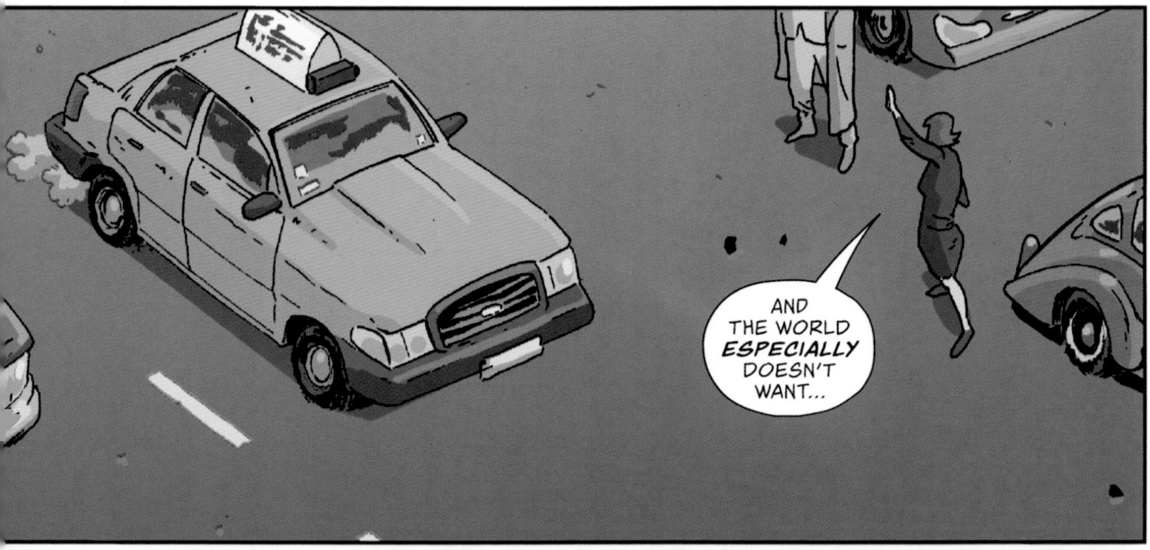
AND THE WORLD ESPECIALLY DOESN'T WANT...

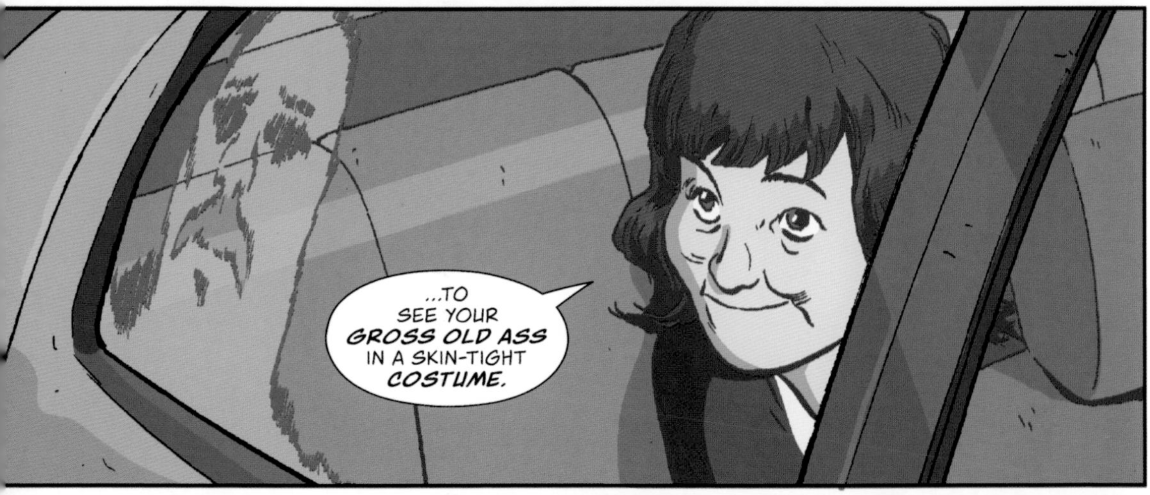
...TO SEE YOUR GROSS OLD ASS IN A SKIN-TIGHT COSTUME.

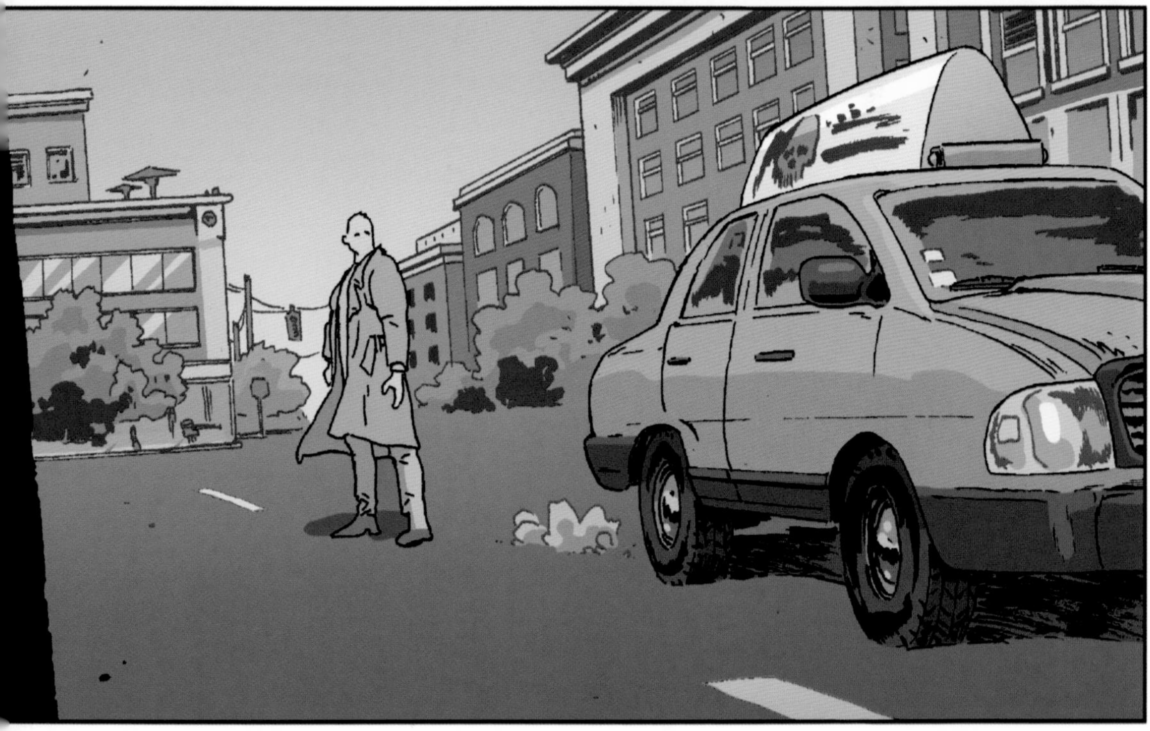

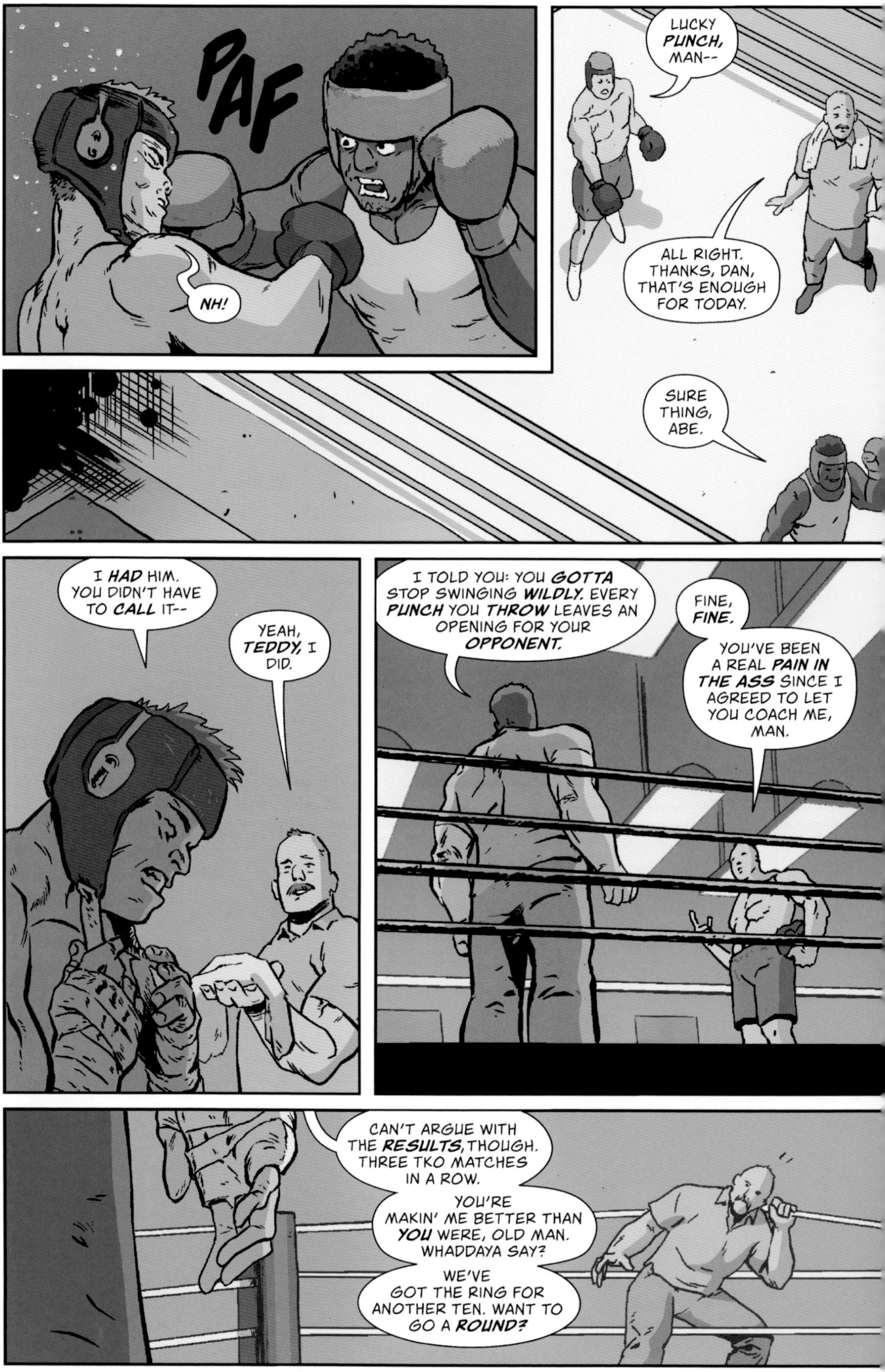
PAF
NH!
LUCKY PUNCH, MAN--
ALL RIGHT. THANKS, DAN, THAT'S ENOUGH FOR TODAY.
SURE THING, ABE.
I HAD HIM. YOU DIDN'T HAVE TO CALL IT--
YEAH, TEDDY, I DID.
I TOLD YOU: YOU GOTTA STOP SWINGING WILDLY. EVERY PUNCH YOU THROW LEAVES AN OPENING FOR YOUR OPPONENT.
FINE, FINE.
YOU'VE BEEN A REAL PAIN IN THE ASS SINCE I AGREED TO LET YOU COACH ME, MAN.
CAN'T ARGUE WITH THE RESULTS, THOUGH. THREE TKO MATCHES IN A ROW.
YOU'RE MAKIN' ME BETTER THAN YOU WERE, OLD MAN. WHADDAYA SAY?
WE'VE GOT THE RING FOR ANOTHER TEN. WANT TO GO A ROUND?

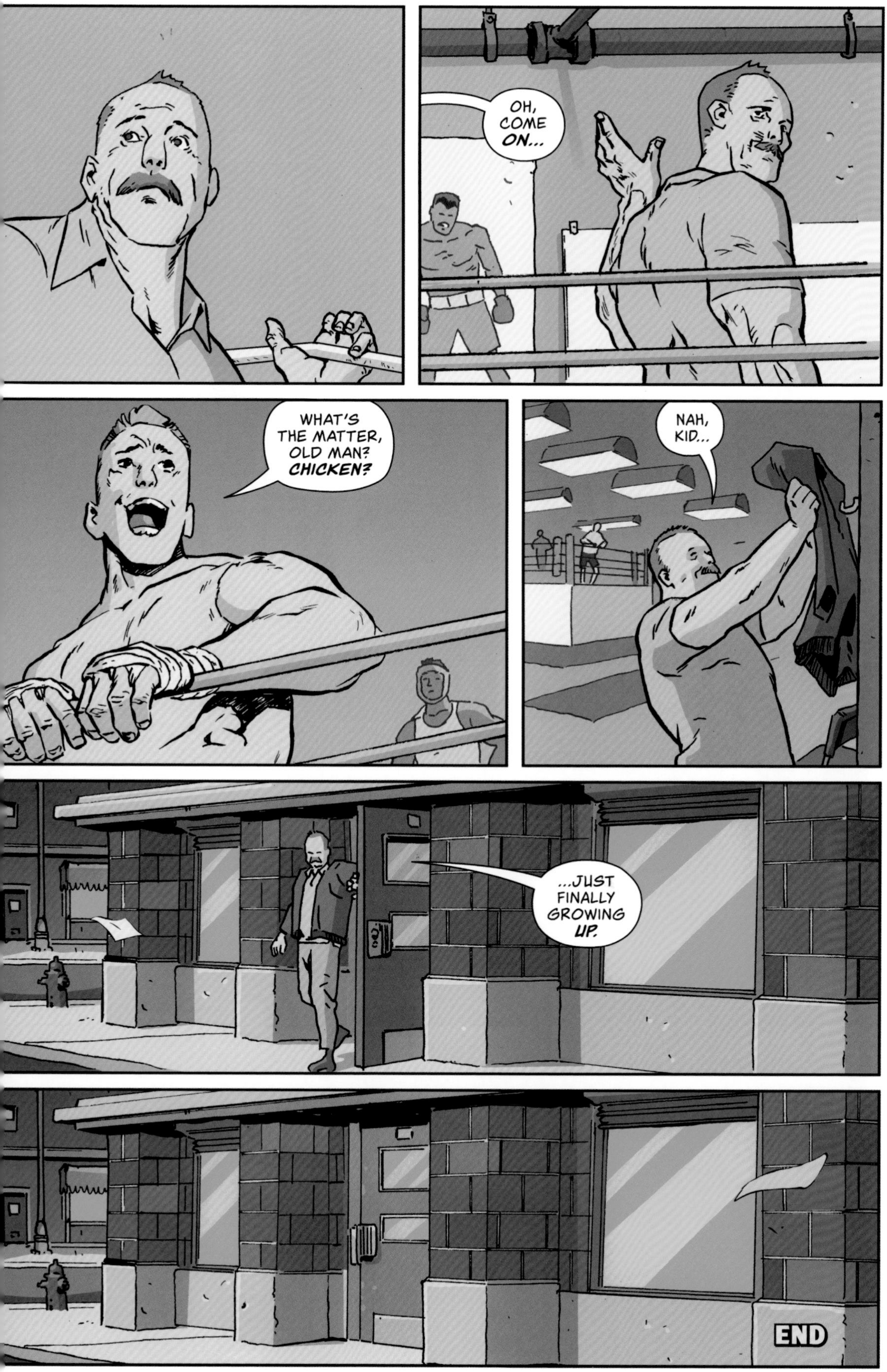
OH, COME ON...
WHAT'S THE MATTER, OLD MAN? CHICKEN?
NAH, KID...
...JUST FINALLY GROWING UP.
END

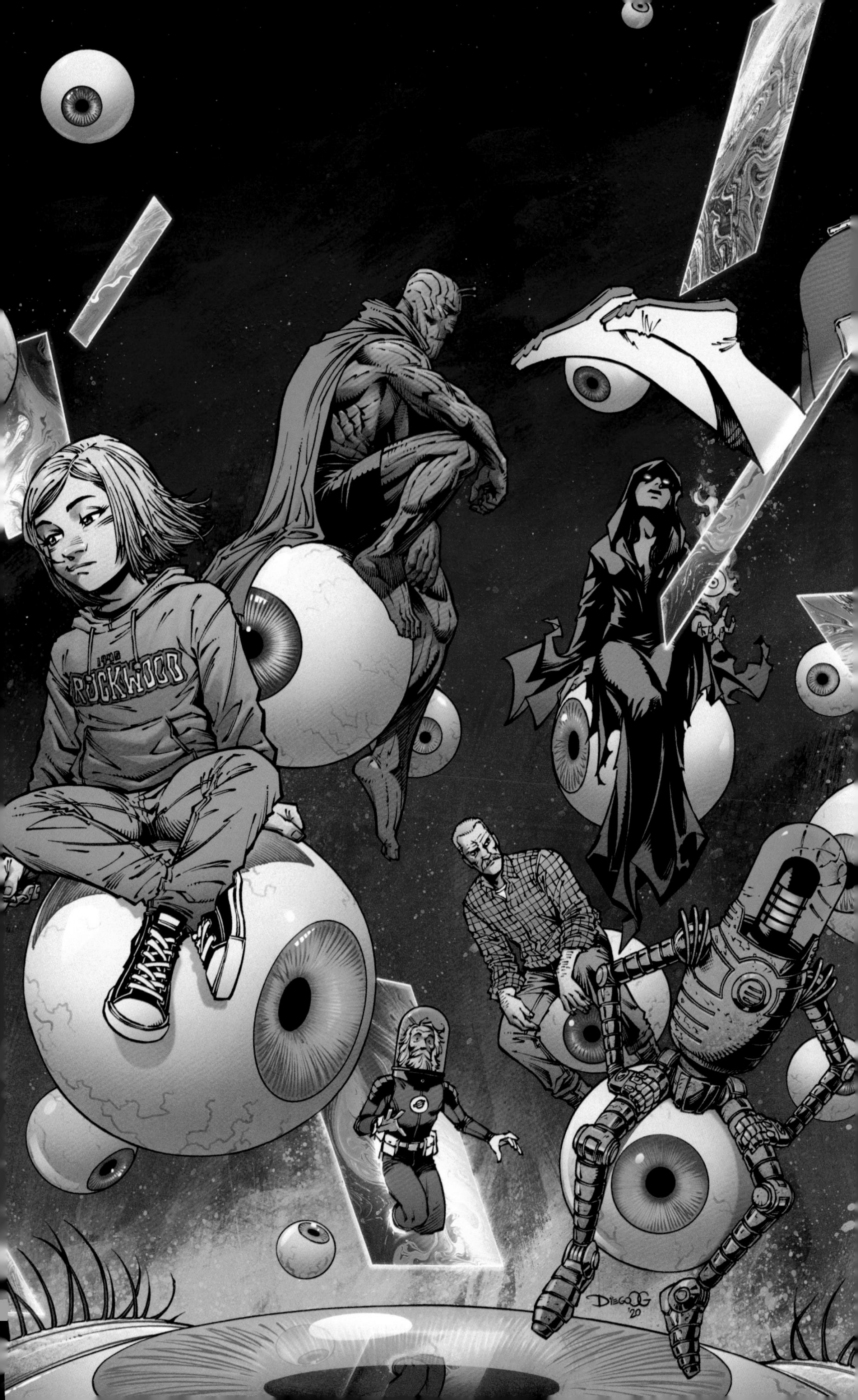
ROCKWOOD

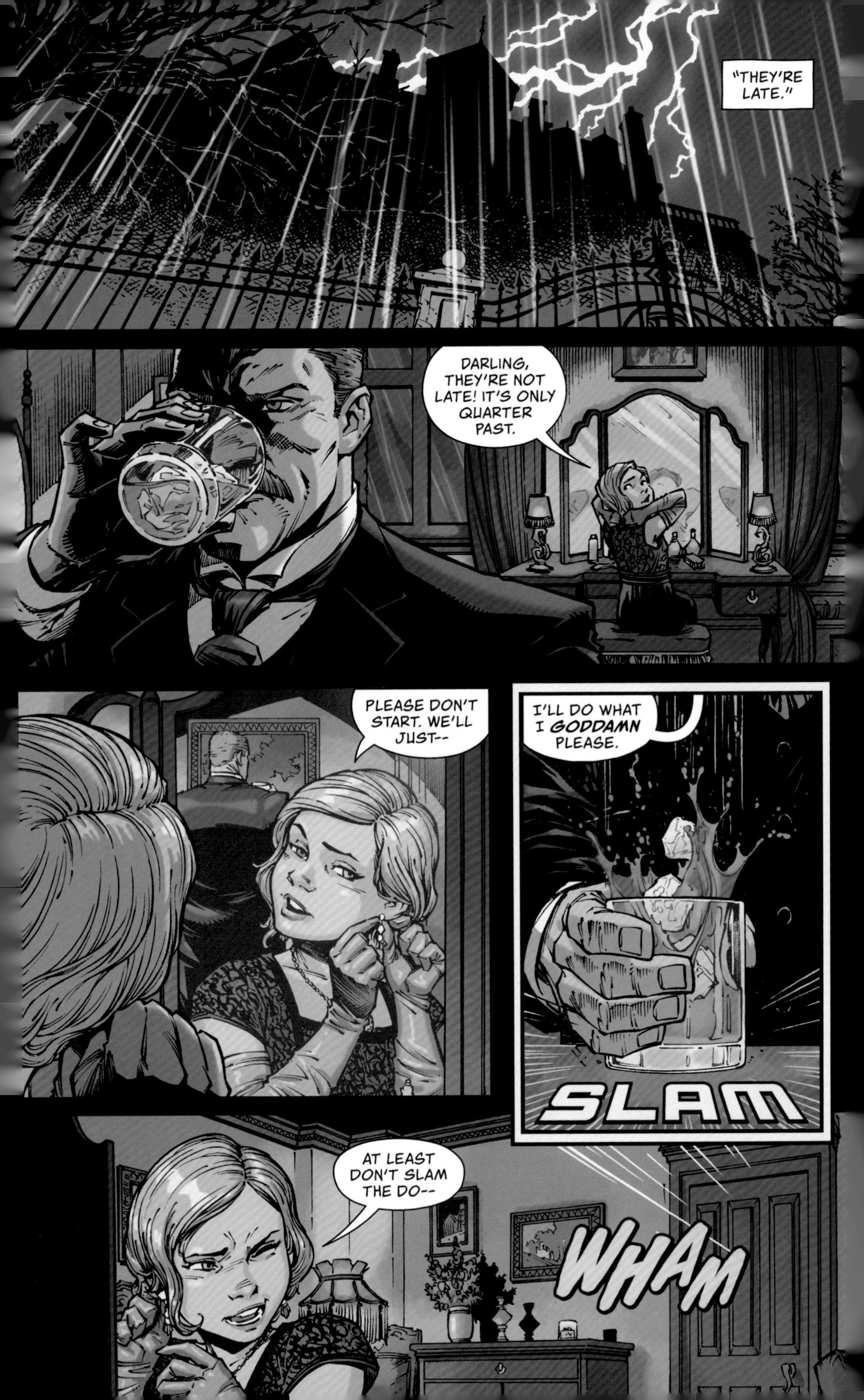
"THEY'RE LATE."
DARLING, THEY'RE NOT LATE! IT'S ONLY QUARTER PAST.
PLEASE DON'T START. WE'LL JUST--
I'LL DO WHAT I *GODDAMN* PLEASE.
SLAM
AT LEAST DON'T SLAM THE DO--
WHAM

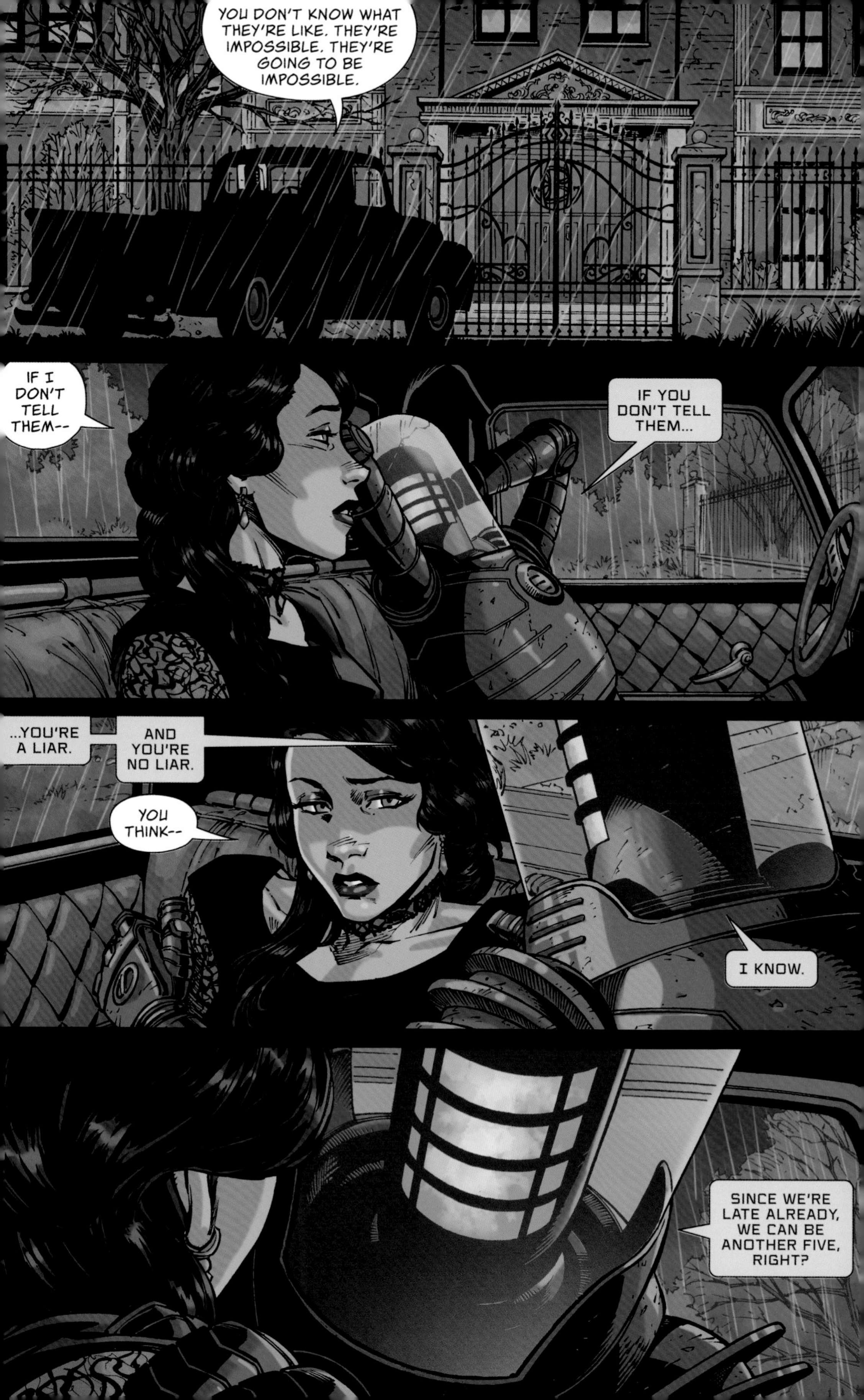
YOU DON'T KNOW WHAT THEY'RE LIKE. THEY'RE IMPOSSIBLE. THEY'RE GOING TO BE IMPOSSIBLE.
IF I DON'T TELL THEM--
IF YOU DON'T TELL THEM...
...YOU'RE A LIAR.
AND YOU'RE NO LIAR.
YOU THINK--
I KNOW.
SINCE WE'RE LATE ALREADY, WE CAN BE ANOTHER FIVE, RIGHT?

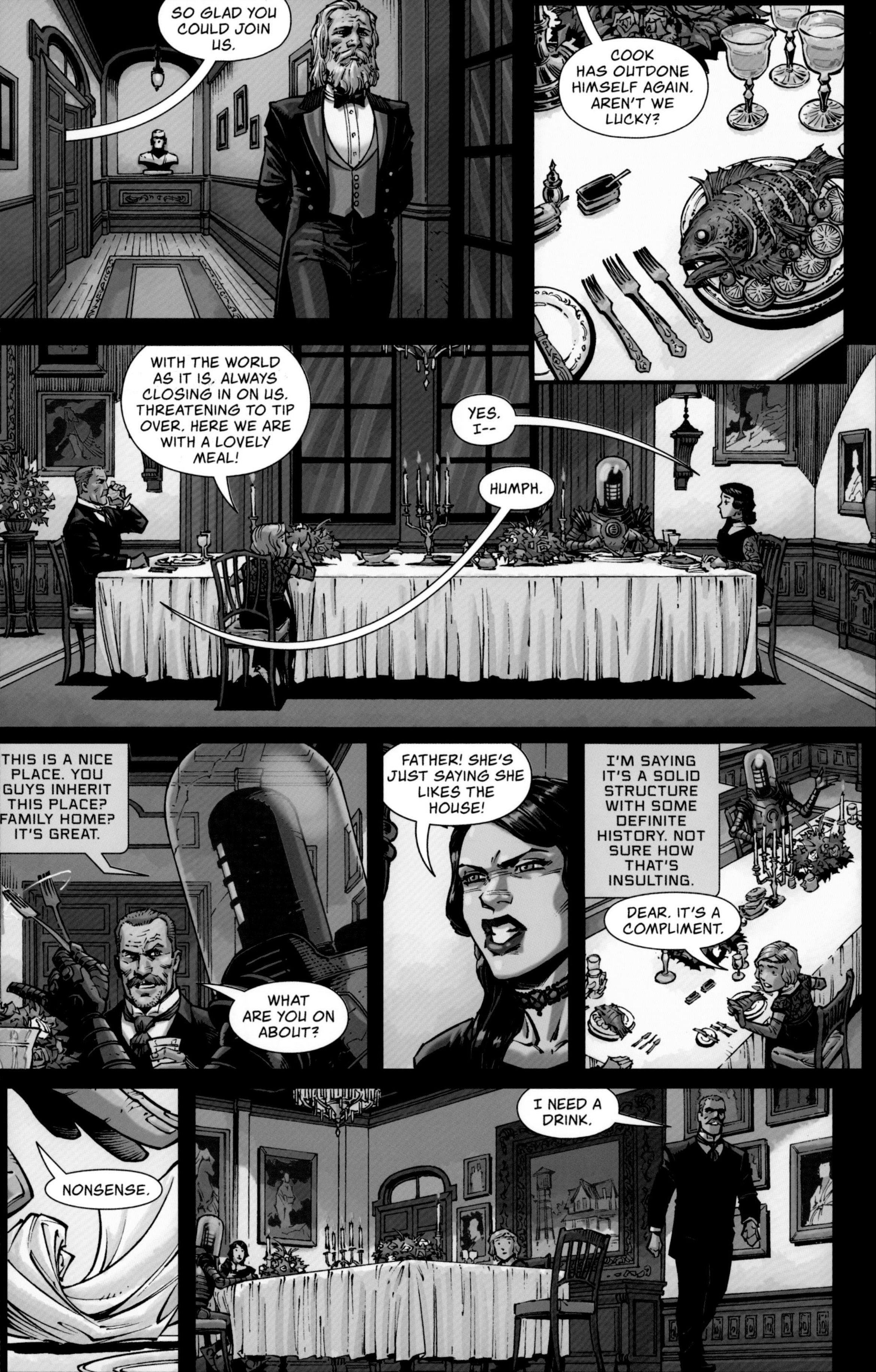
SO GLAD YOU COULD JOIN US.
COOK HAS OUTDONE HIMSELF AGAIN. AREN'T WE LUCKY?
WITH THE WORLD AS IT IS. ALWAYS CLOSING IN ON US. THREATENING TO TIP OVER. HERE WE ARE WITH A LOVELY MEAL!
YES. I--
HUMPH.
THIS IS A NICE PLACE. YOU GUYS INHERIT THIS PLACE? FAMILY HOME? IT'S GREAT.
WHAT ARE YOU ON ABOUT?
FATHER! SHE'S JUST SAYING SHE LIKES THE HOUSE!
I'M SAYING IT'S A SOLID STRUCTURE WITH SOME DEFINITE HISTORY. NOT SURE HOW THAT'S INSULTING.
DEAR. IT'S A COMPLIMENT.
NONSENSE.
I NEED A DRINK.

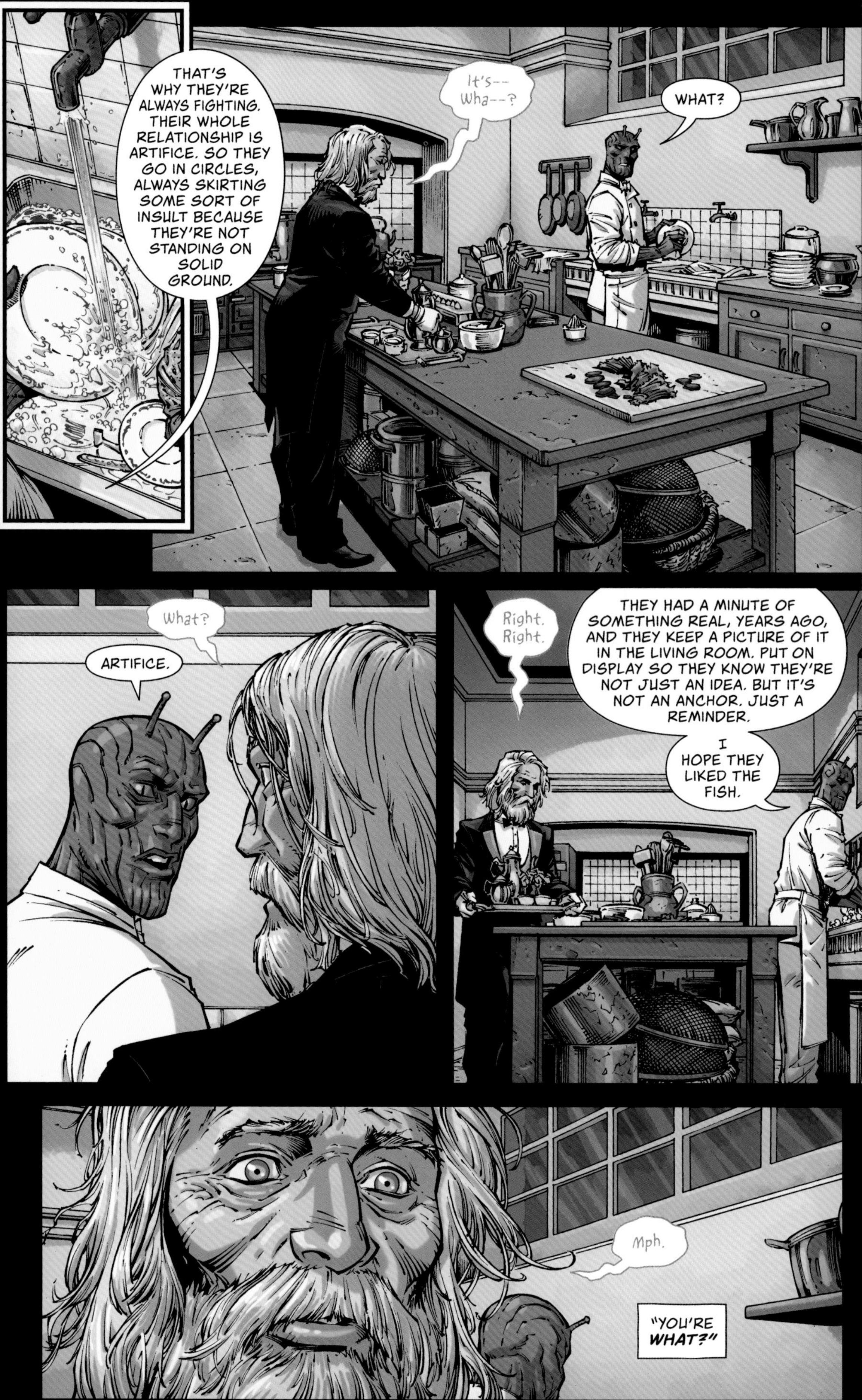
THAT'S WHY THEY'RE ALWAYS FIGHTING. THEIR WHOLE RELATIONSHIP IS ARTIFICE. SO THEY GO IN CIRCLES, ALWAYS SKIRTING SOME SORT OF INSULT BECAUSE THEY'RE NOT STANDING ON SOLID GROUND.
It's-- Wha--?
WHAT?
ARTIFICE.
What?
Right. Right.
THEY HAD A MINUTE OF SOMETHING REAL, YEARS AGO, AND THEY KEEP A PICTURE OF IT IN THE LIVING ROOM. PUT ON DISPLAY SO THEY KNOW THEY'RE NOT JUST AN IDEA. BUT IT'S NOT AN ANCHOR. JUST A REMINDER.
I HOPE THEY LIKED THE FISH.
Mph.
"YOU'RE *WHAT?*"

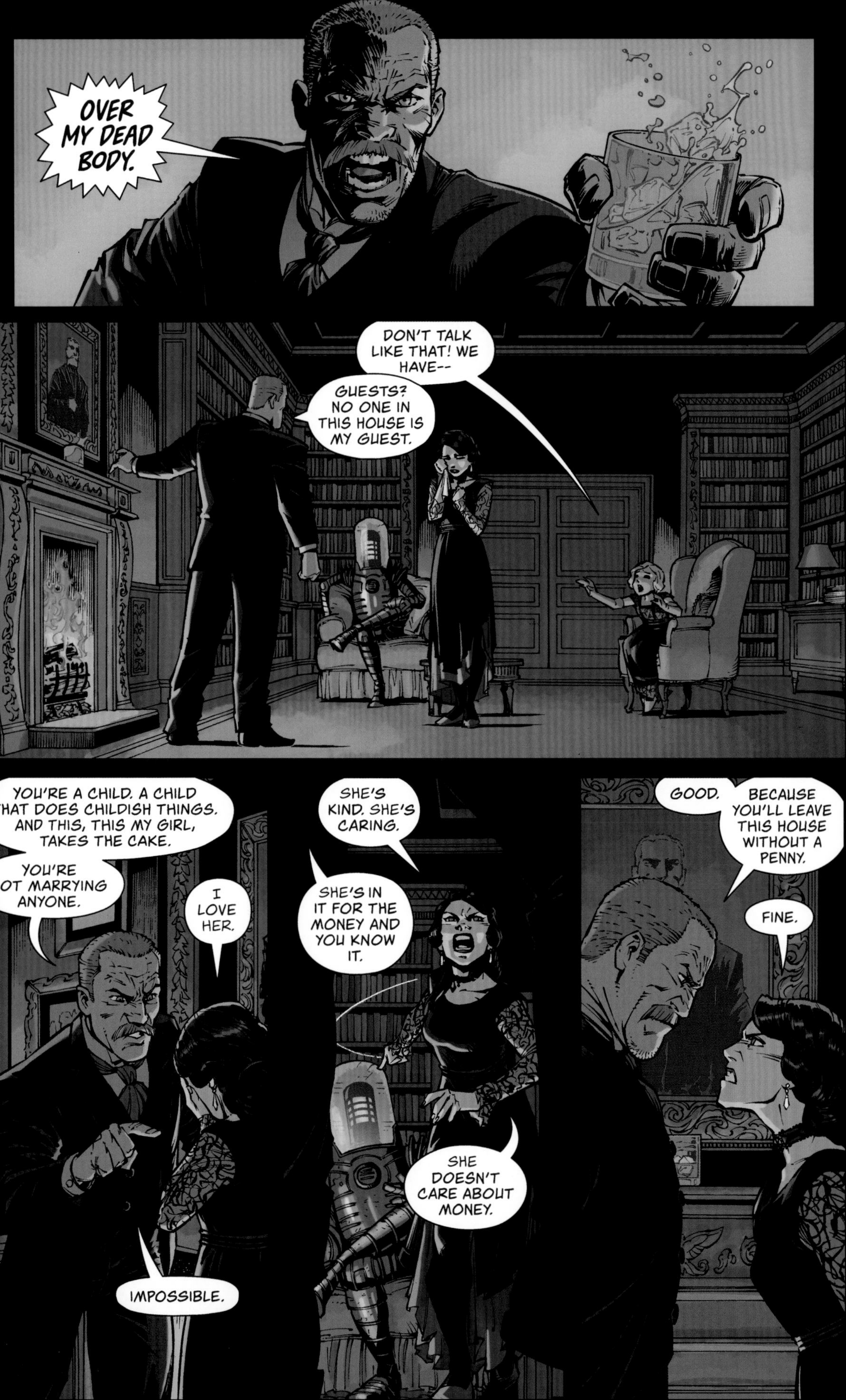
OVER MY DEAD BODY.
DON'T TALK LIKE THAT! WE HAVE--
GUESTS? NO ONE IN THIS HOUSE IS MY GUEST.
YOU'RE A CHILD. A CHILD THAT DOES CHILDISH THINGS. AND THIS, THIS MY GIRL, TAKES THE CAKE.
YOU'RE OT MARRYING ANYONE.
I LOVE HER.
IMPOSSIBLE.
SHE'S KIND. SHE'S CARING.
SHE'S IN IT FOR THE MONEY AND YOU KNOW IT.
SHE DOESN'T CARE ABOUT MONEY.
GOOD.
BECAUSE YOU'LL LEAVE THIS HOUSE WITHOUT A PENNY.
FINE.

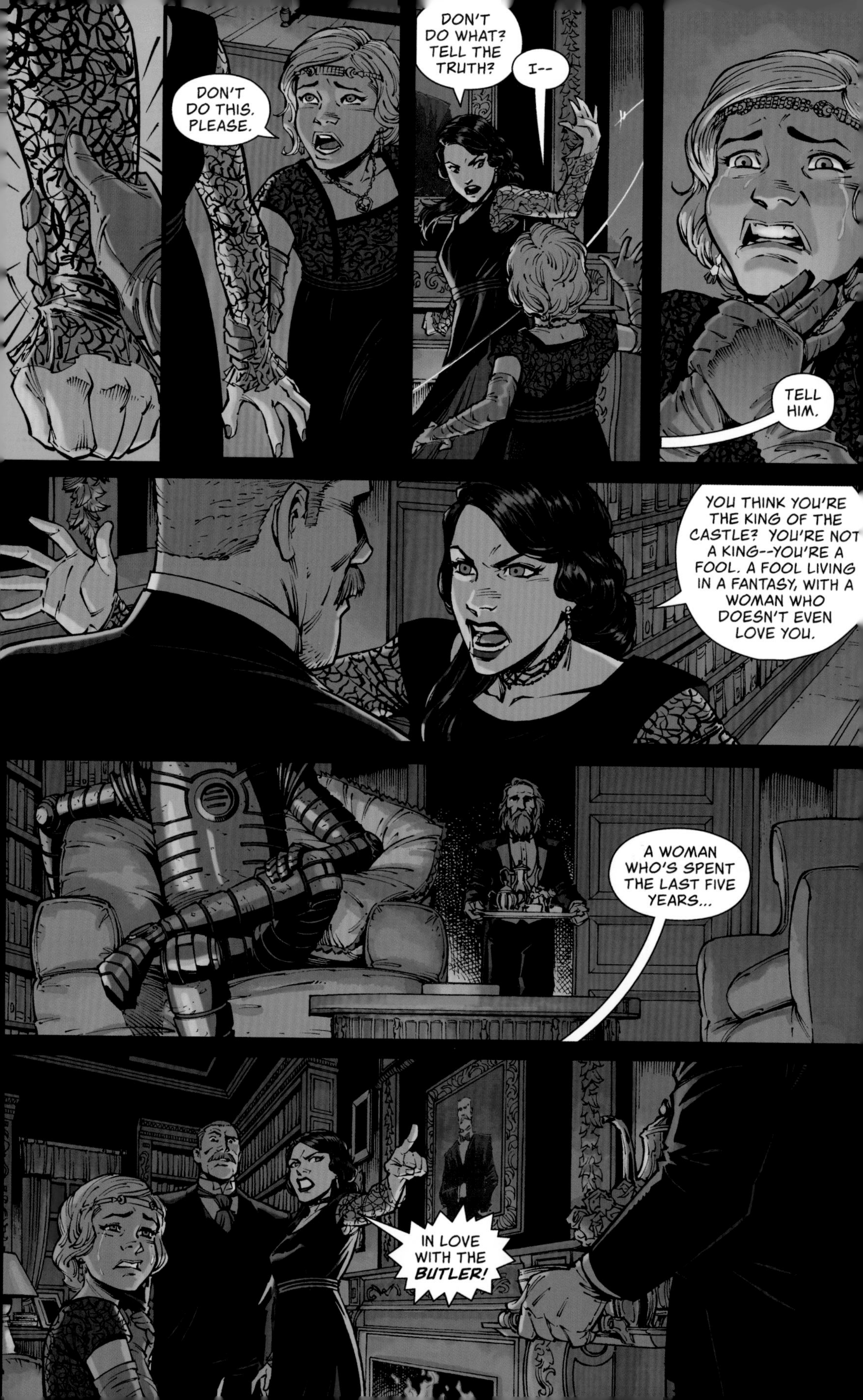
DON'T
DO THIS.
PLEASE.
DON'T
DO WHAT?
TELL THE
TRUTH?
I--
TELL
HIM.
YOU THINK YOU'RE THE KING OF THE CASTLE? YOU'RE NOT A KING--YOU'RE A FOOL. A FOOL LIVING IN A FANTASY, WITH A WOMAN WHO DOESN'T EVEN LOVE YOU.
A WOMAN WHO'S SPENT THE LAST FIVE YEARS...
IN LOVE WITH THE *BUTLER!*

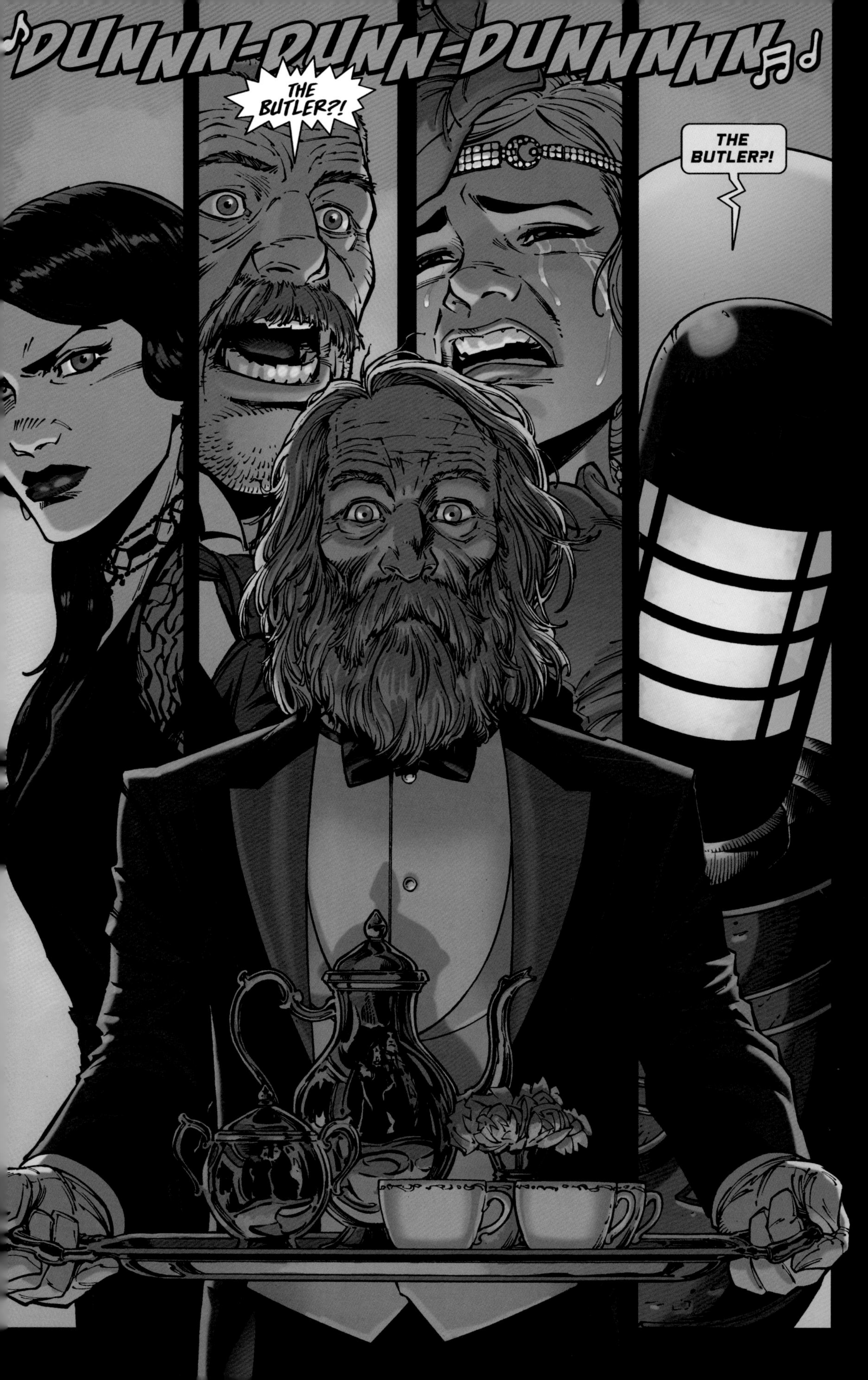
DUNNN-DUNN-DUNNNNN
THE BUTLER?!
THE BUTLER?!

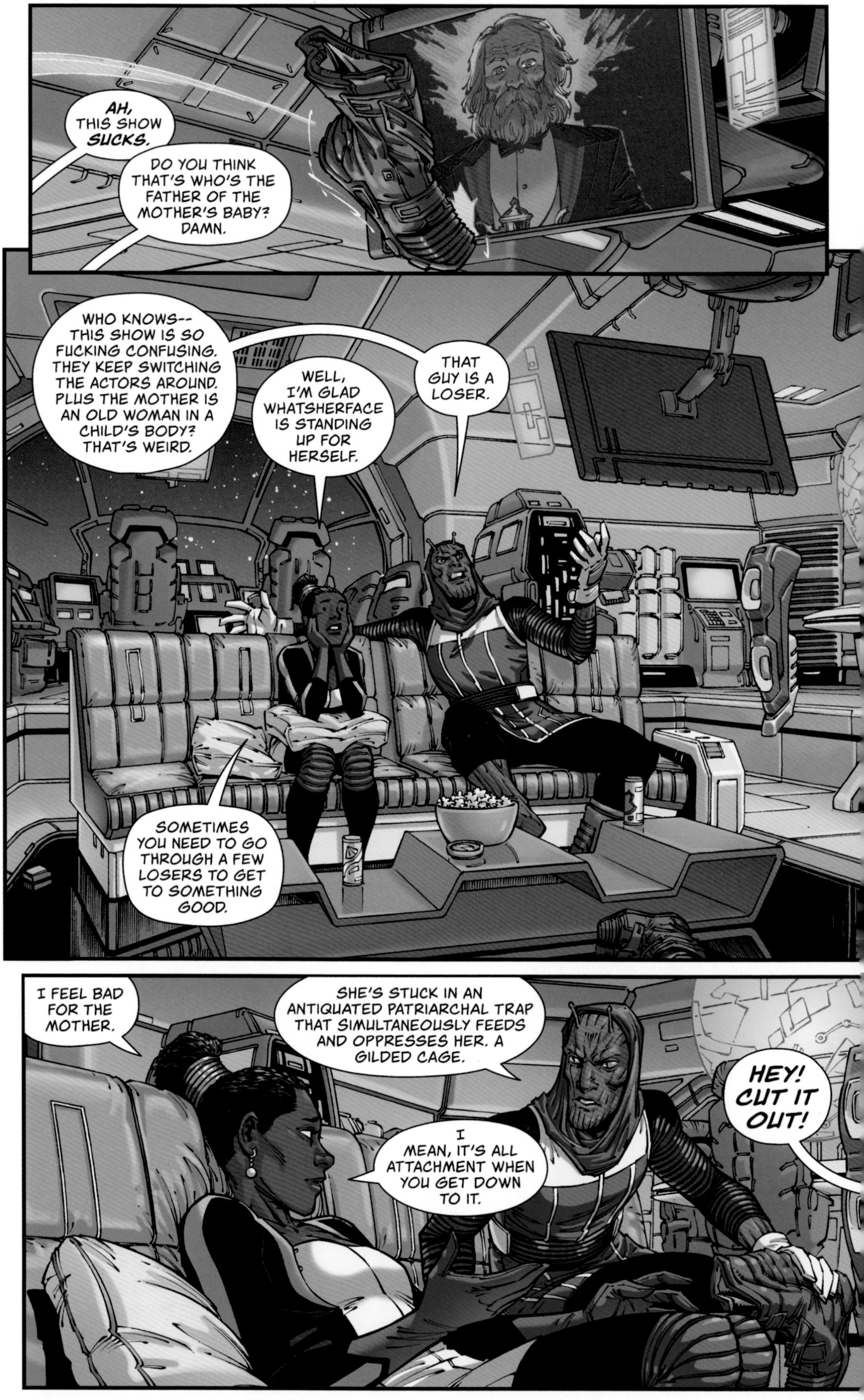
AH, THIS SHOW SUCKS.
DO YOU THINK THAT'S WHO'S THE FATHER OF THE MOTHER'S BABY? DAMN.
WHO KNOWS-- THIS SHOW IS SO FUCKING CONFUSING. THEY KEEP SWITCHING THE ACTORS AROUND. PLUS THE MOTHER IS AN OLD WOMAN IN A CHILD'S BODY? THAT'S WEIRD.
WELL, I'M GLAD WHATSHERFACE IS STANDING UP FOR HERSELF.
THAT GUY IS A LOSER.
SOMETIMES YOU NEED TO GO THROUGH A FEW LOSERS TO GET TO SOMETHING GOOD.
I FEEL BAD FOR THE MOTHER.
SHE'S STUCK IN AN ANTIQUATED PATRIARCHAL TRAP THAT SIMULTANEOUSLY FEEDS AND OPPRESSES HER. A GILDED CAGE.
I MEAN, IT'S ALL ATTACHMENT WHEN YOU GET DOWN TO IT.
HEY! CUT IT OUT!

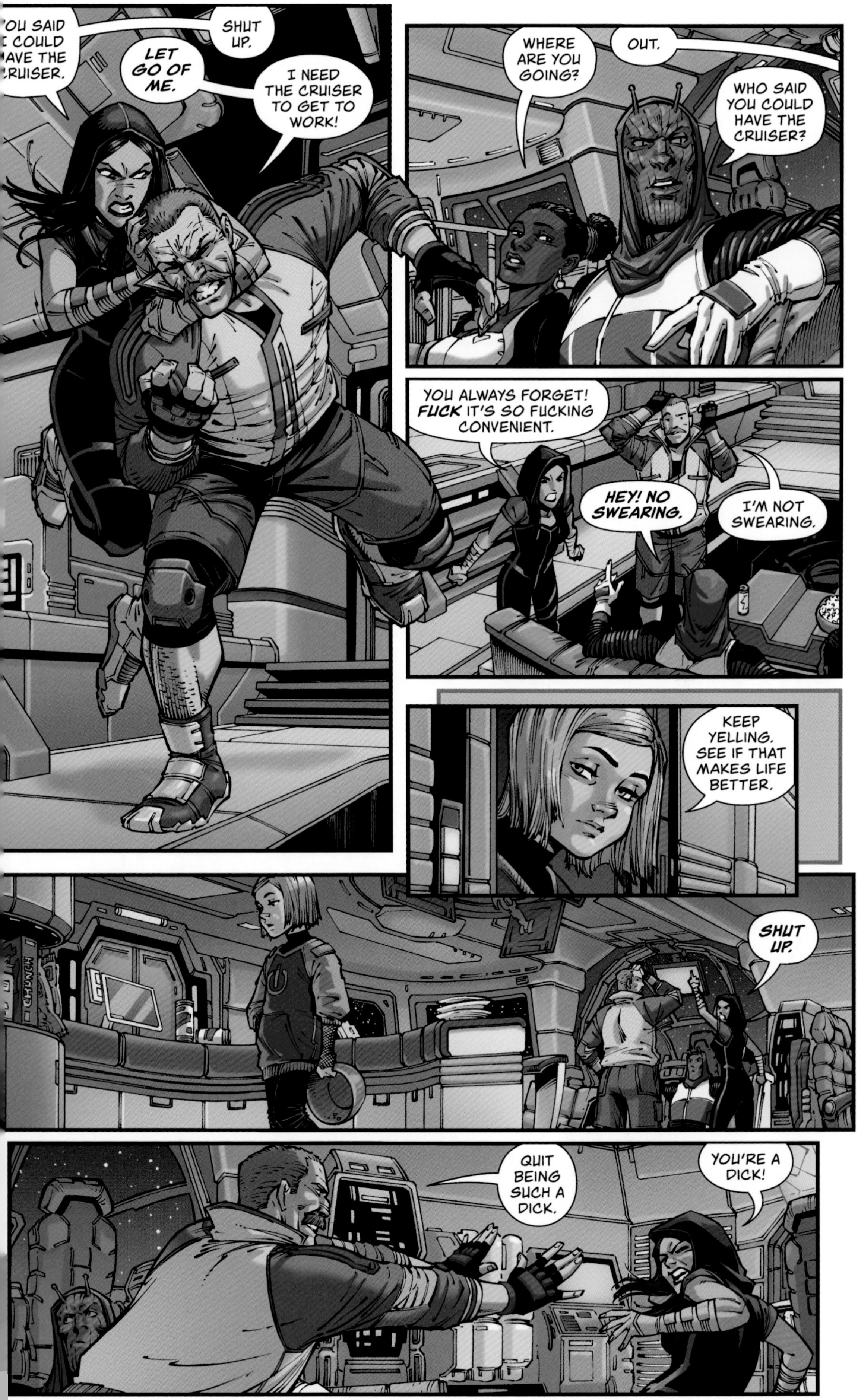
OU SAID COULD AVE THE RUISER.
SHUT UP.
LET GO OF ME.
I NEED THE CRUISER TO GET TO WORK!
WHERE ARE YOU GOING?
OUT.
WHO SAID YOU COULD HAVE THE CRUISER?
YOU ALWAYS FORGET! FUCK IT'S SO FUCKING CONVENIENT.
HEY! NO SWEARING.
I'M NOT SWEARING.
KEEP YELLING. SEE IF THAT MAKES LIFE BETTER.
SHUT UP.
QUIT BEING SUCH A DICK.
YOU'RE A DICK!

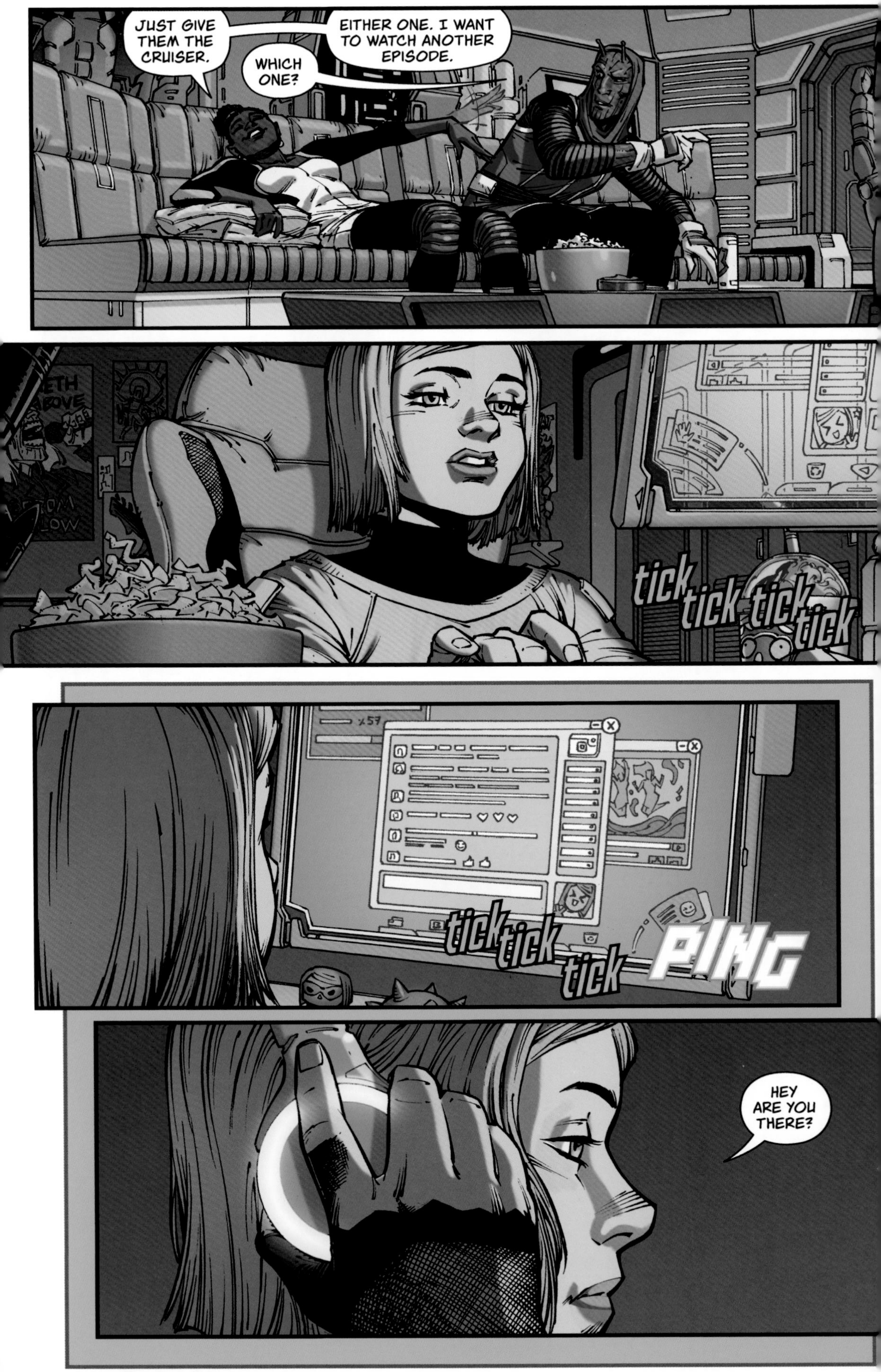
JUST GIVE THEM THE CRUISER.
WHICH ONE?
EITHER ONE. I WANT TO WATCH ANOTHER EPISODE.
tick tick tick tick
tick tick tick
PING
HEY ARE YOU THERE?

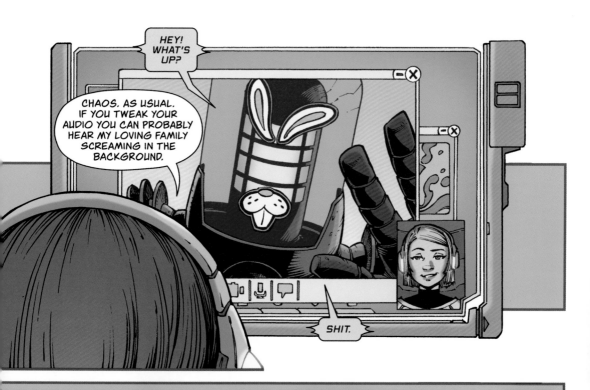

HEY! WHAT'S UP?

CHAOS. AS USUAL. IF YOU TWEAK YOUR AUDIO YOU CAN PROBABLY HEAR MY LOVING FAMILY SCREAMING IN THE BACKGROUND.

SHIT.

MAYBE EVERYONE IN THE WHOLE GALAXY IS AN ASSHOLE AND MY FAMILY ARE JUST SPECIAL SPECIMENS OF ULTRA ASSHOLES?

POSSIBLY.

I'M HOPING THEY GET LOST IN A BLACK HOLE AND DIE AND I'LL NEVER SEE THEM AGAIN.

I SUPPORT THAT HOPE.

DID YOU EVER READ THAT STORY ABOUT THE KID AND THE SUNBEAM WHEN YOU WERE LITTLE?

LIKE WHO'S THE SUNBEAM AND WHO'S THE CLOUD?

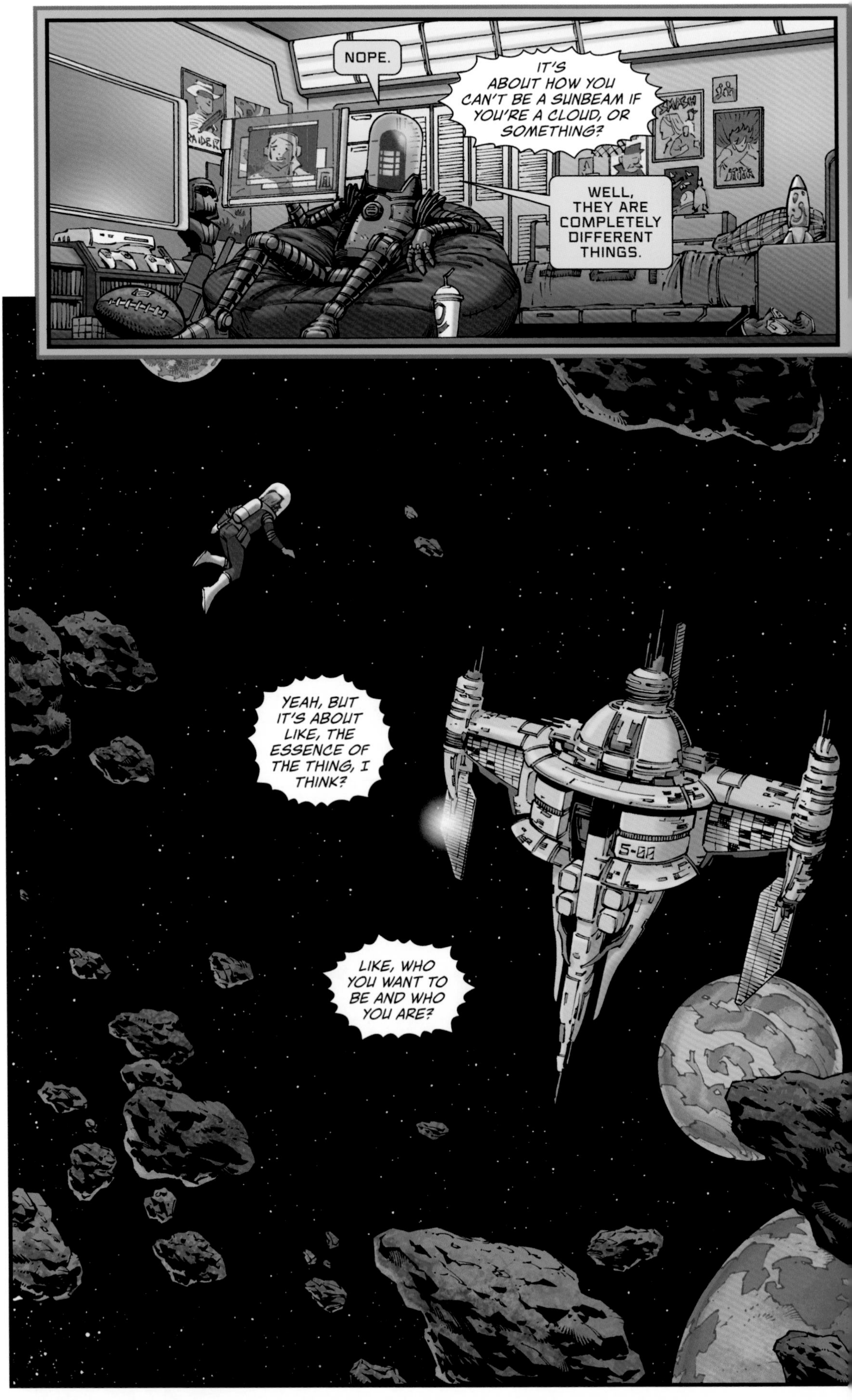
NOPE.
IT'S ABOUT HOW YOU CAN'T BE A SUNBEAM IF YOU'RE A CLOUD, OR SOMETHING?
WELL, THEY ARE COMPLETELY DIFFERENT THINGS.
YEAH, BUT IT'S ABOUT LIKE, THE ESSENCE OF THE THING, I THINK?
LIKE, WHO YOU WANT TO BE AND WHO YOU ARE?

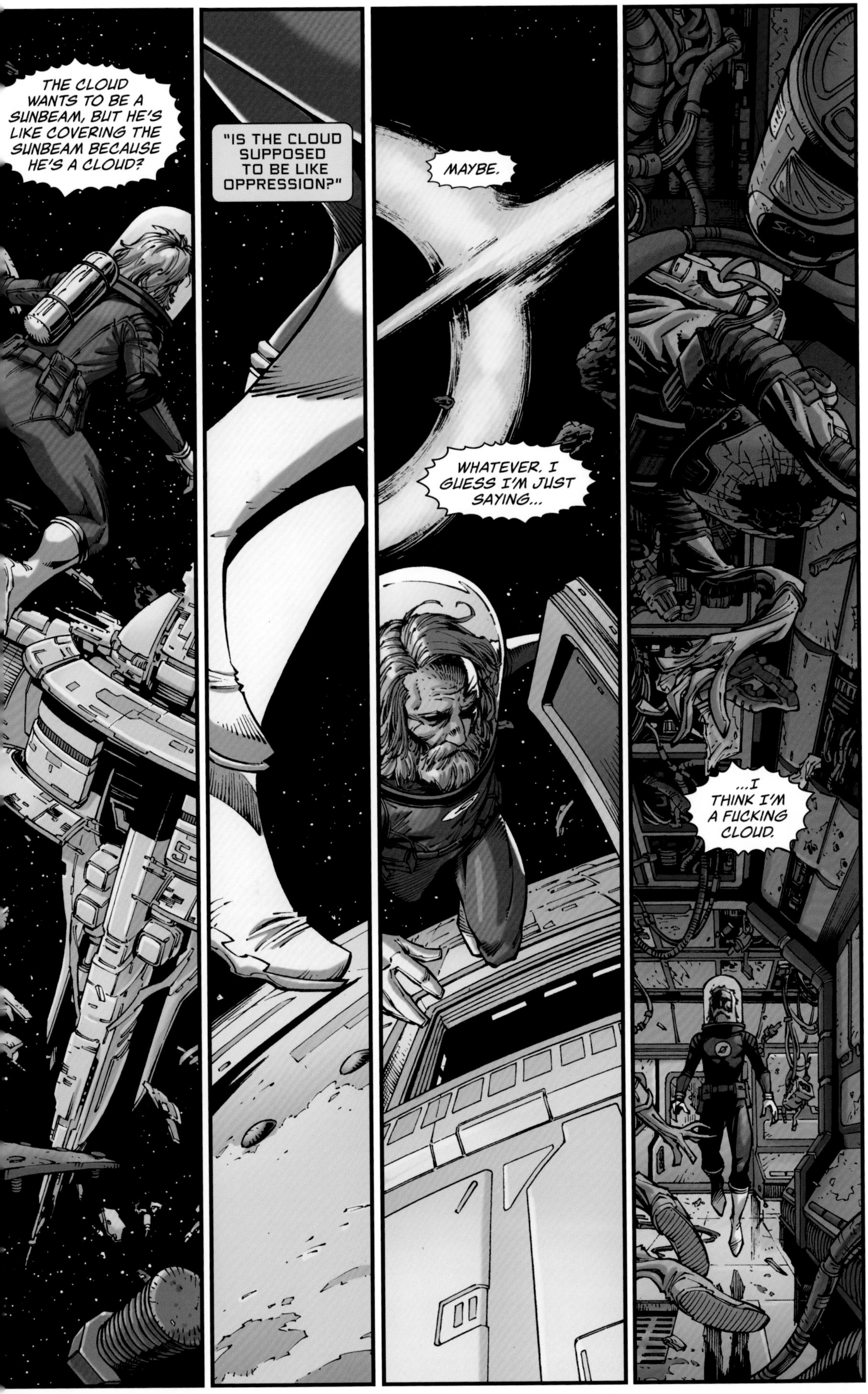
THE CLOUD WANTS TO BE A SUNBEAM, BUT HE'S LIKE COVERING THE SUNBEAM BECAUSE HE'S A CLOUD?
"IS THE CLOUD SUPPOSED TO BE LIKE OPPRESSION?"
MAYBE.
WHATEVER. I GUESS I'M JUST SAYING...
...I THINK I'M A FUCKING CLOUD.

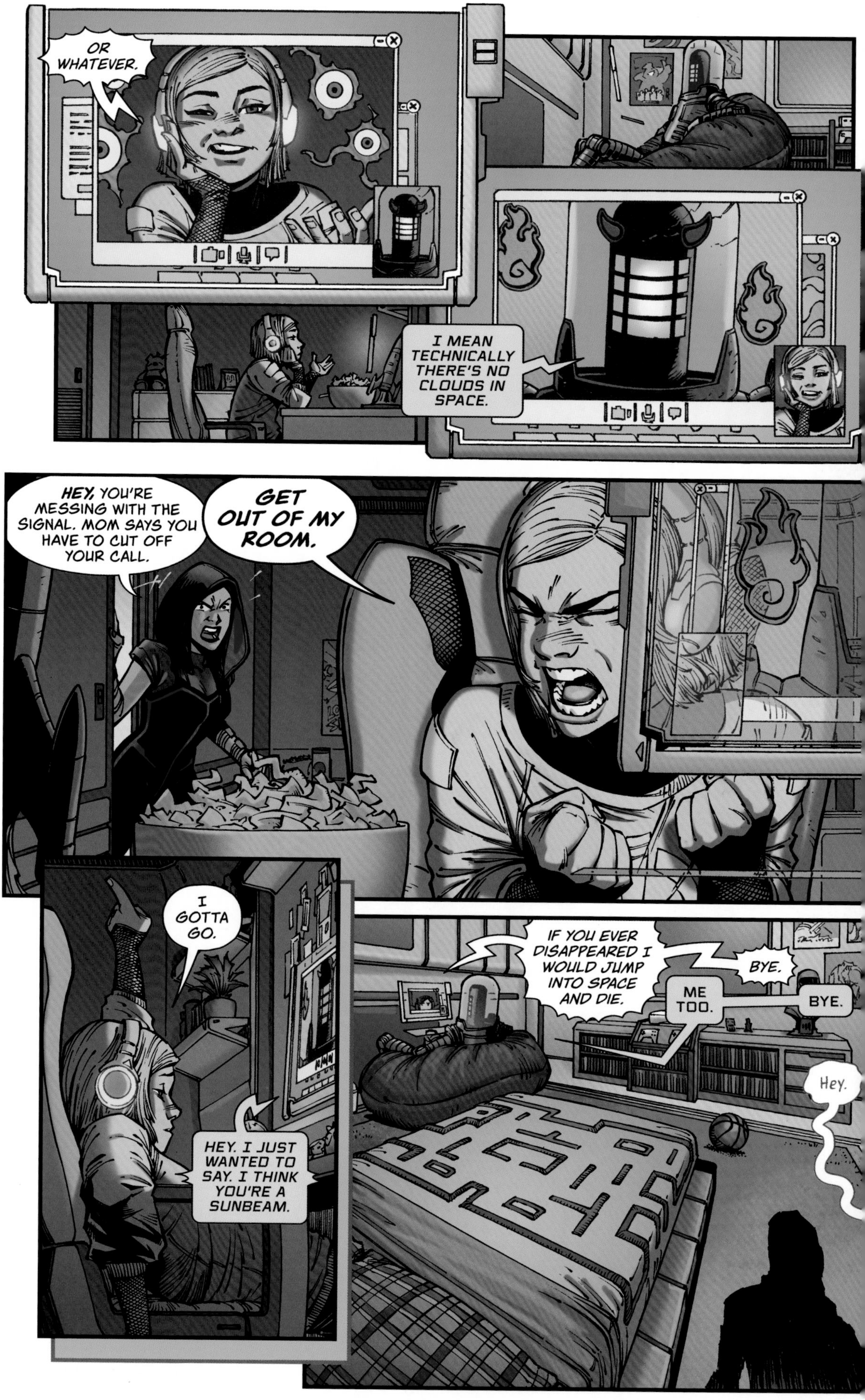
OR WHATEVER.
I MEAN TECHNICALLY THERE'S NO CLOUDS IN SPACE.
HEY, YOU'RE MESSING WITH THE SIGNAL. MOM SAYS YOU HAVE TO CUT OFF YOUR CALL.
GET OUT OF MY ROOM.
I GOTTA GO.
HEY. I JUST WANTED TO SAY. I THINK YOU'RE A SUNBEAM.
IF YOU EVER DISAPPEARED I WOULD JUMP INTO SPACE AND DIE.
ME TOO.
BYE.
BYE.
Hey.

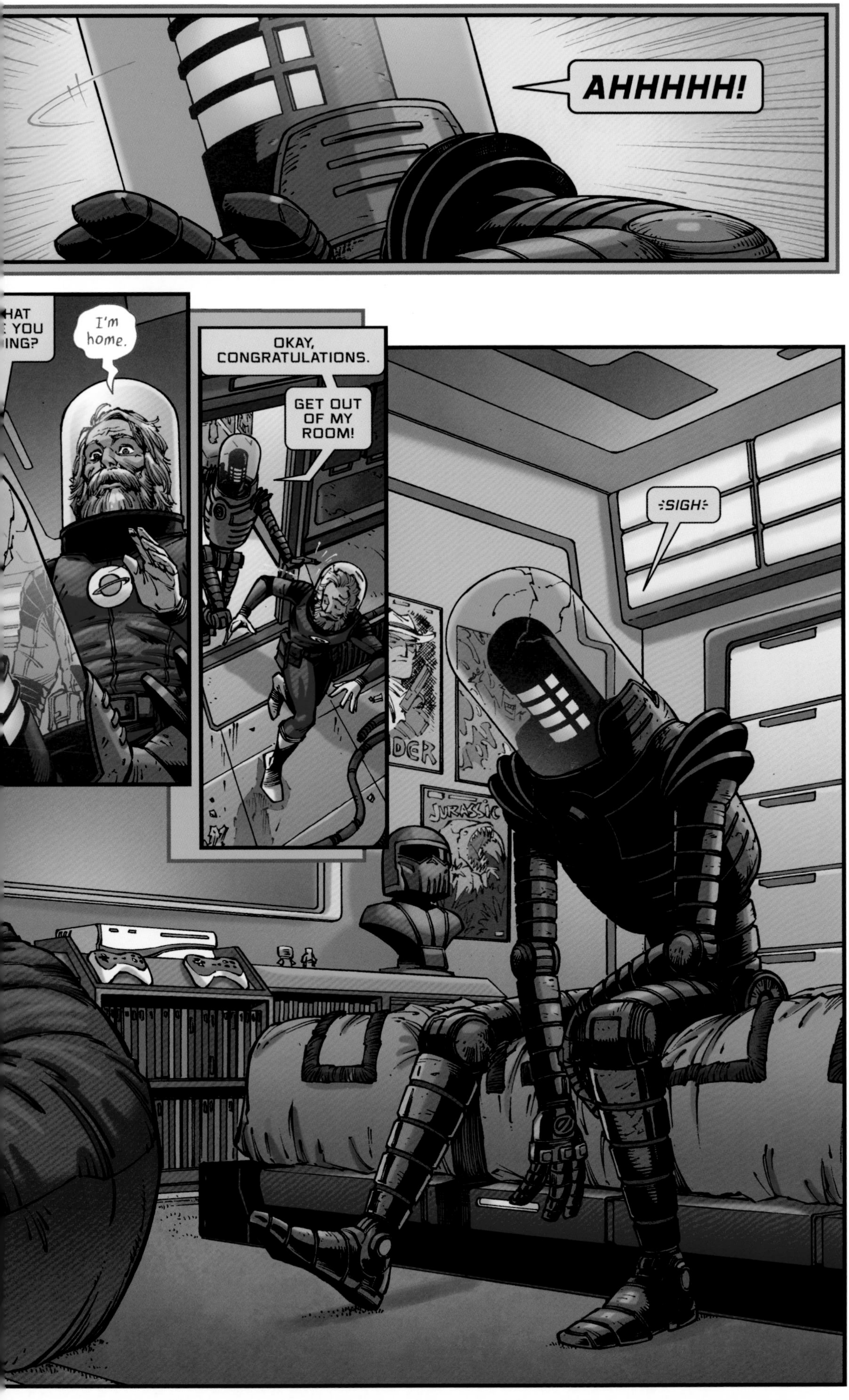
AHHHHH!
HAT
E YOU
ING?
I'm home.
OKAY, CONGRATULATIONS.
GET OUT OF MY ROOM!
JURASSIC
SIGH

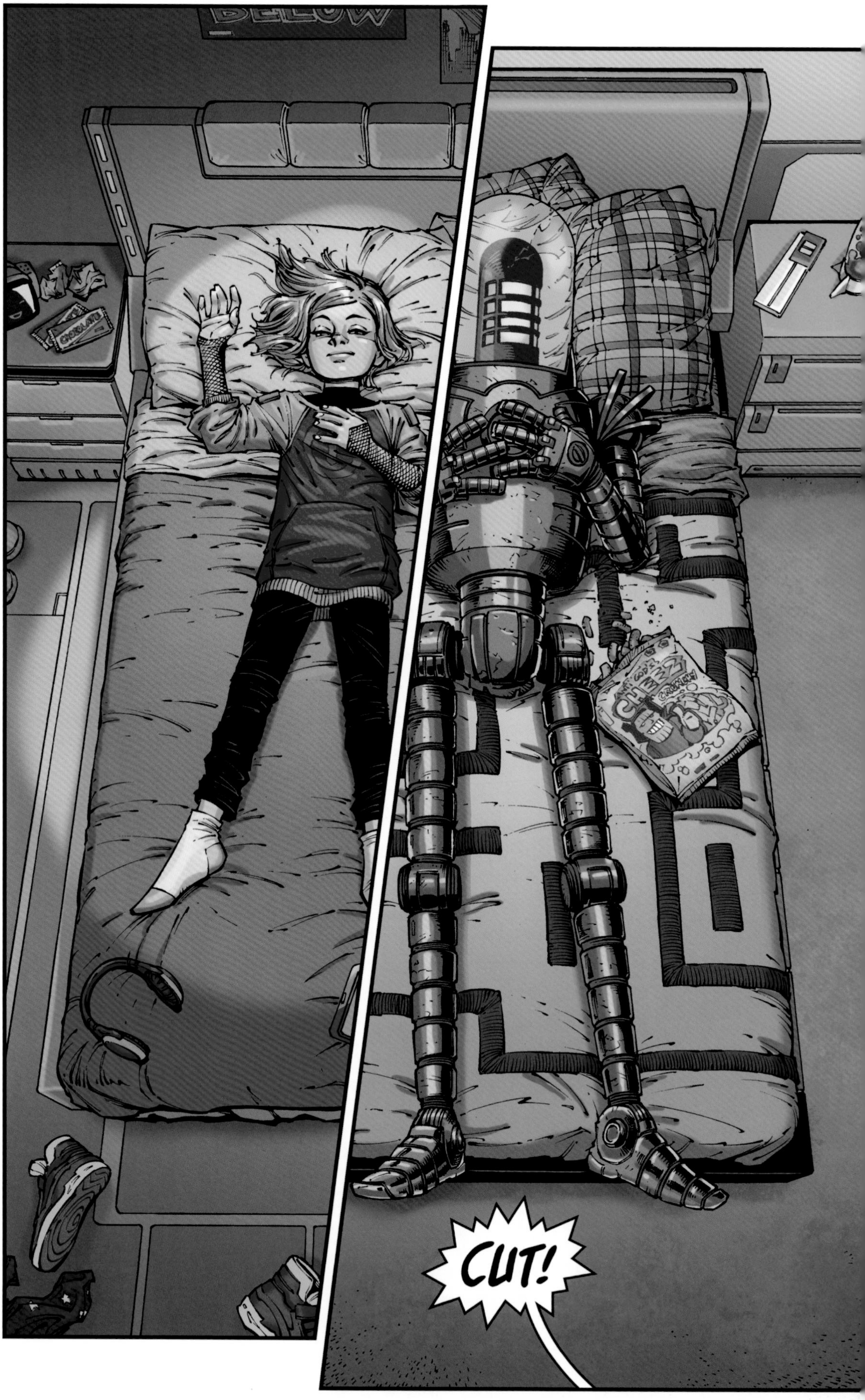
BELOW
CUT!

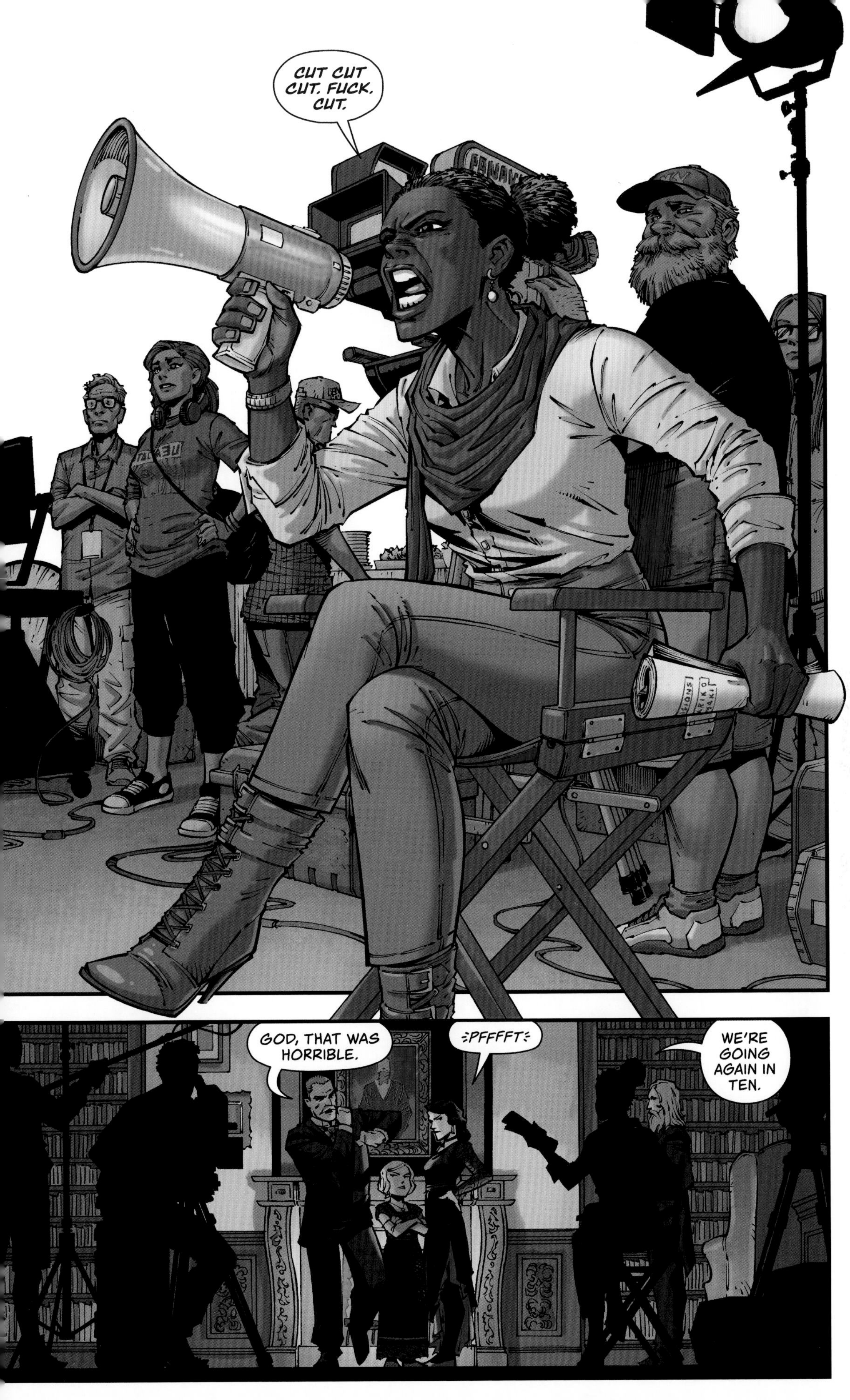
CUT CUT CUT. FUCK. CUT.
GOD, THAT WAS HORRIBLE.
PFFFFT
WE'RE GOING AGAIN IN TEN.

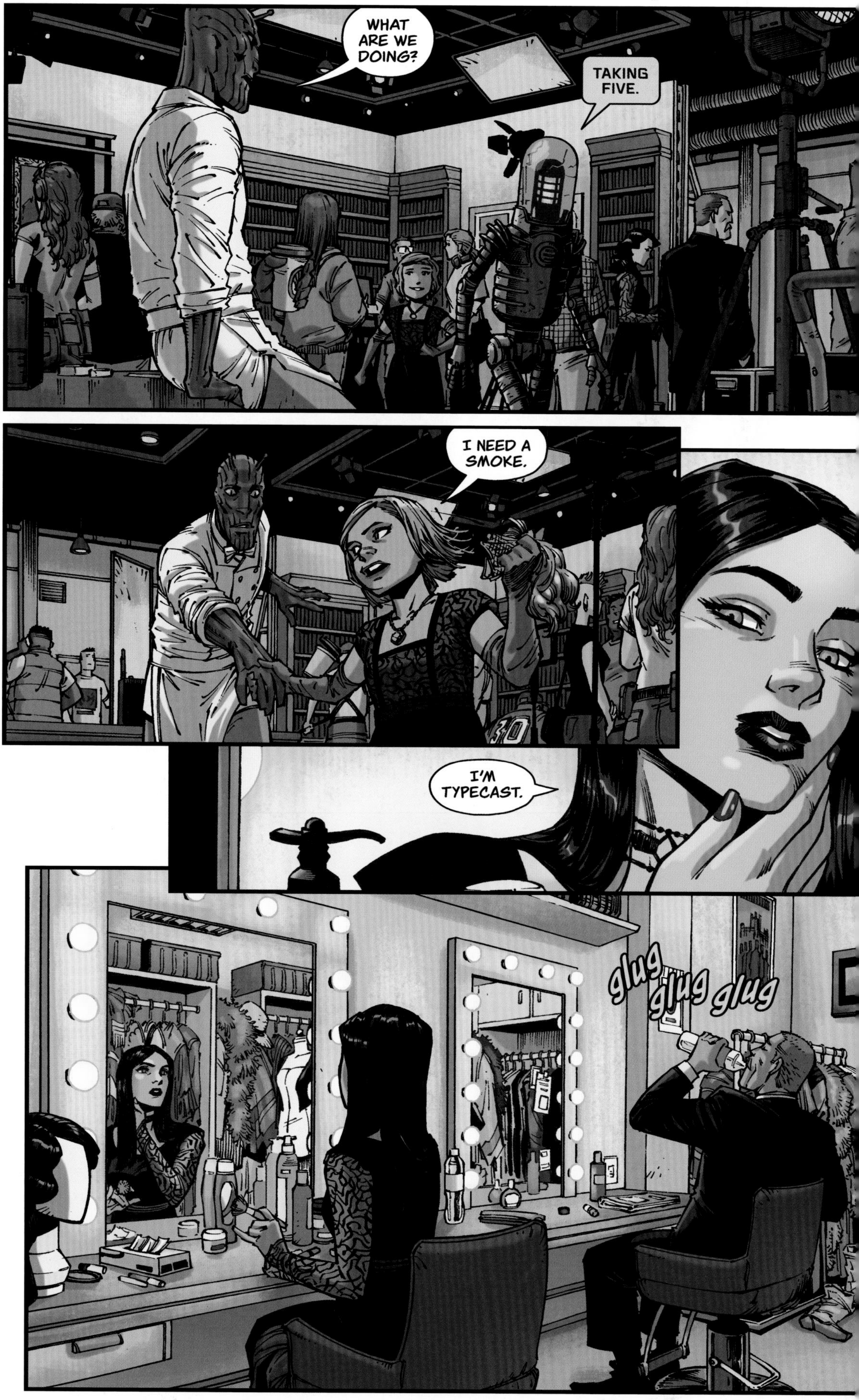
WHAT ARE WE DOING?
TAKING FIVE.
I NEED A SMOKE.
I'M TYPECAST.
glug glug glug

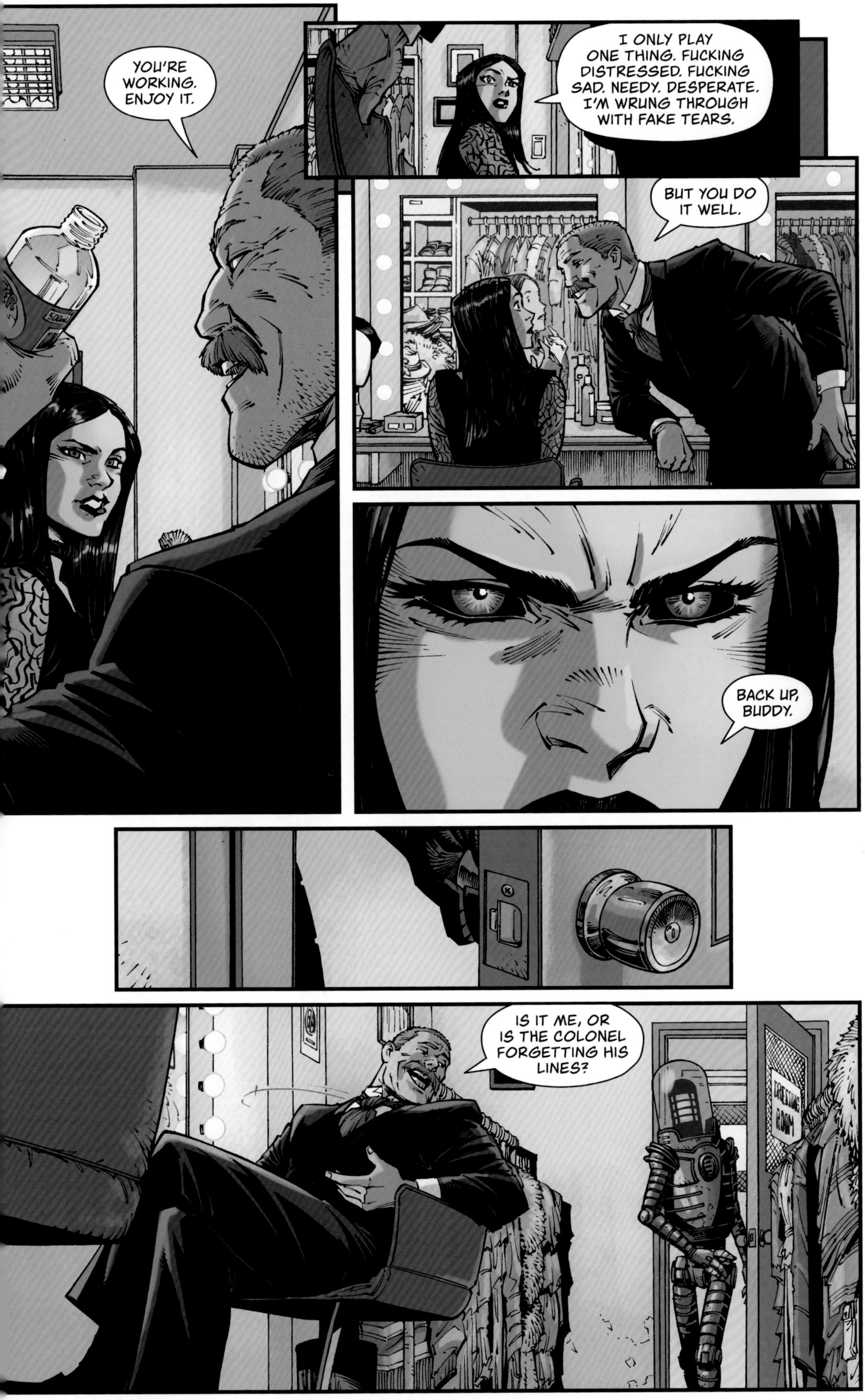
YOU'RE WORKING. ENJOY IT.
I ONLY PLAY ONE THING. FUCKING DISTRESSED. FUCKING SAD. NEEDY. DESPERATE. I'M WRUNG THROUGH WITH FAKE TEARS.
BUT YOU DO IT WELL.
BACK UP, BUDDY.
IS IT ME, OR IS THE COLONEL FORGETTING HIS LINES?
DRESSING ROOM

IT'S COMPLETELY POSSIBLE THE OLD MAN HAS NO IDEA HE'S EVEN ON A TELEVISION SHOW.

MFFF.

STAGE 04

HE FORGOT A LINE TODAY.

CRAP. REALLY?

WE JUST LOOKED AT EACH OTHER. FOR A MINUTE. LIKE A WHOLE MINUTE OF JUST HIM STARING AT ME.

DAMN.

I'M NOT GOING BACK IN THERE. LET THEM WORK AROUND WHAT THEY'VE ALREADY SHOT. I CAN'T DO THIS SHIT ANYMORE.

LET'S GET A DONUT.

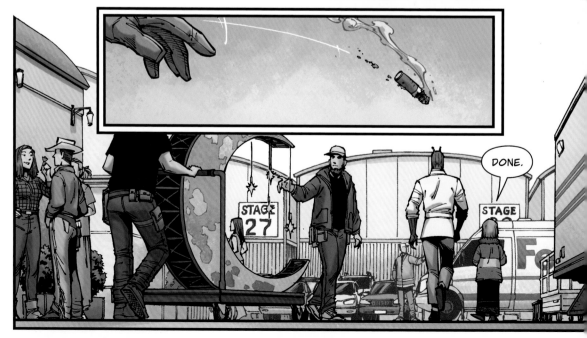

STAGE 27

DONE.

STAGE

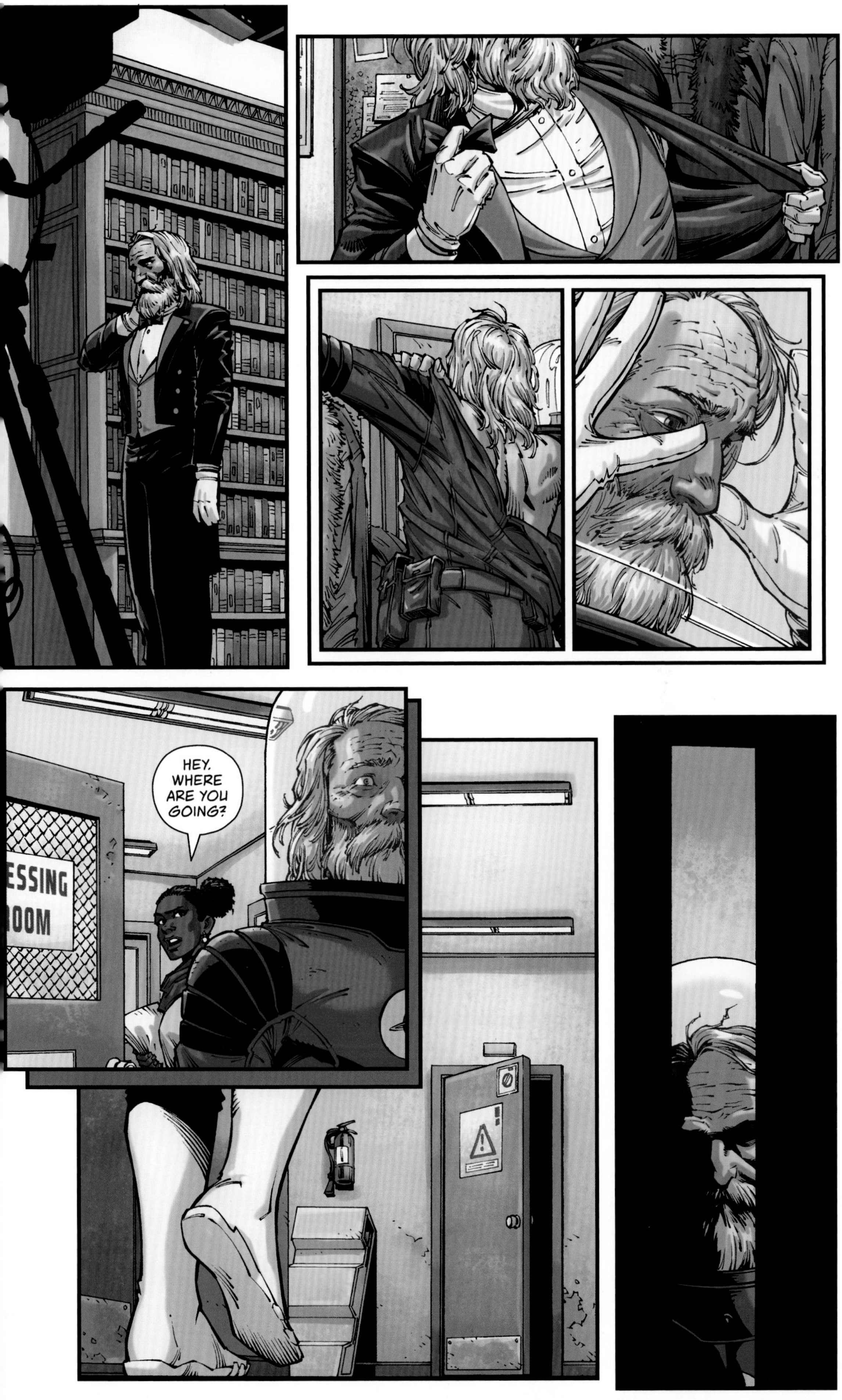
HEY. WHERE ARE YOU GOING?
ESSING
ROOM

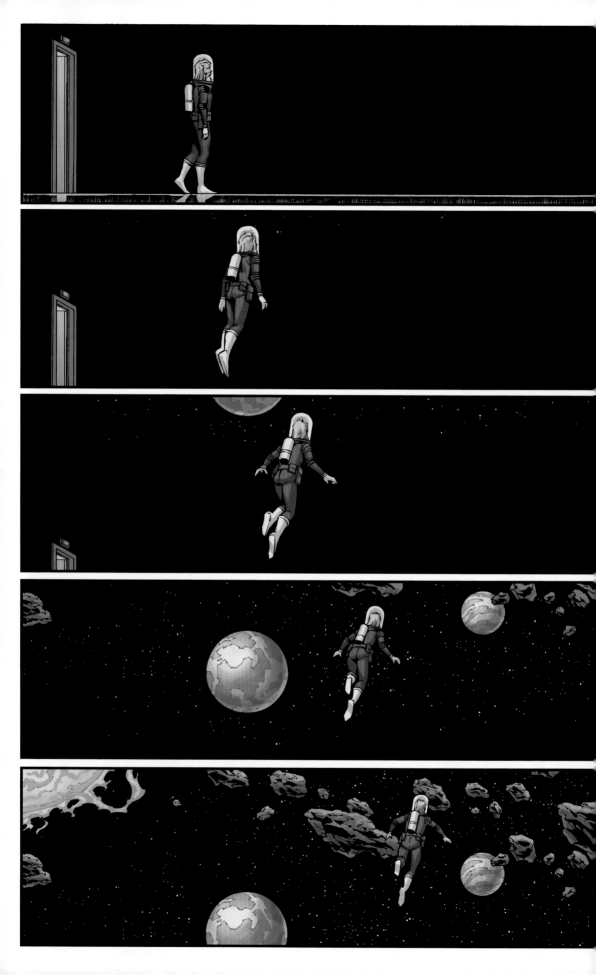

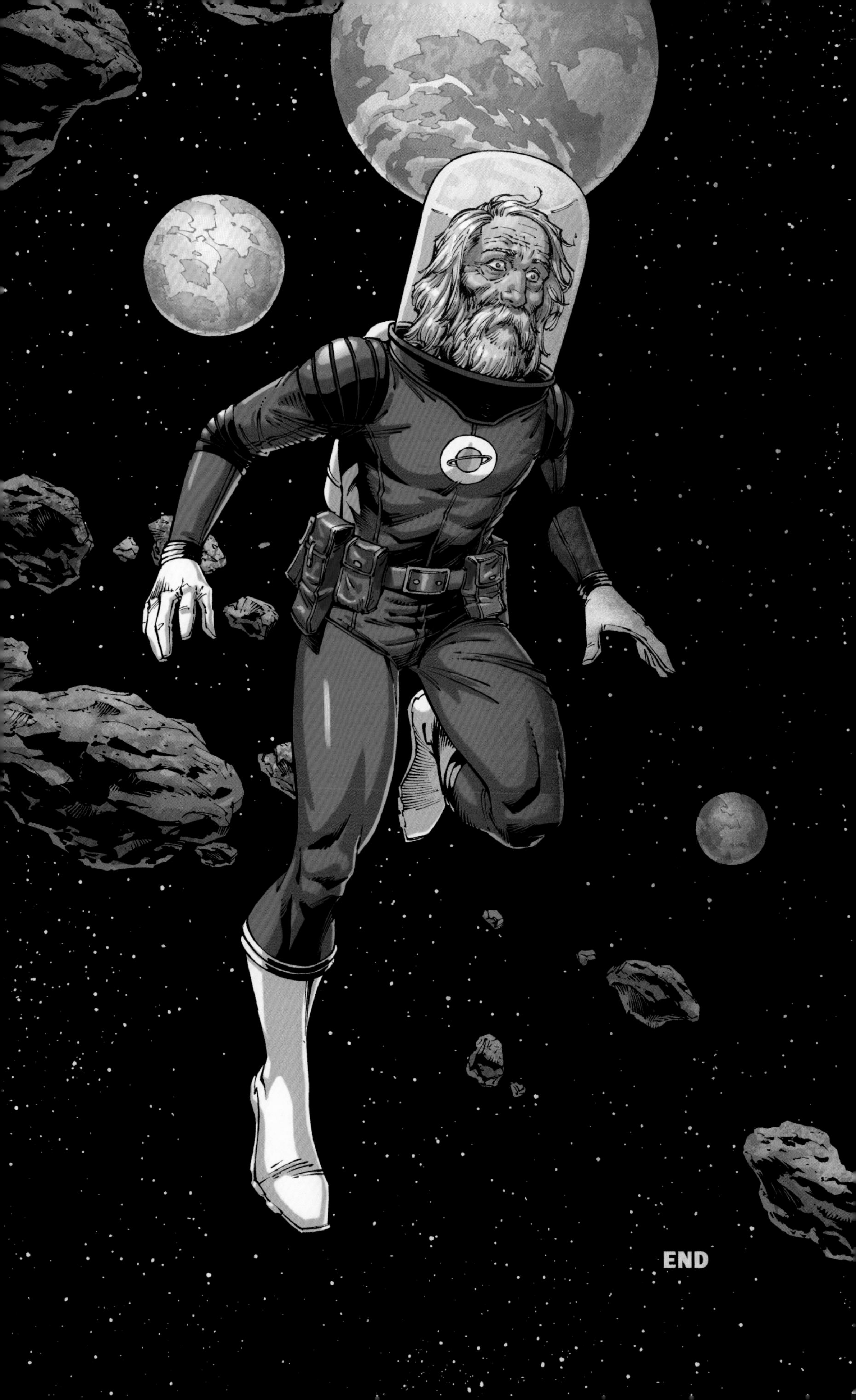
END

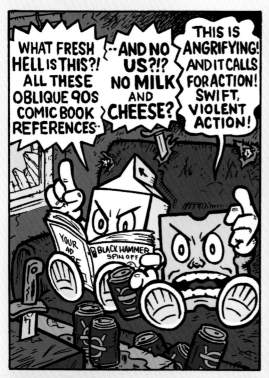

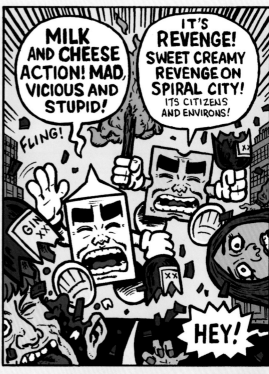

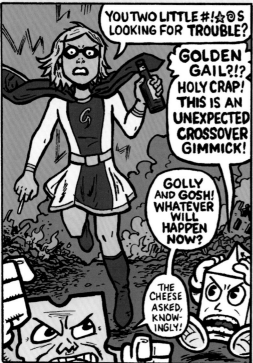

WHAT FRESH HELL IS THIS?! ALL THESE OBLIQUE 90S COMIC BOOK REFERENCES--
--AND NO US?!? NO MILK AND CHEESE?
THIS IS ANGRIFYING! AND IT CALLS FOR ACTION! SWIFT, VIOLENT ACTION!
BLACK HAMMER SPIN OFF
MILK AND CHEESE ACTION! MAD, VICIOUS AND STUPID!
IT'S REVENGE! SWEET CREAMY REVENGE ON SPIRAL CITY! ITS CITIZENS AND ENVIRONS!
FLING!
HEY!
YOU TWO LITTLE #!☆@S LOOKING FOR TROUBLE?
GOLDEN GAIL?!? HOLY CRAP! THIS IS AN UNEXPECTED CROSSOVER GIMMICK!
GOLLY AND GOSH! WHATEVER WILL HAPPEN NOW?
THE CHEESE ASKED, KNOW-INGLY!
TO THE NEXT PANEL →
ONE CONVENIENT OFF-PANEL CONVERSATION LATER--
ZAFRAM!
ZAFRAM LIKE @☆#?! CRAZY!
HA-HA! SHE'S OUR KIND OF MANIAC!
ENJOY YOUR COMIC!

Black Hammer: Visions #1 Cover B by Evan Dorkin with Sarah Dyer

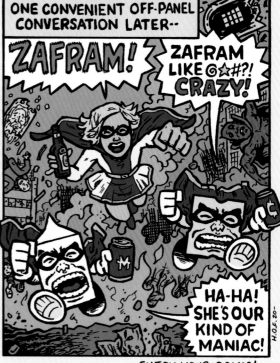

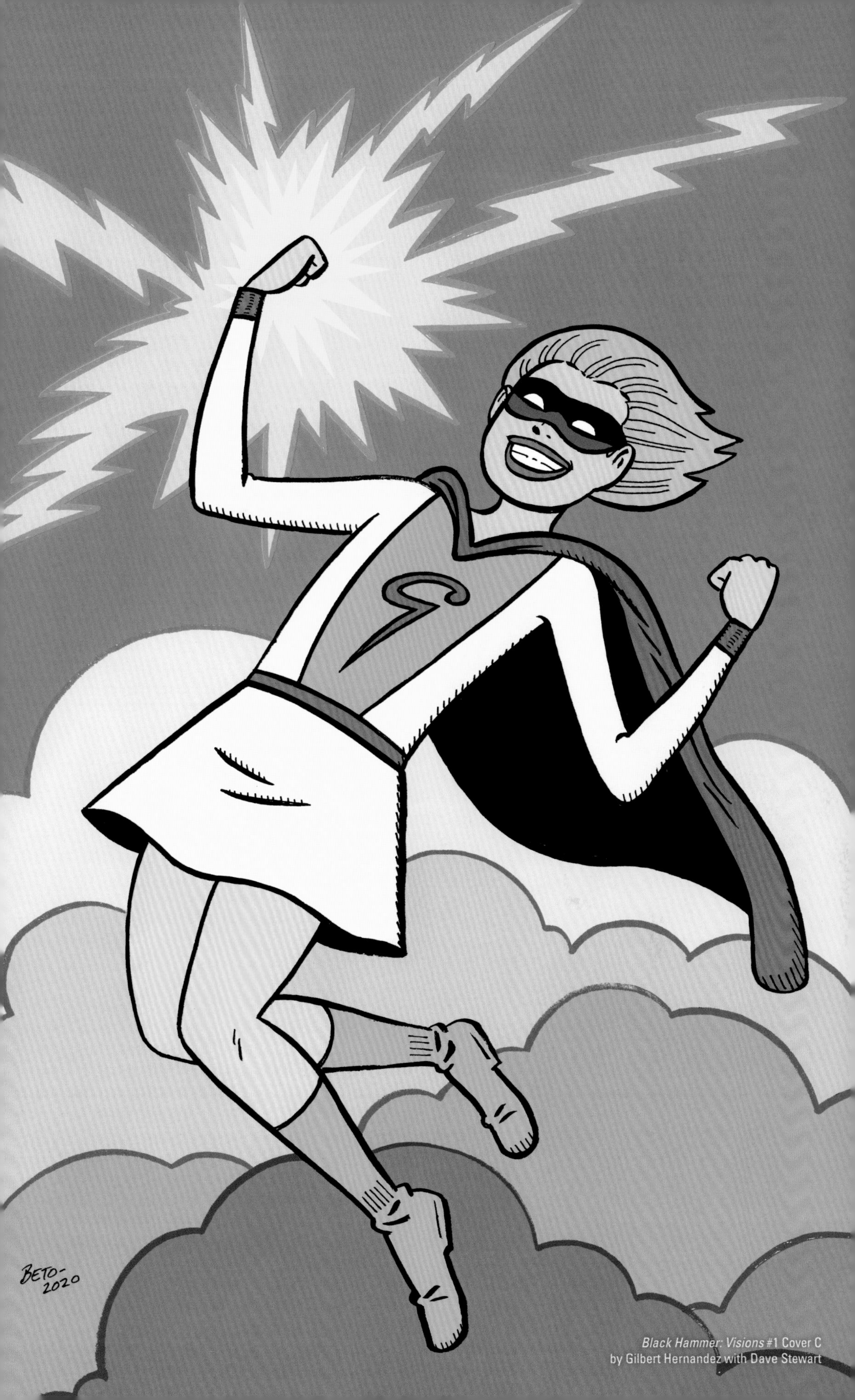
BETO-
2020

Black Hammer: Visions #1 Cover C
by Gilbert Hernandez with Dave Stewart

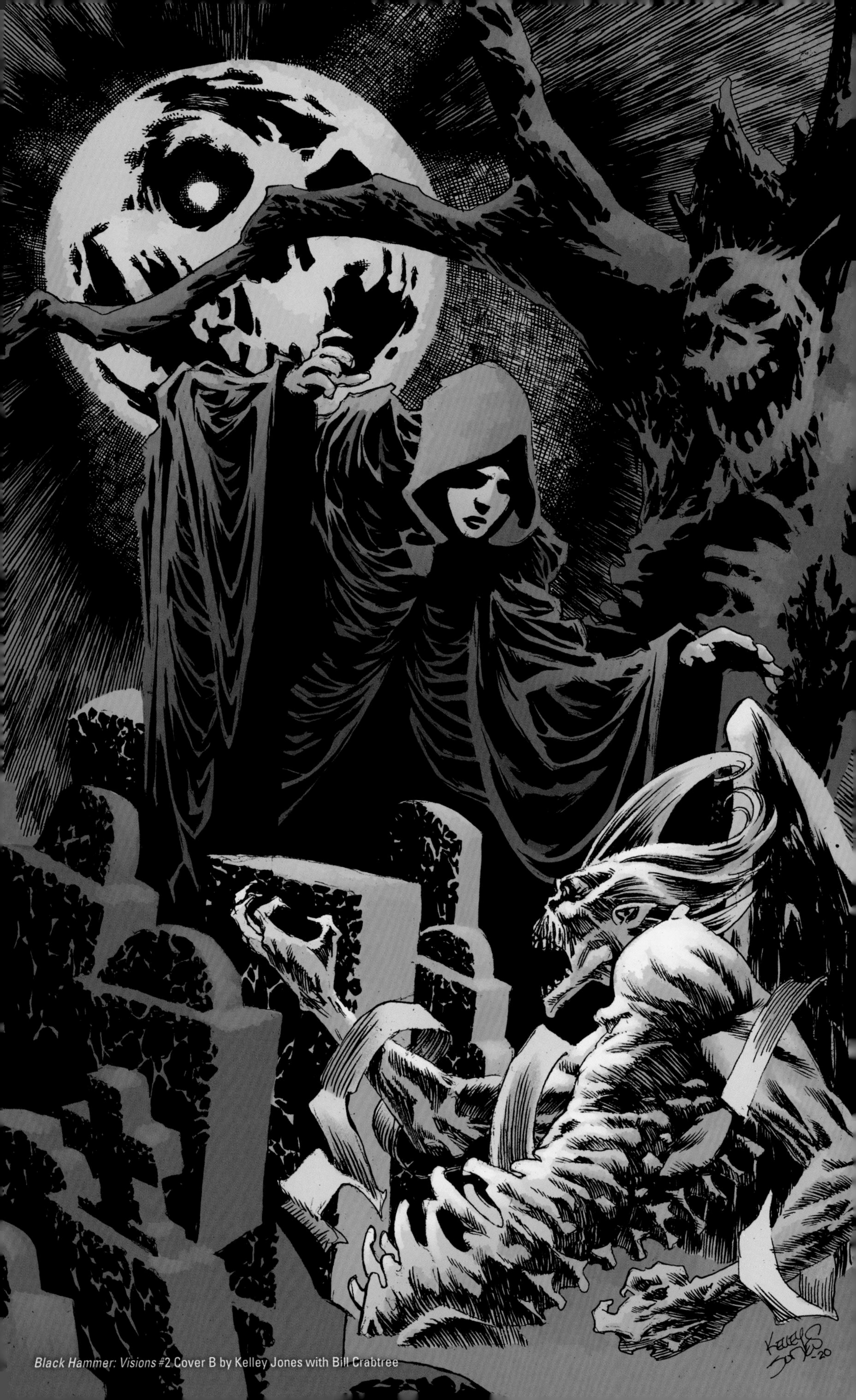

Black Hammer: Visions #2 Cover B by Kelley Jones with Bill Crabtree

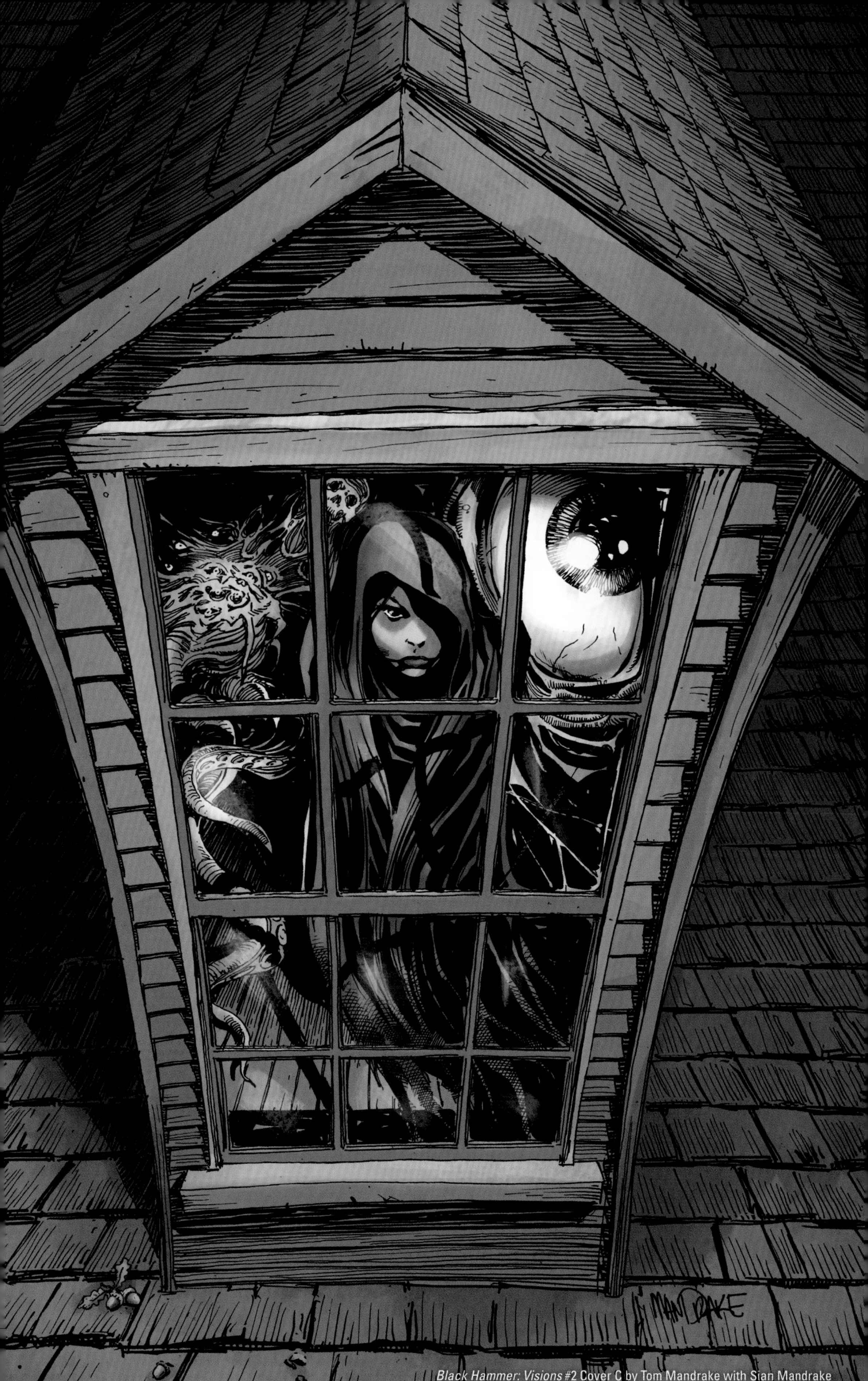
MANDRAKE

Black Hammer: Visions #2 Cover C by Tom Mandrake with Sian Mandrake

Black Hammer: Visions #3 Cover B by Jason Loo

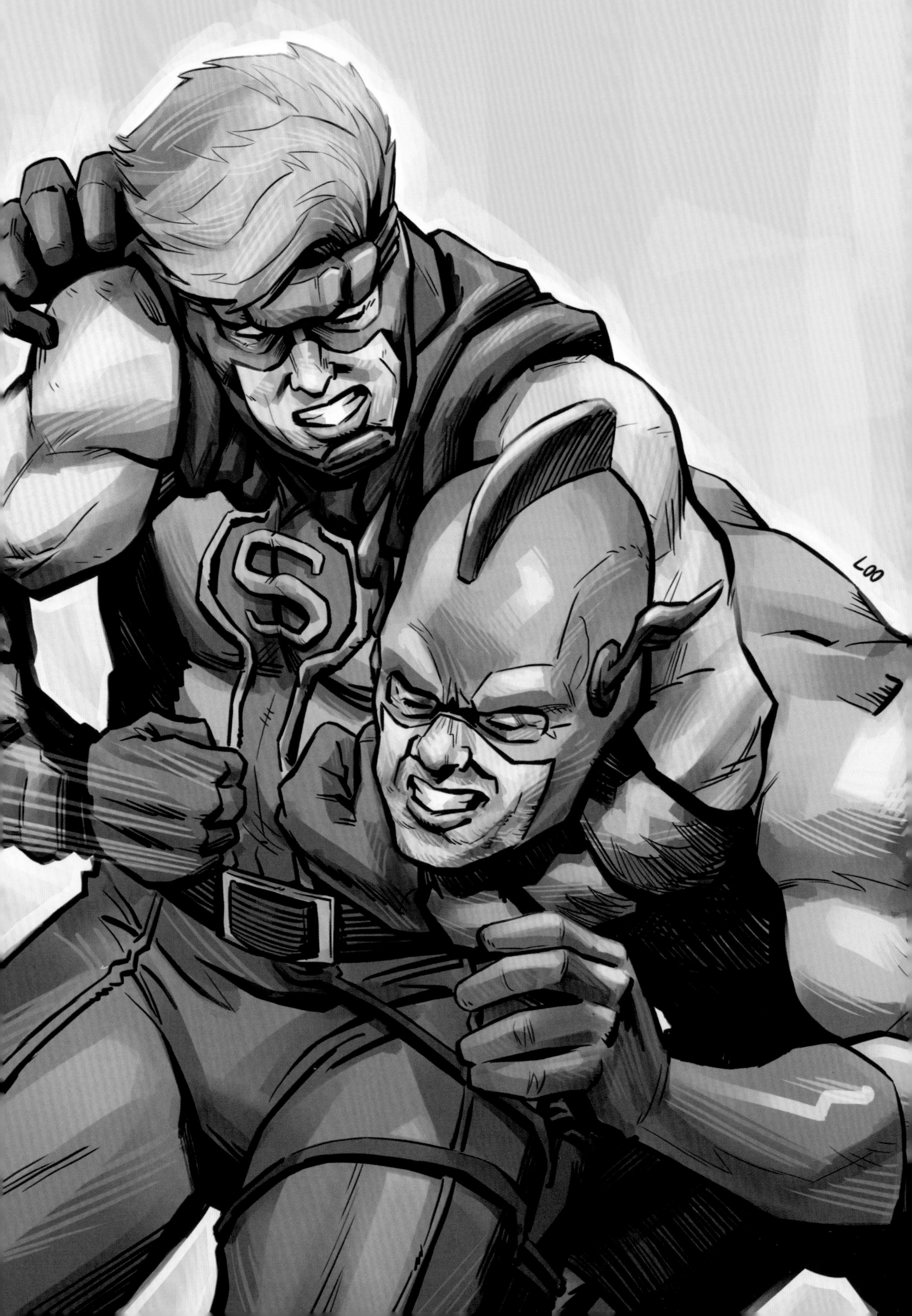

Black Hammer: Visions #3 Cover C by Gerardo Zaffino

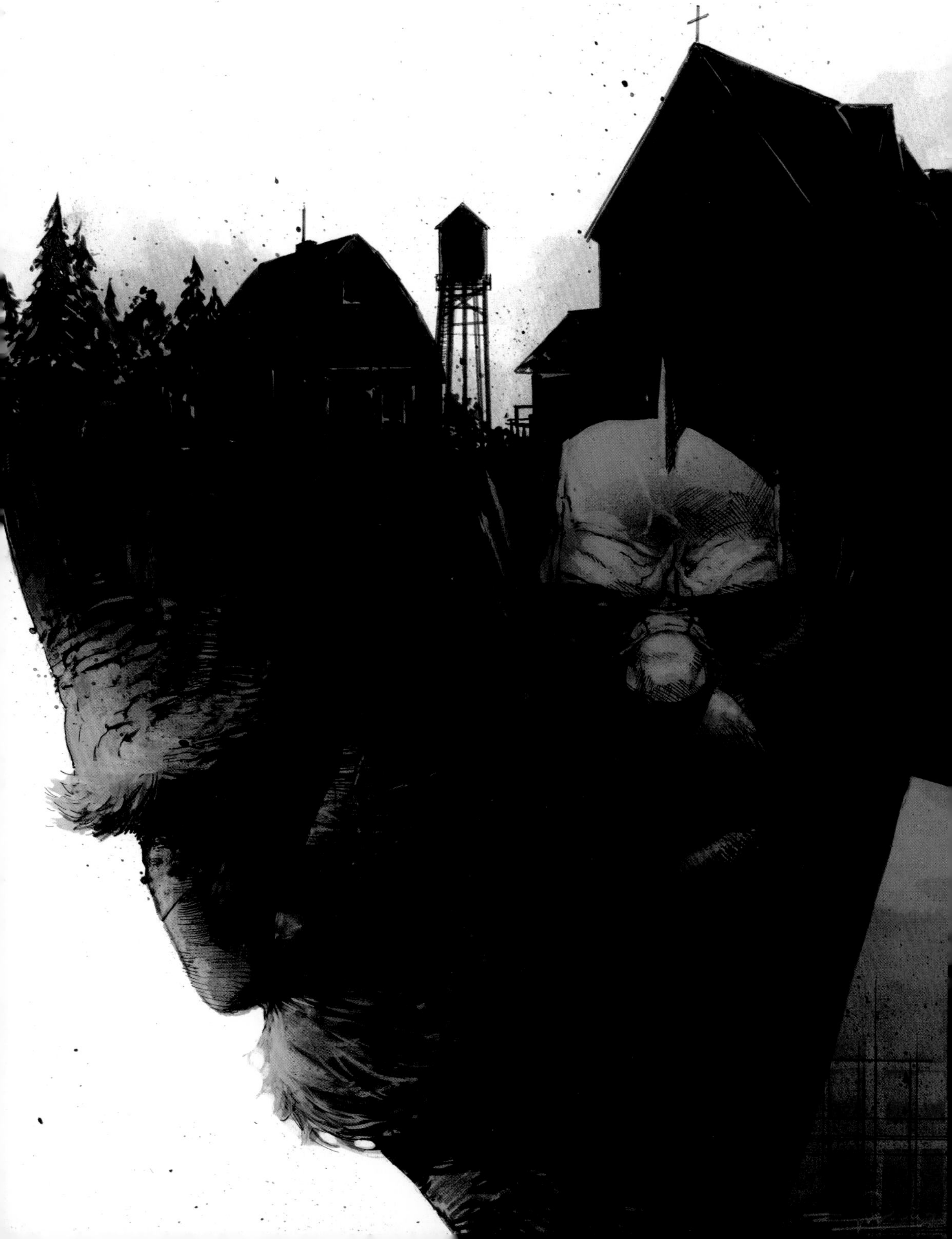

Black Hammer: Visions #4 Cover B by Patricia Martin

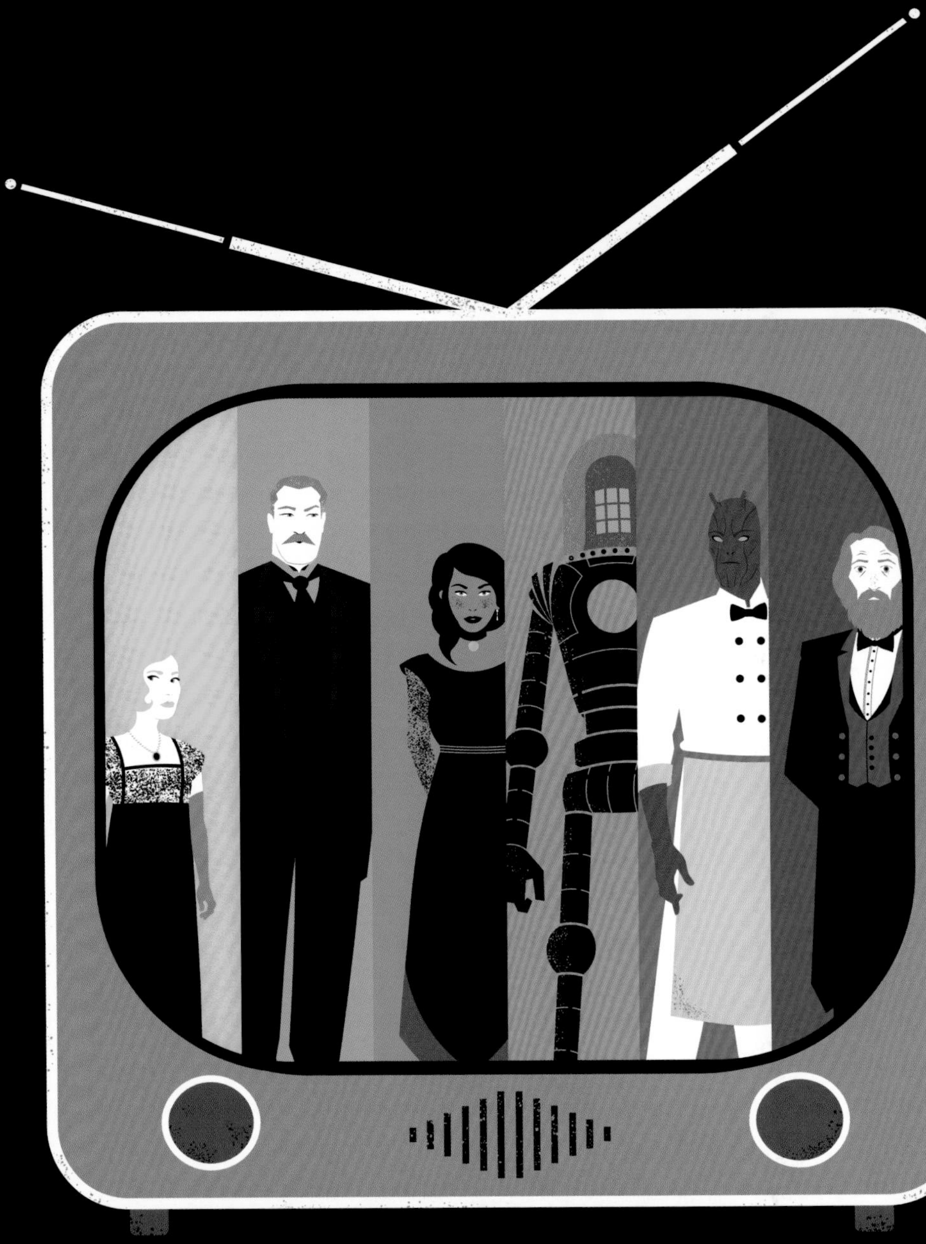

Black Hammer: Visions #4 Cover C by Christina Chung

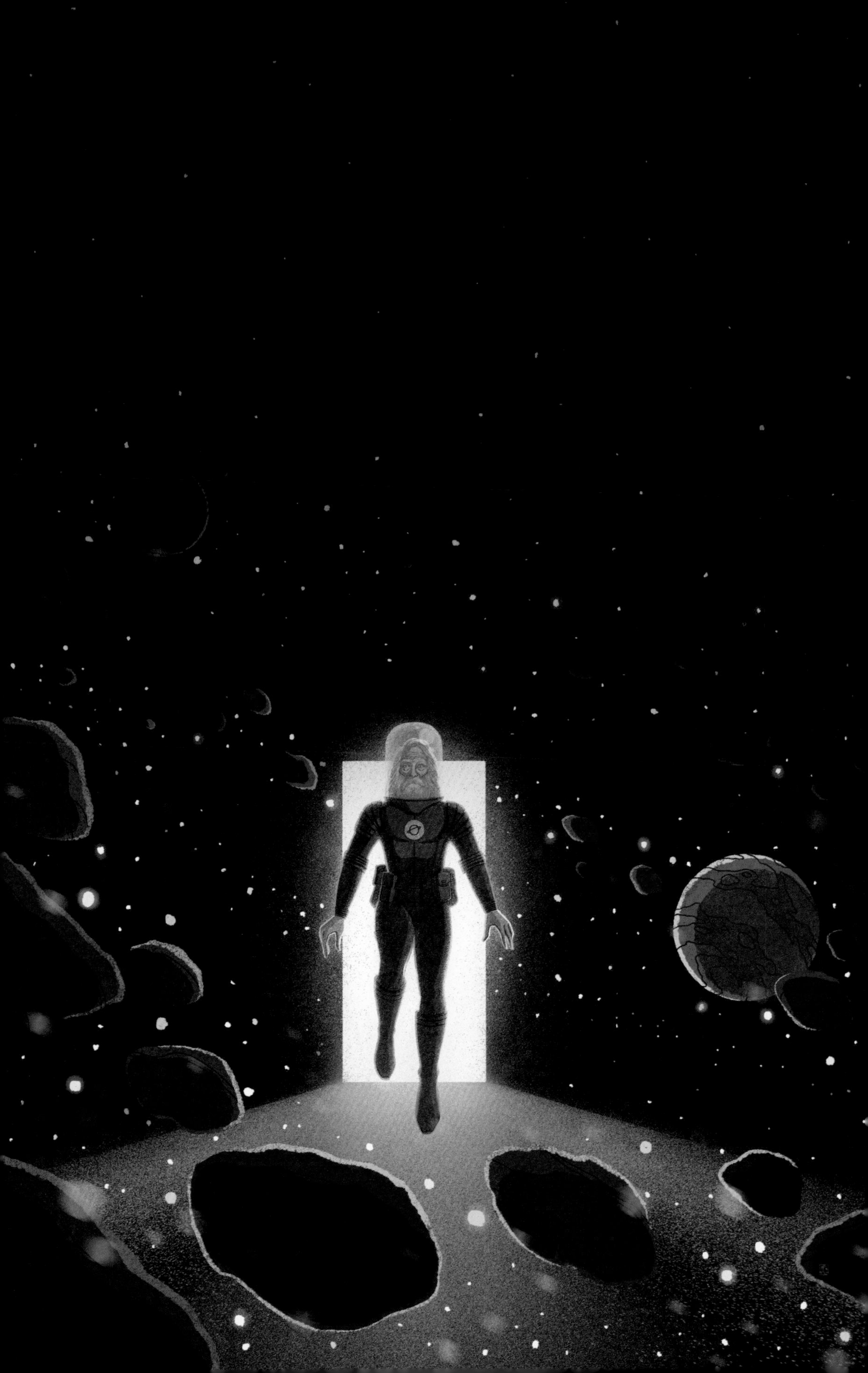

BLACK HAMMER VISIONS
VOLUME 1 SKETCHBOOK

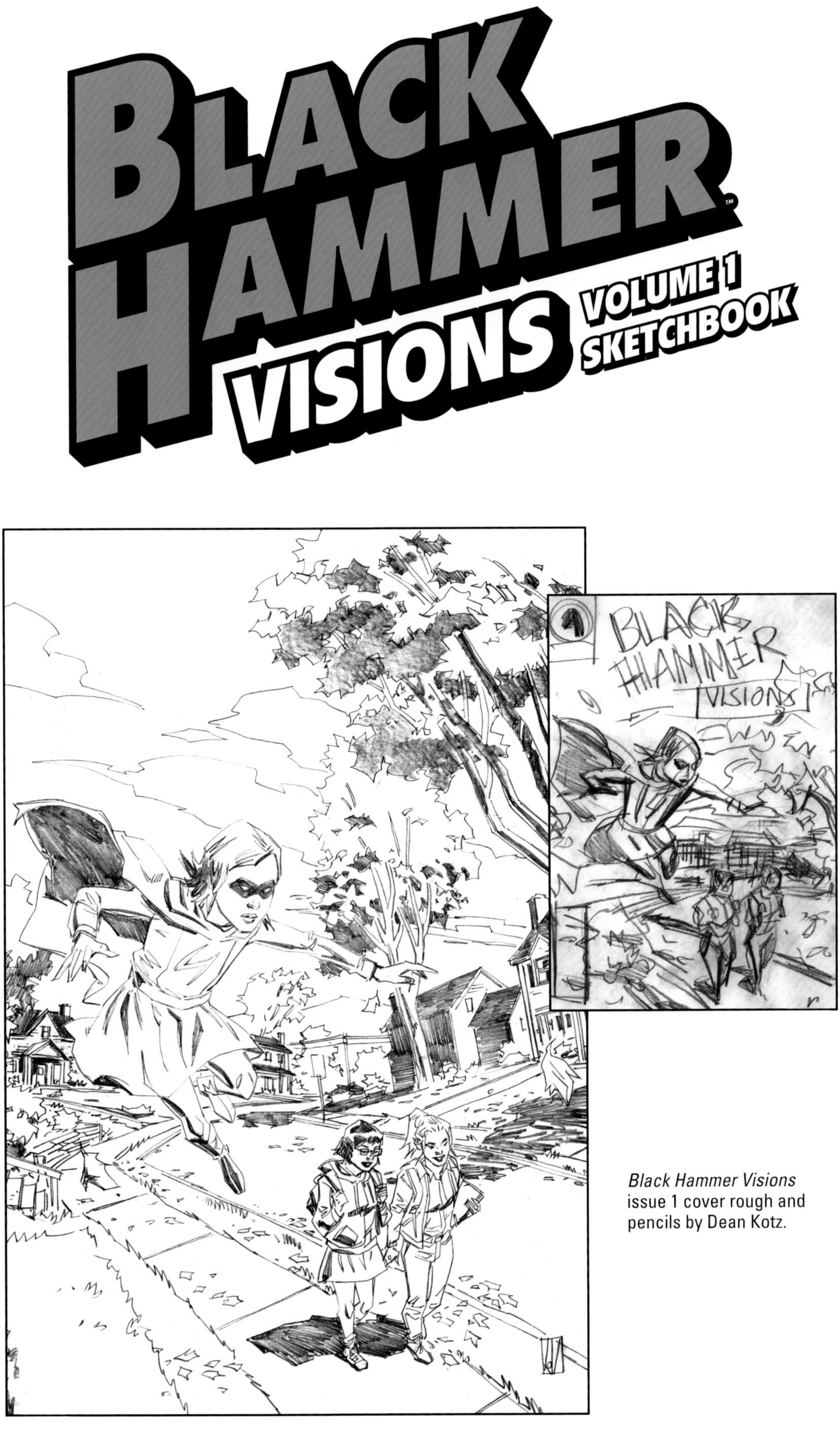
BLACK HAMMER
VISIONS

Black Hammer Visions issue 1 cover rough and pencils by Dean Kotz.

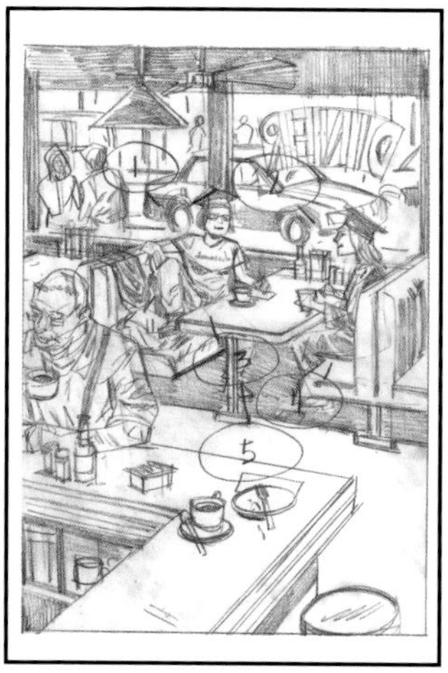

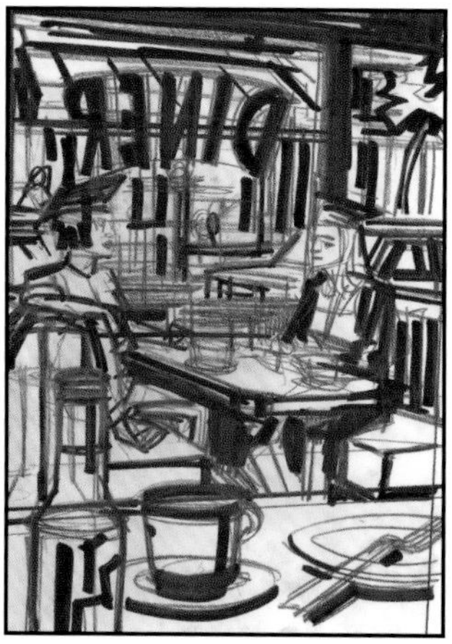

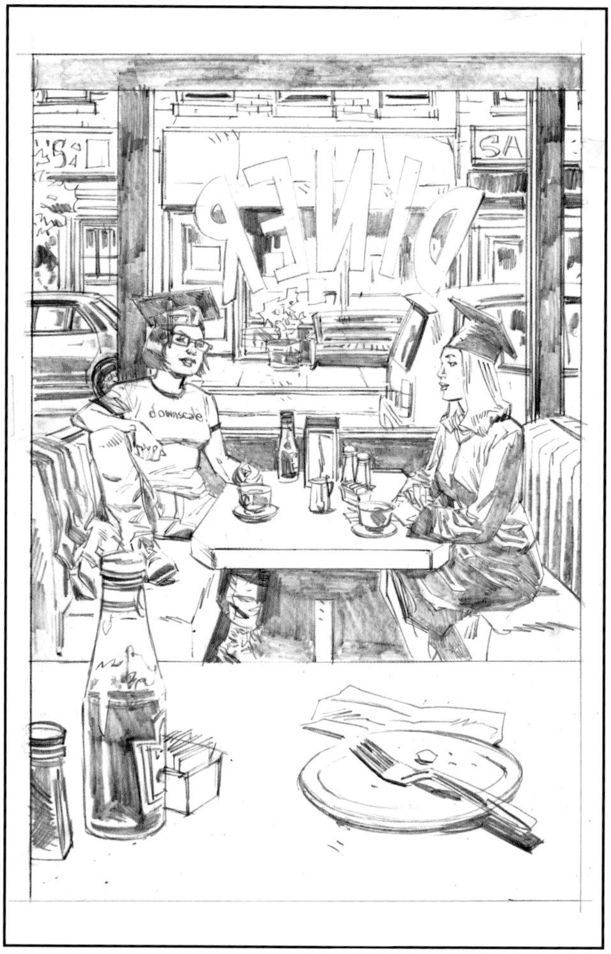

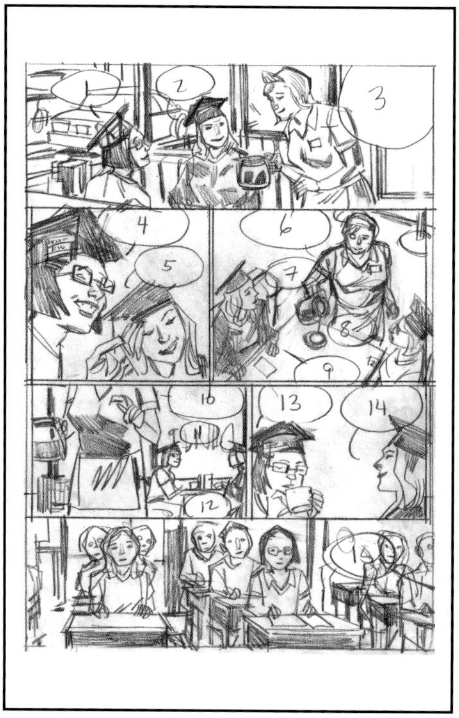

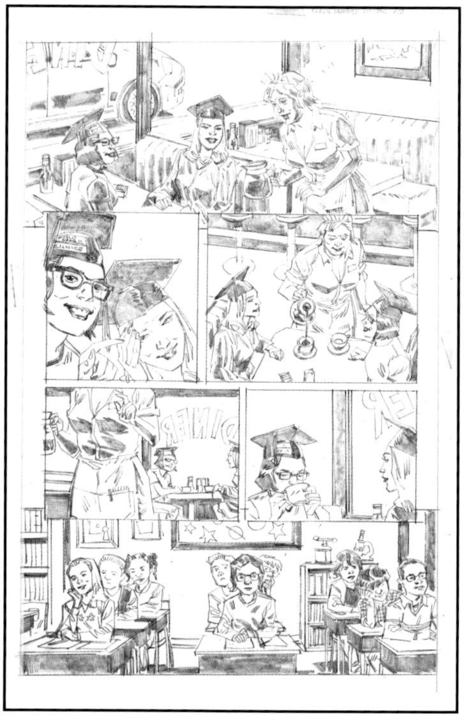

Black Hammer Visions issue 1, page 1 and 2 roughs and pencils by Dean Kotz.

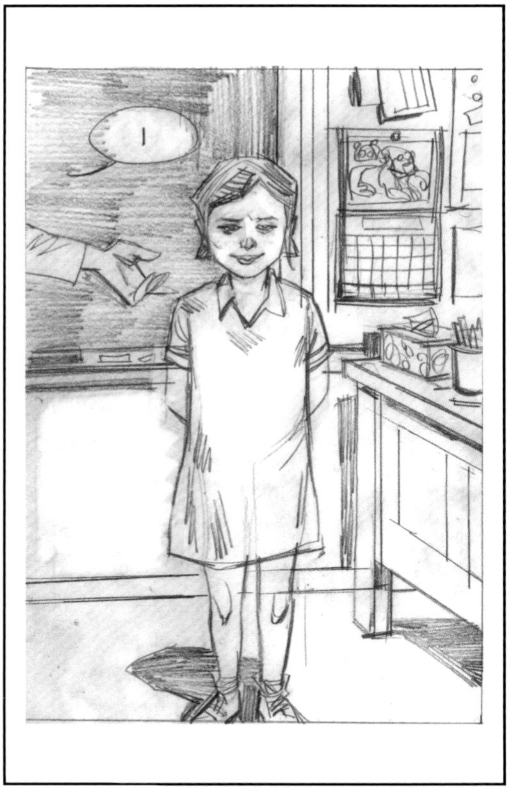
1

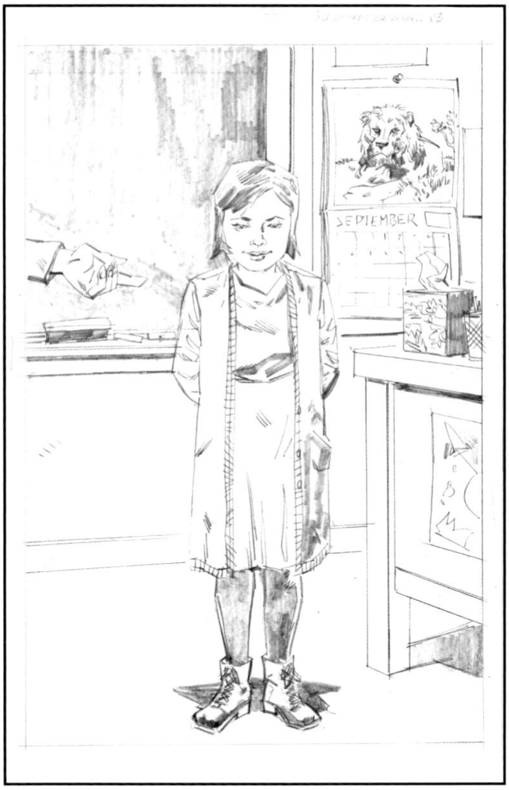
SEPTEMBER

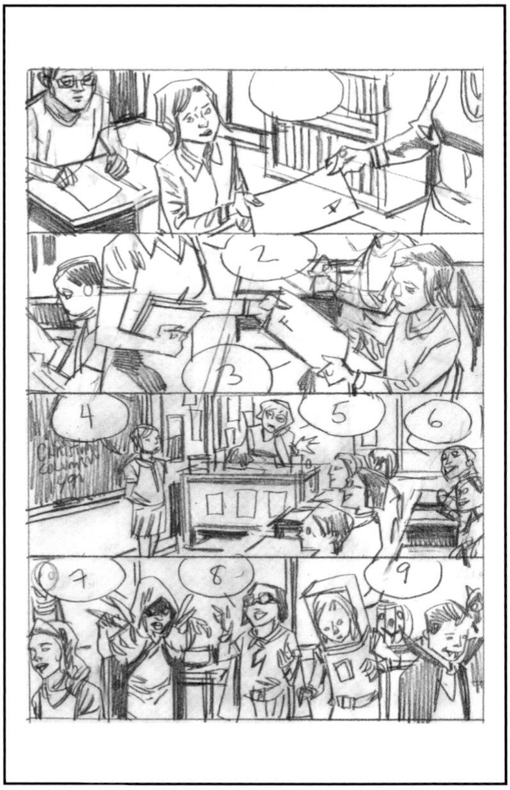
2
3
4
5
6
7
8
9

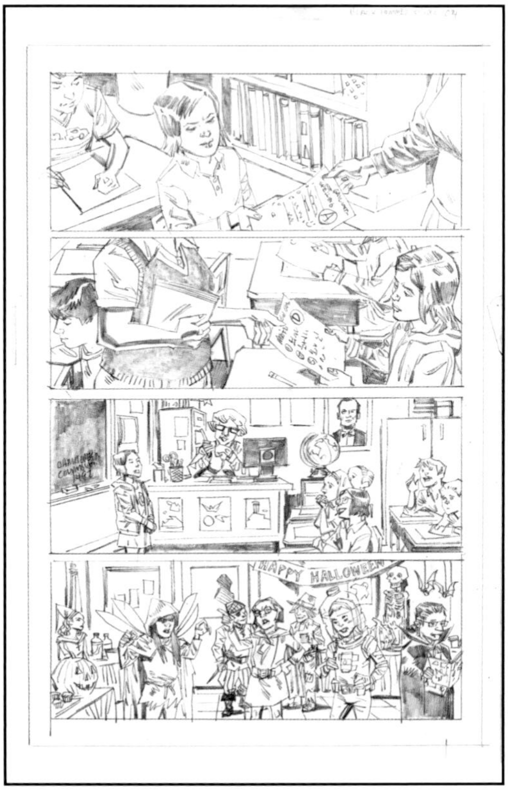
HAPPY HALLOWEEN

Black Hammer Visions issue 1, page 3 and 4 roughs and pencils by Dean Kotz.

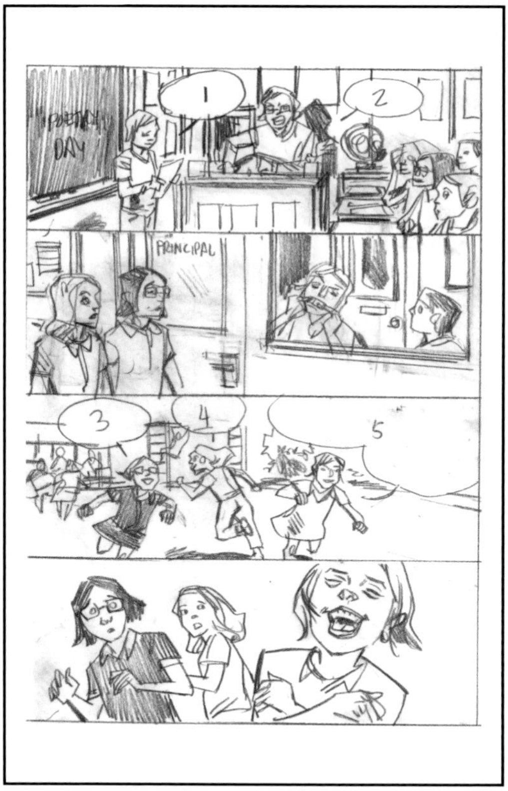
POETRY DAY
1
2
PRINCIPAL
3
4
5

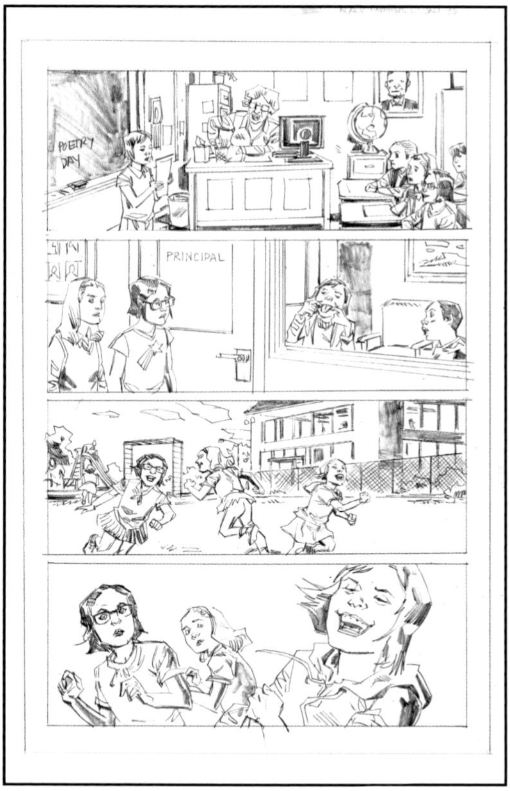
POETRY DAY
PRINCIPAL

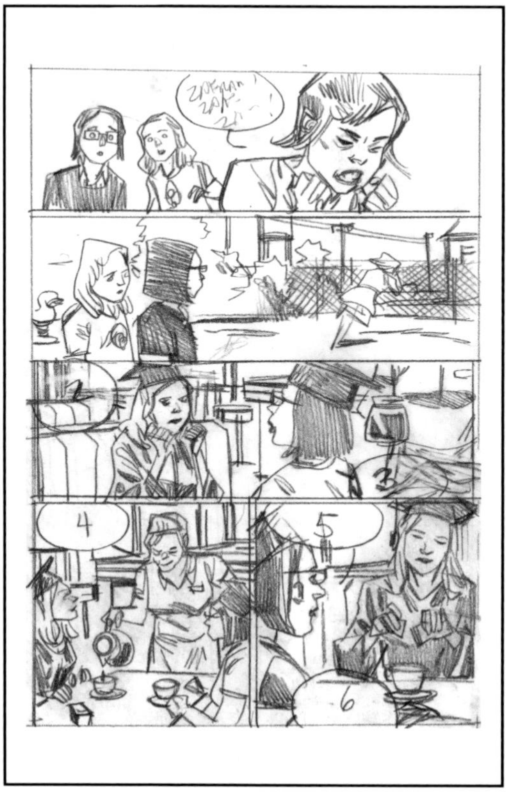
4
5
6

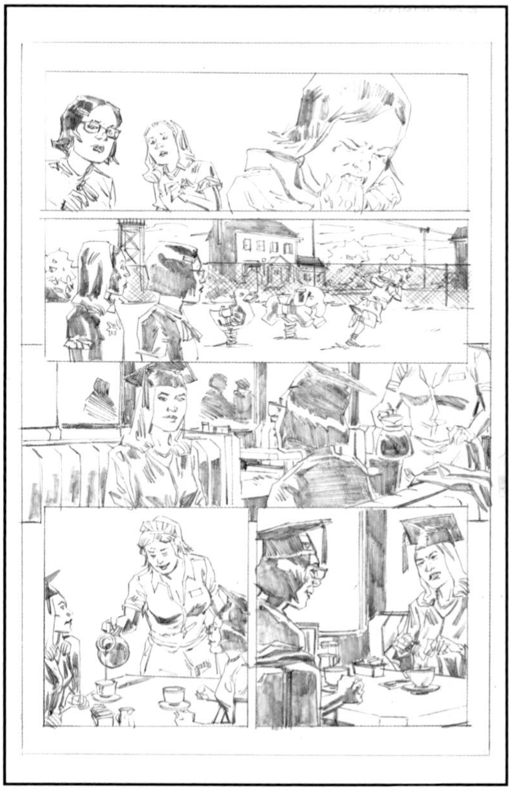

Black Hammer Visions issue 1, page 5 and 6 roughs and pencils by Dean Kotz.

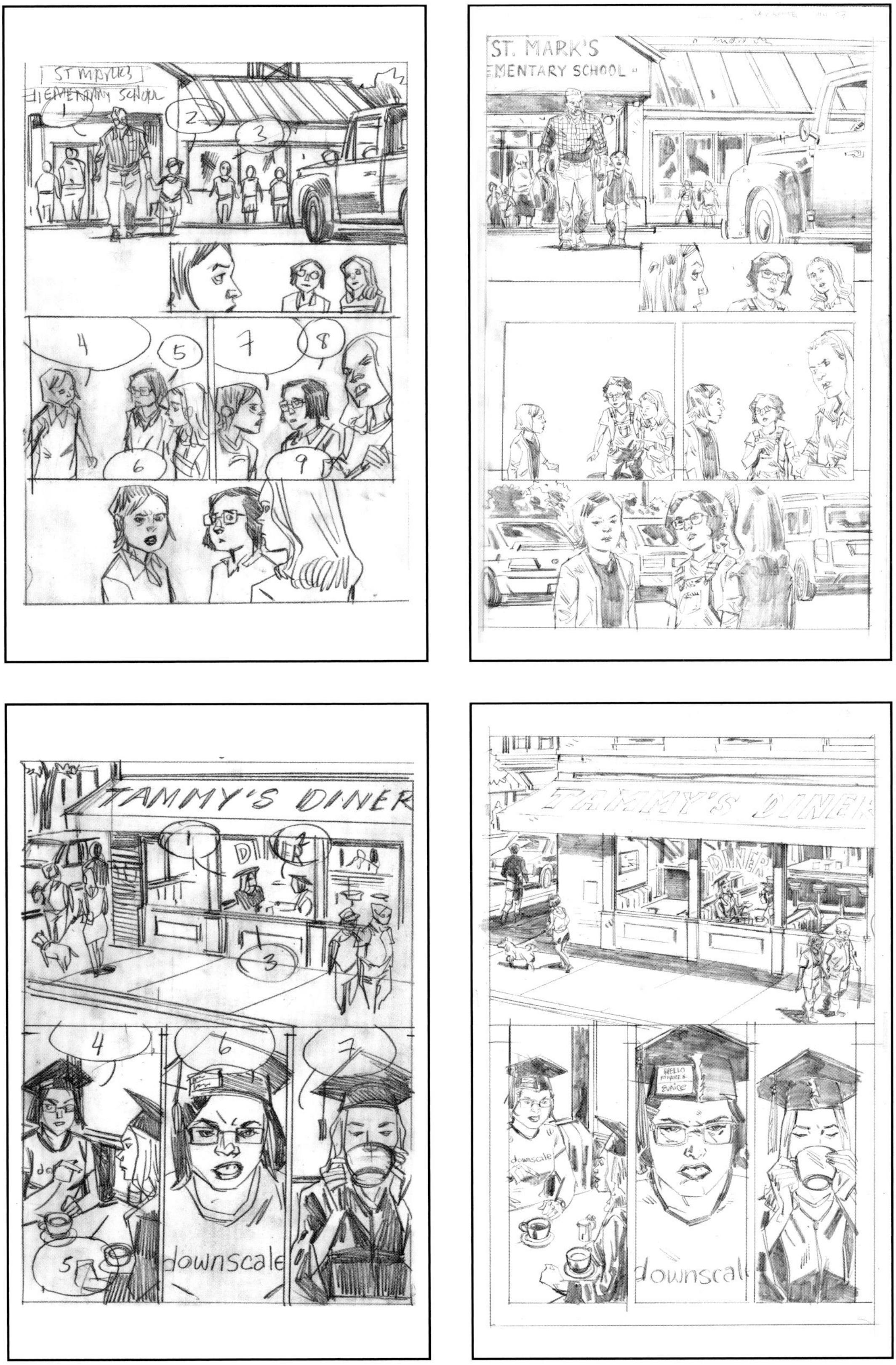
ST. MARK'S
EMENTARY SCHOOL
TAMMY'S DINER
DINER
downscale

Black Hammer Visions issue 1, page 7 and 8 roughs and pencils by Dean Kotz.

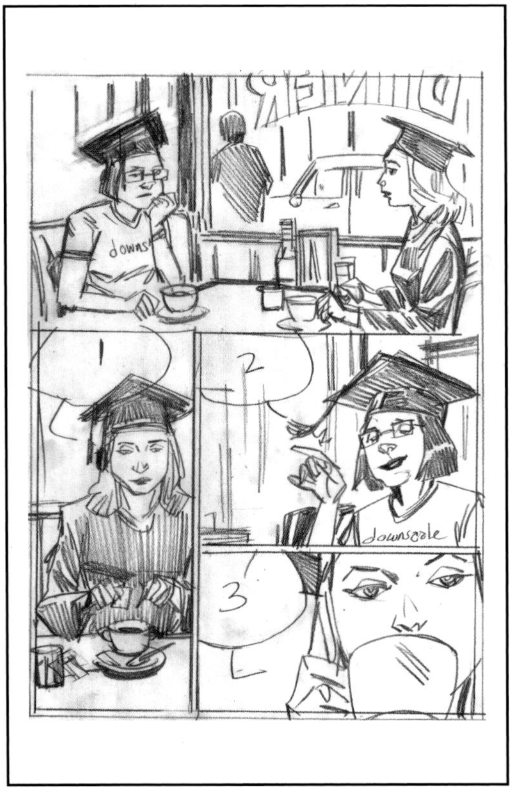
DINER
downsc
1
2
downscale
3

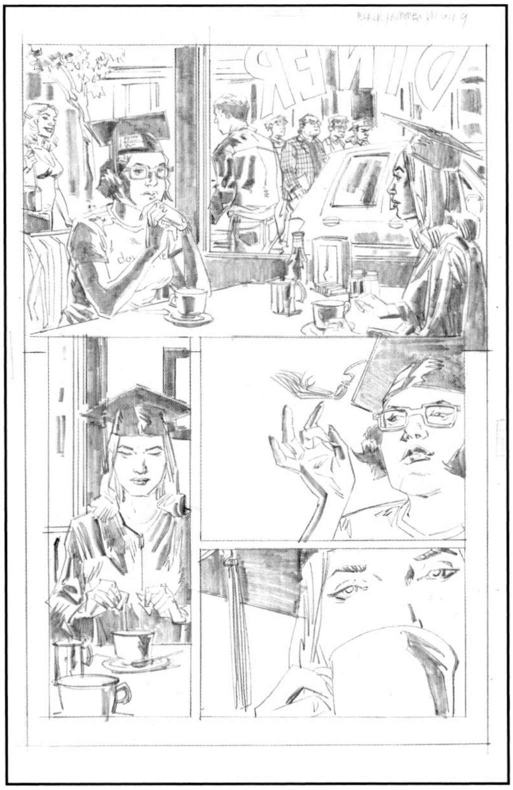
DINER

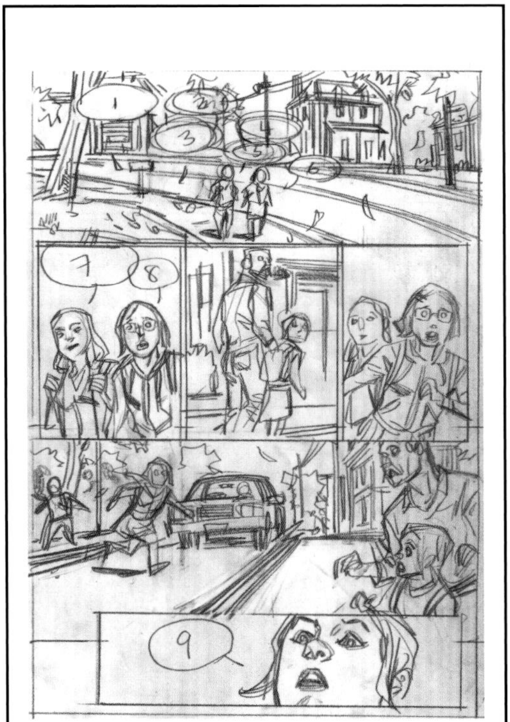
1
2
3
4
5
6
7
8
9

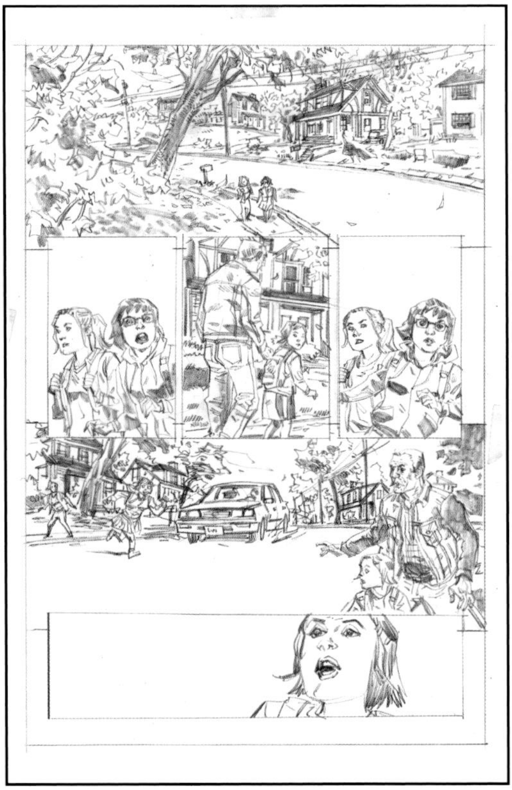

Black Hammer Visions issue 1, page 9 and 10 roughs and pencils by Dean Kotz.

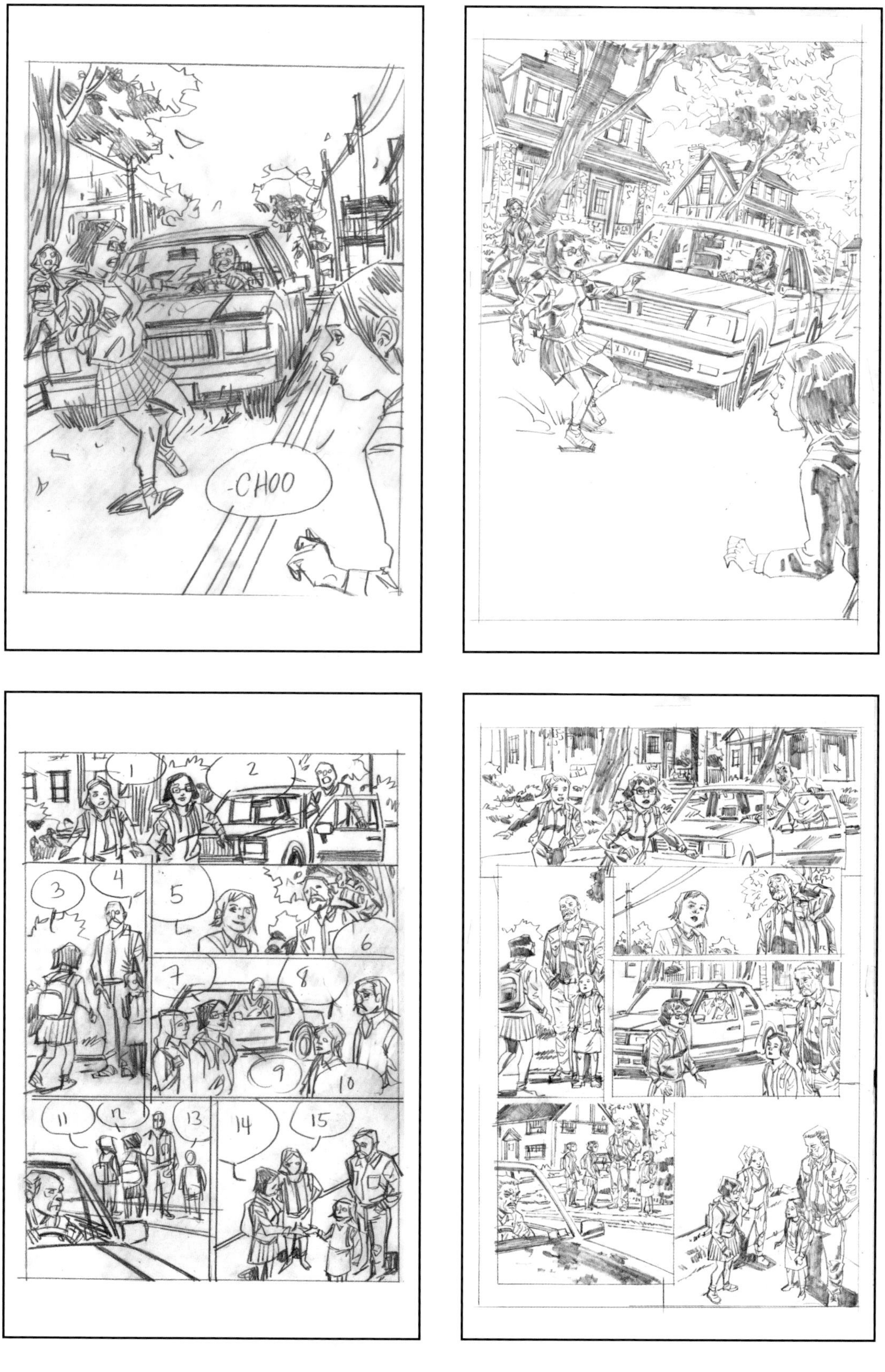
-CHOO
1
2
3
4
5
6
7
8
9
10
11
12
13
14
15

Black Hammer Visions issue 1, page 11 and 12 roughs and pencils by Dean Kotz.

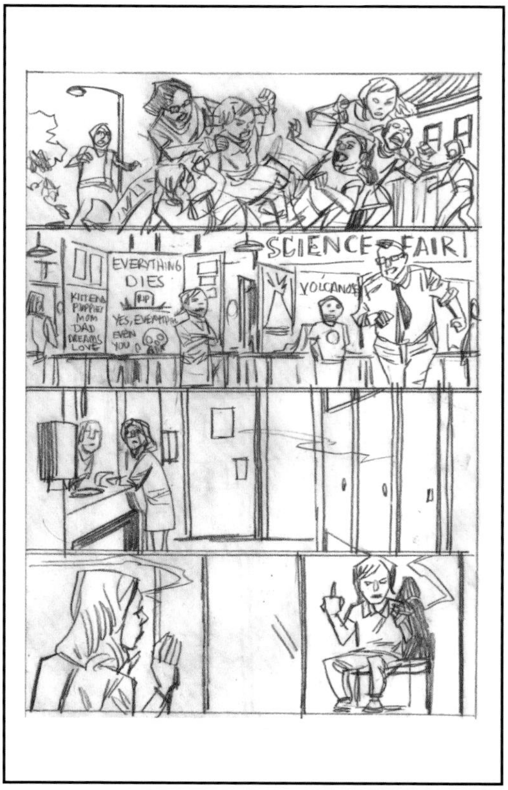
SCIENCE FAIR
EVERYTHING DIES

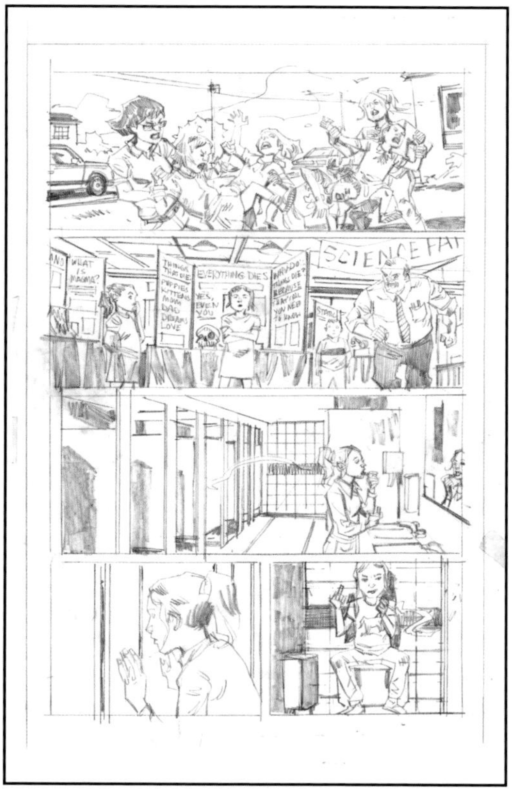
WHAT IS MAGMA?
EVERYTHING DIES
YES, EVEN YOU
SCIENCE FAIR

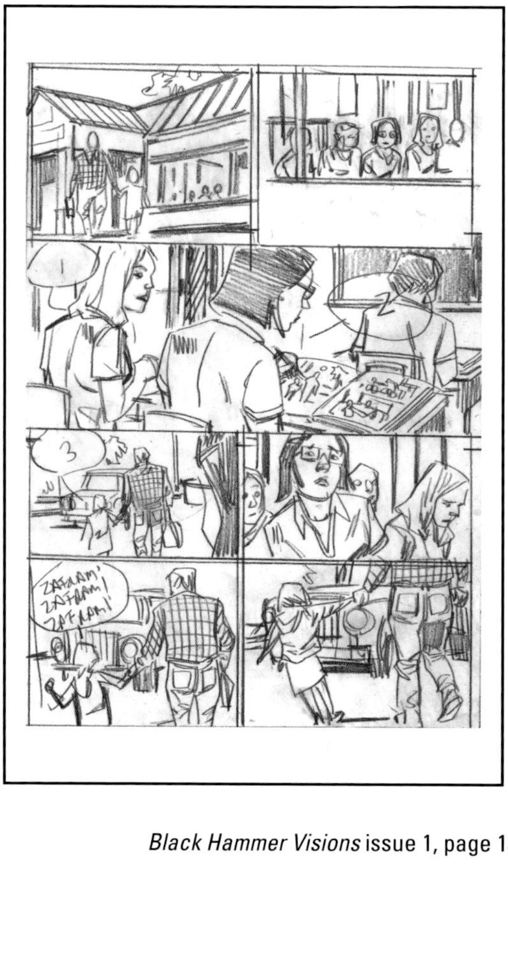

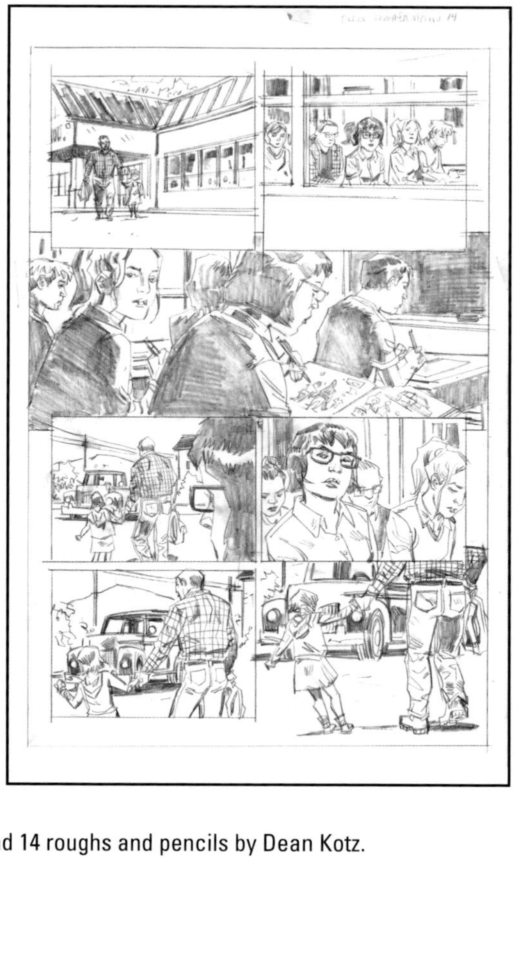

Black Hammer Visions issue 1, page 13 and 14 roughs and pencils by Dean Kotz.

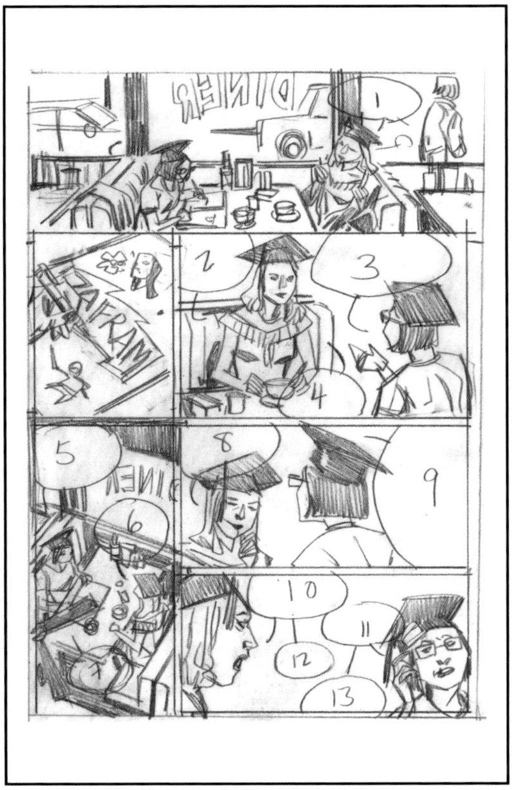
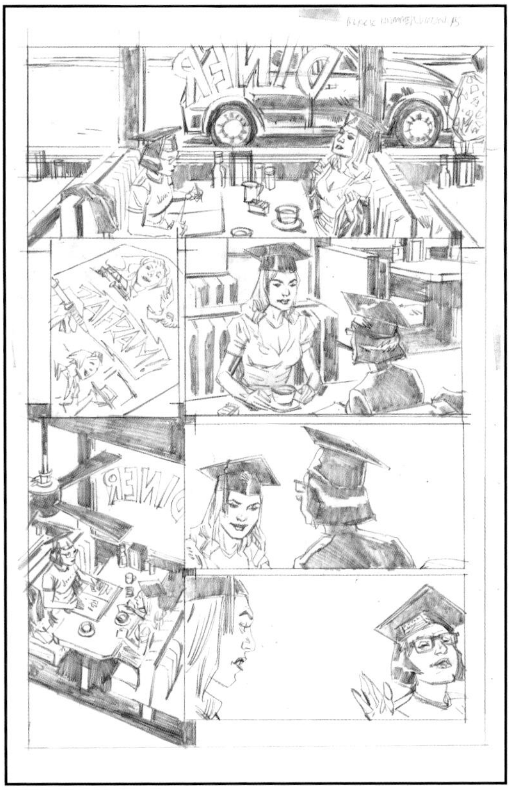
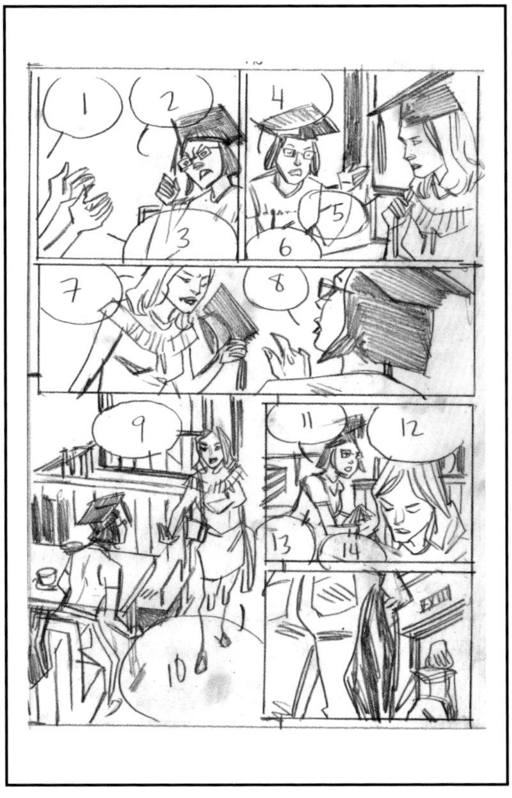
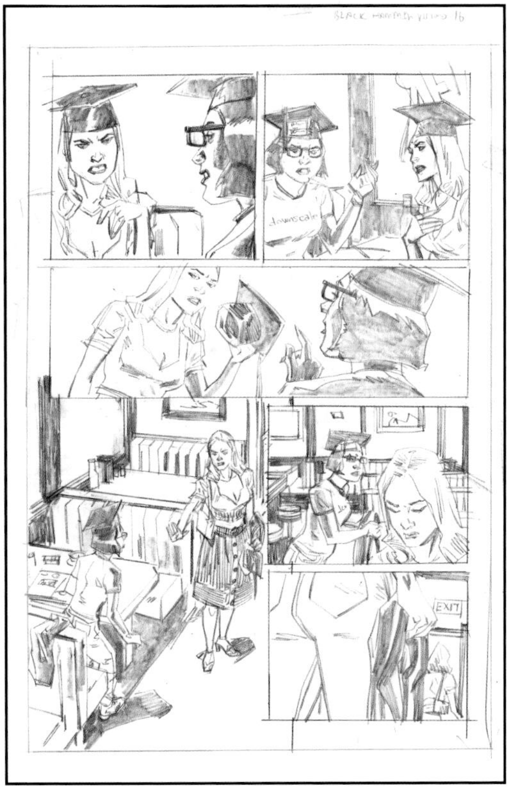

Black Hammer Visions issue 1, page 15 and 16 roughs and pencils by Dean Kotz.

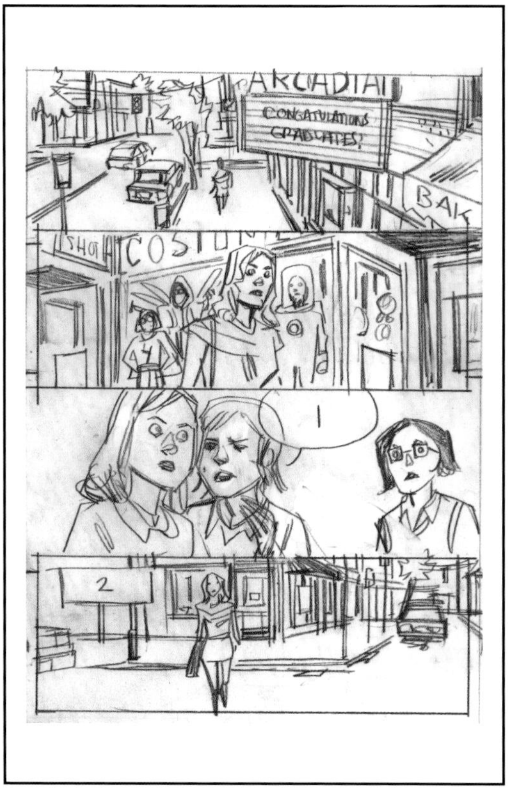
ARCADIA
CONGRATULATIONS GRADUATES!
BAK

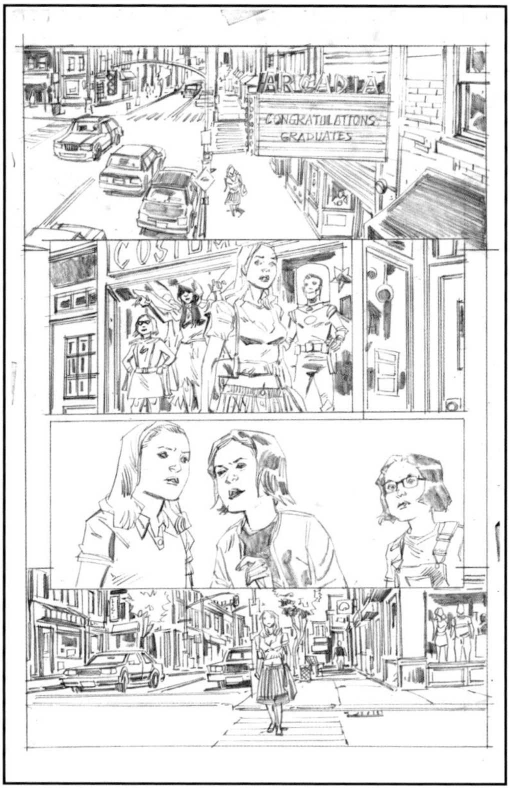
ARCADIA
CONGRATULATIONS GRADUATES

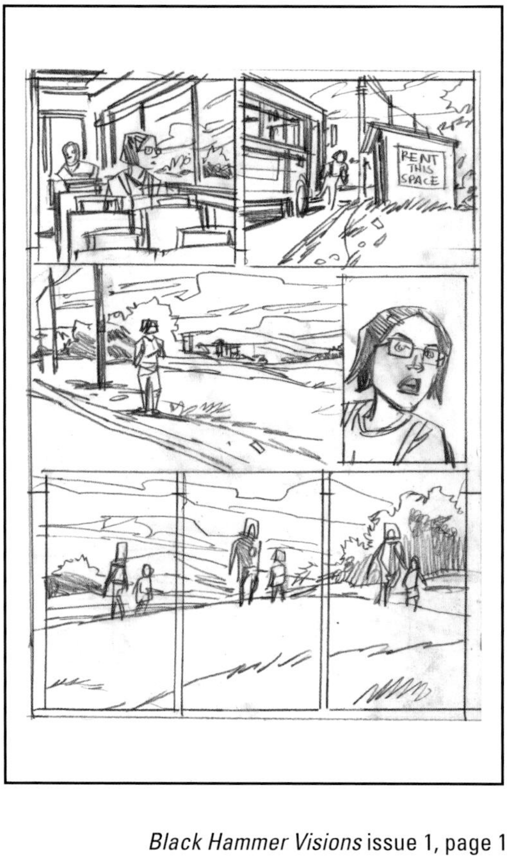
RENT THIS SPACE

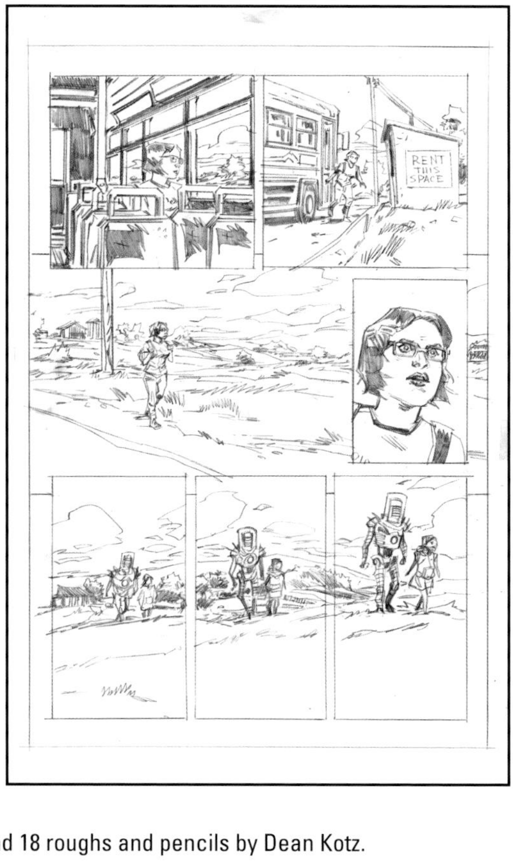
RENT THIS SPACE

Black Hammer Visions issue 1, page 17 and 18 roughs and pencils by Dean Kotz.

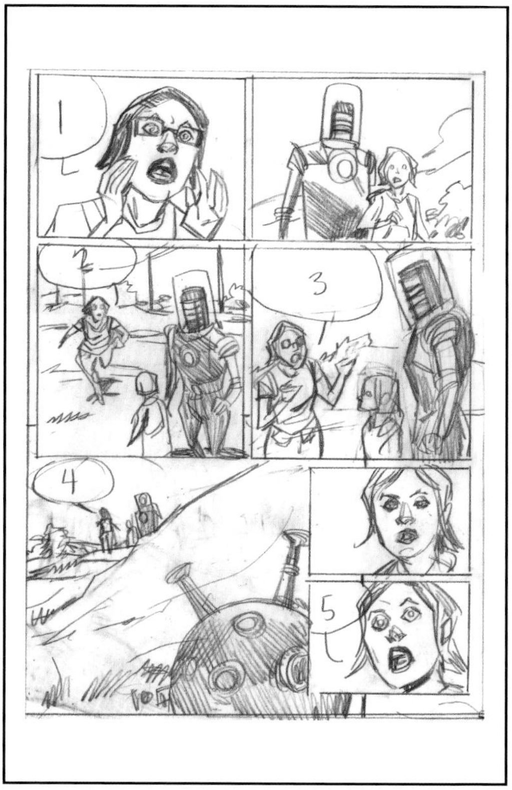
1
2
3
4
5
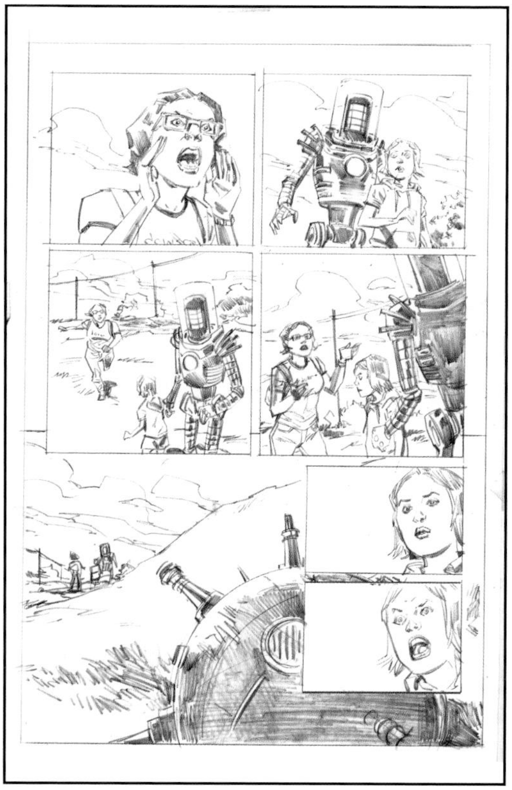
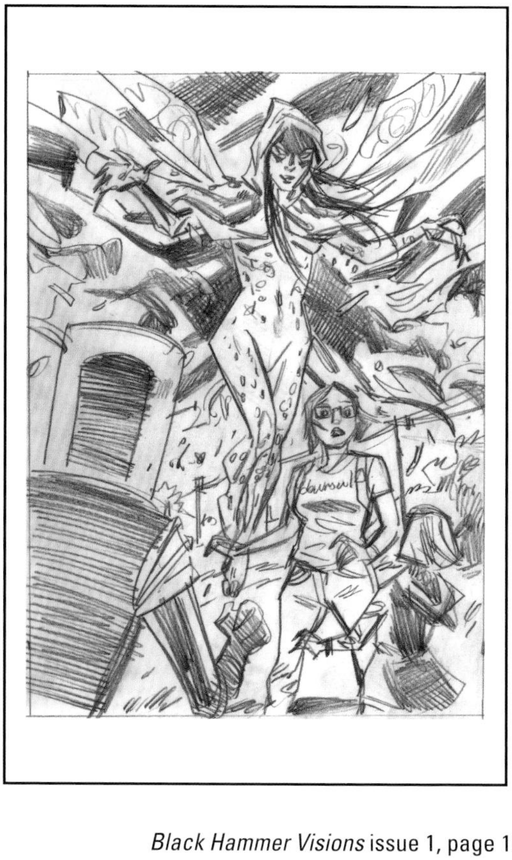
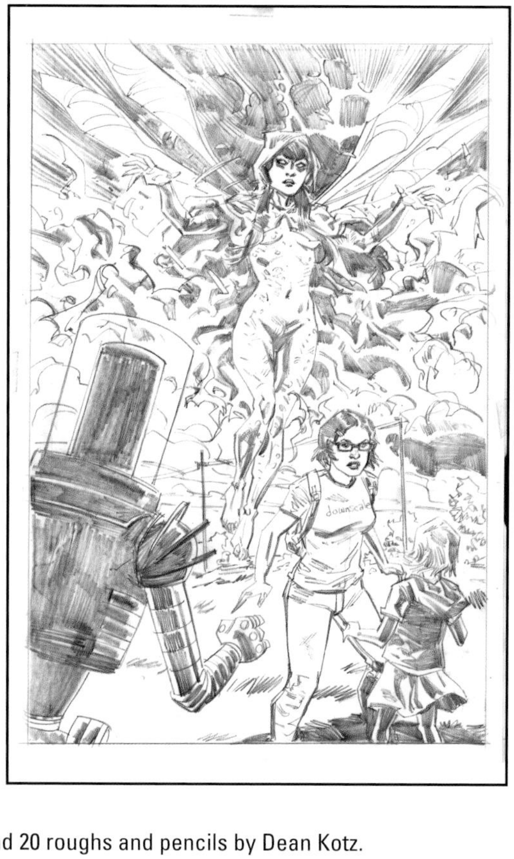

Black Hammer Visions issue 1, page 19 and 20 roughs and pencils by Dean Kotz.

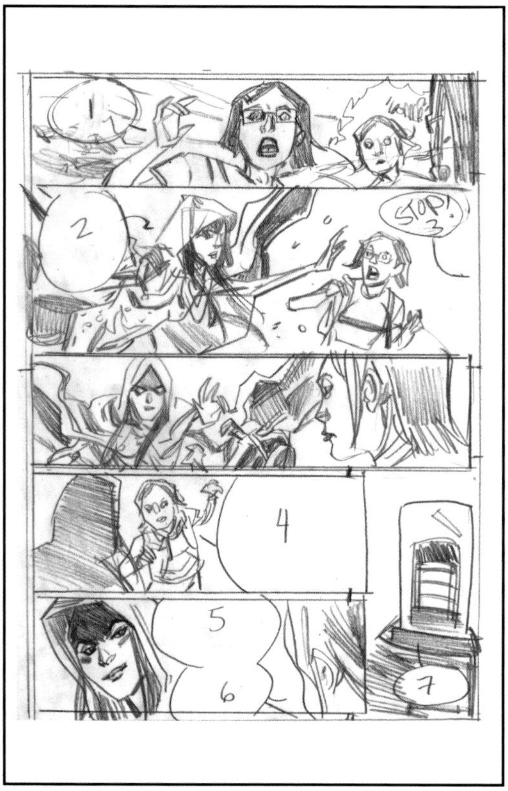
STOP!
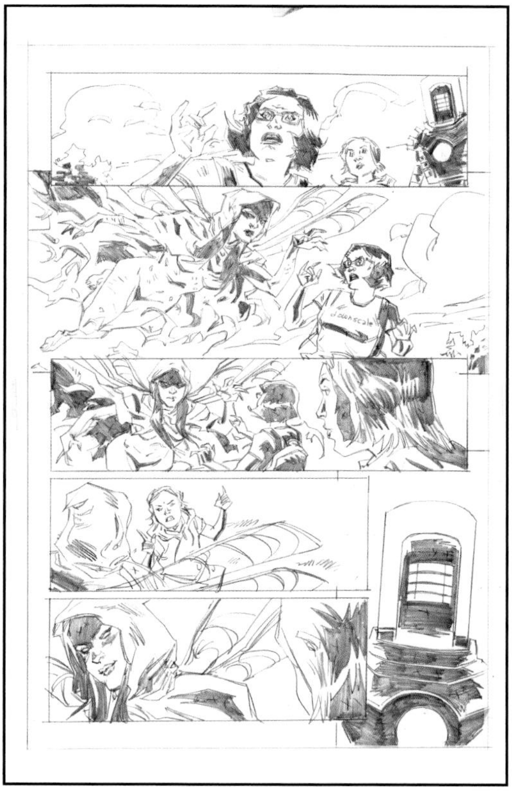
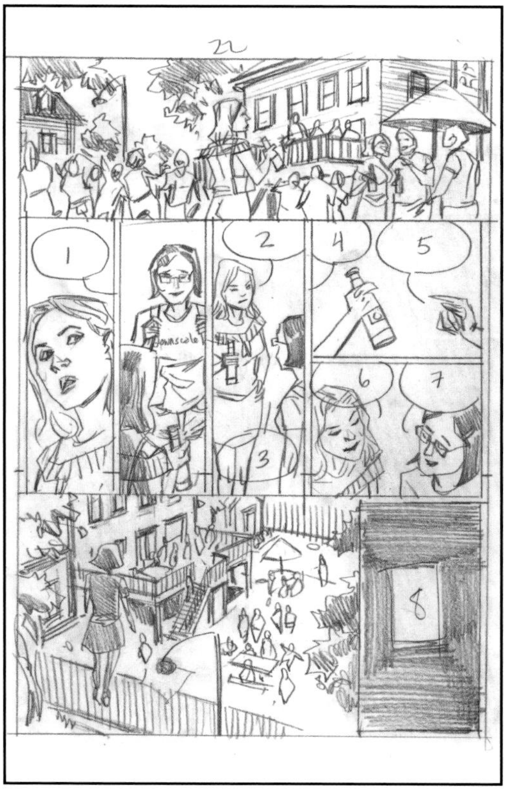
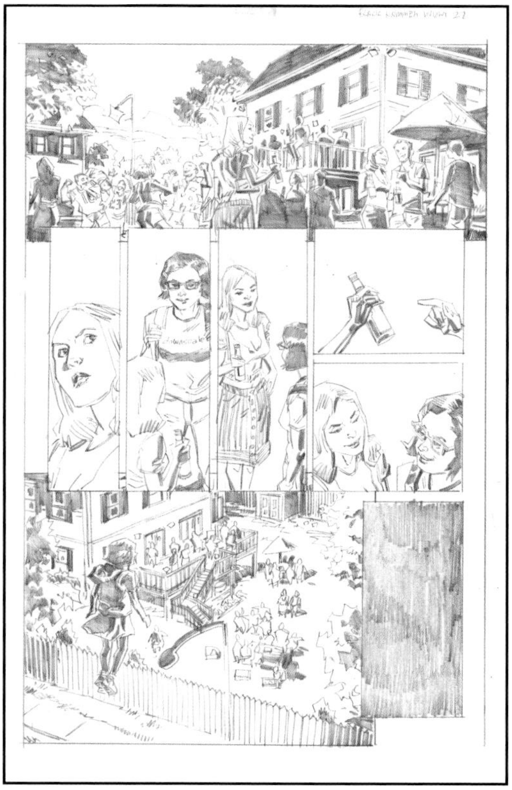

Black Hammer Visions issue 1, page 21 and 22 roughs and pencils by Dean Kotz.

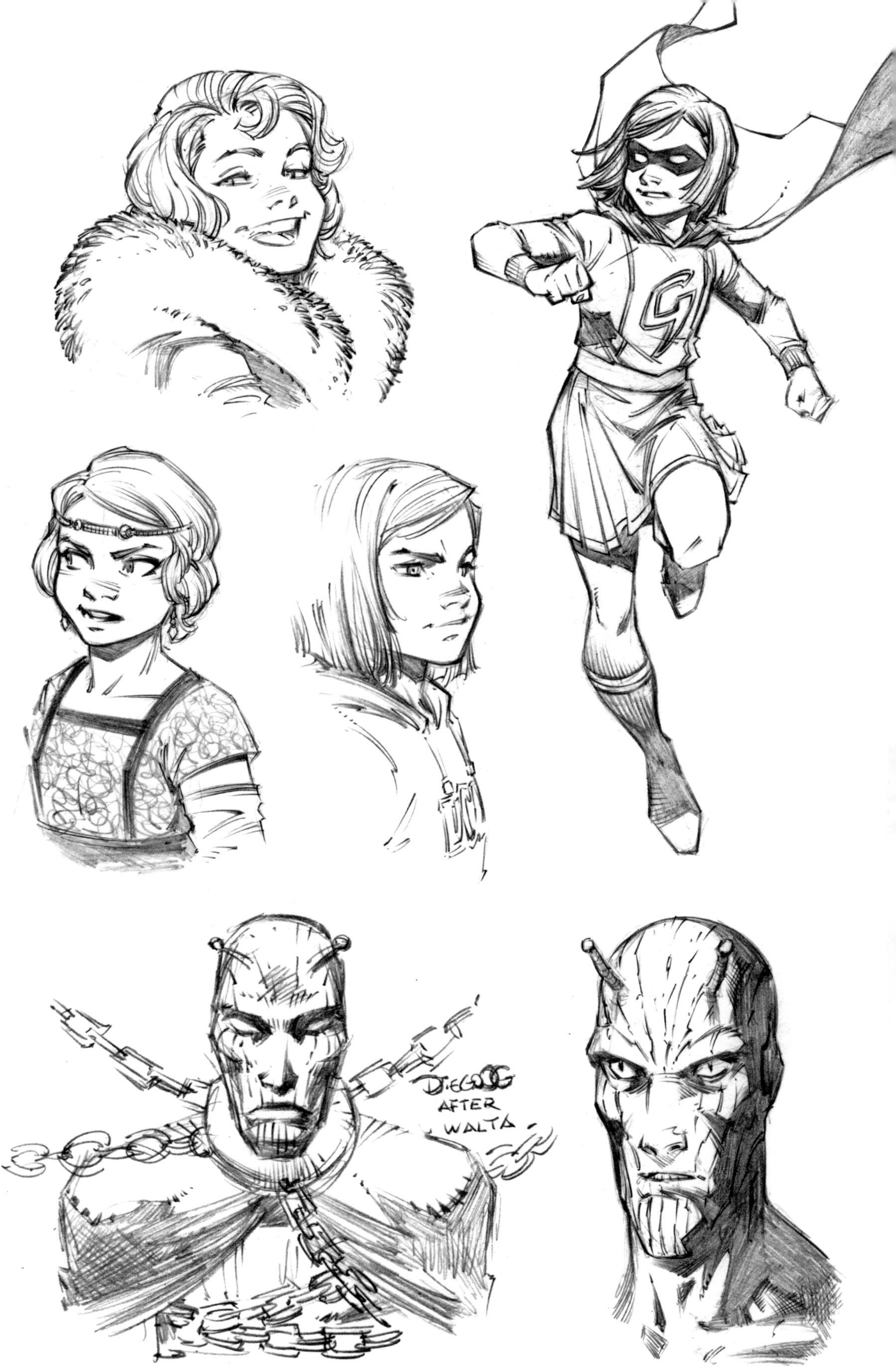
DIEGOOG
AFTER
WALTA

Black Hammer Visions issue 4 character sketches by Diego Olortegui.

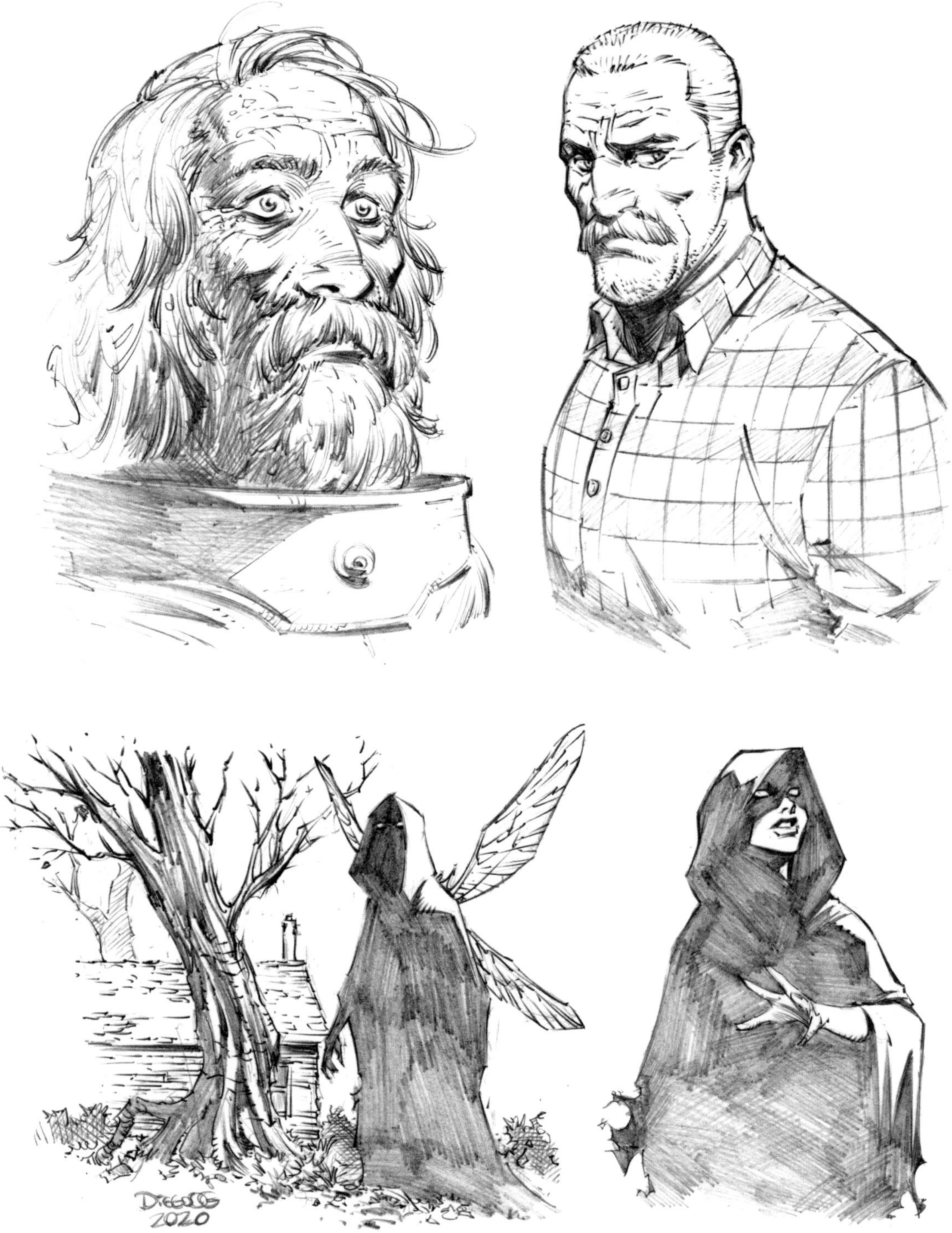

Black Hammer Visions issue 4 character sketches by Diego Olortegui.

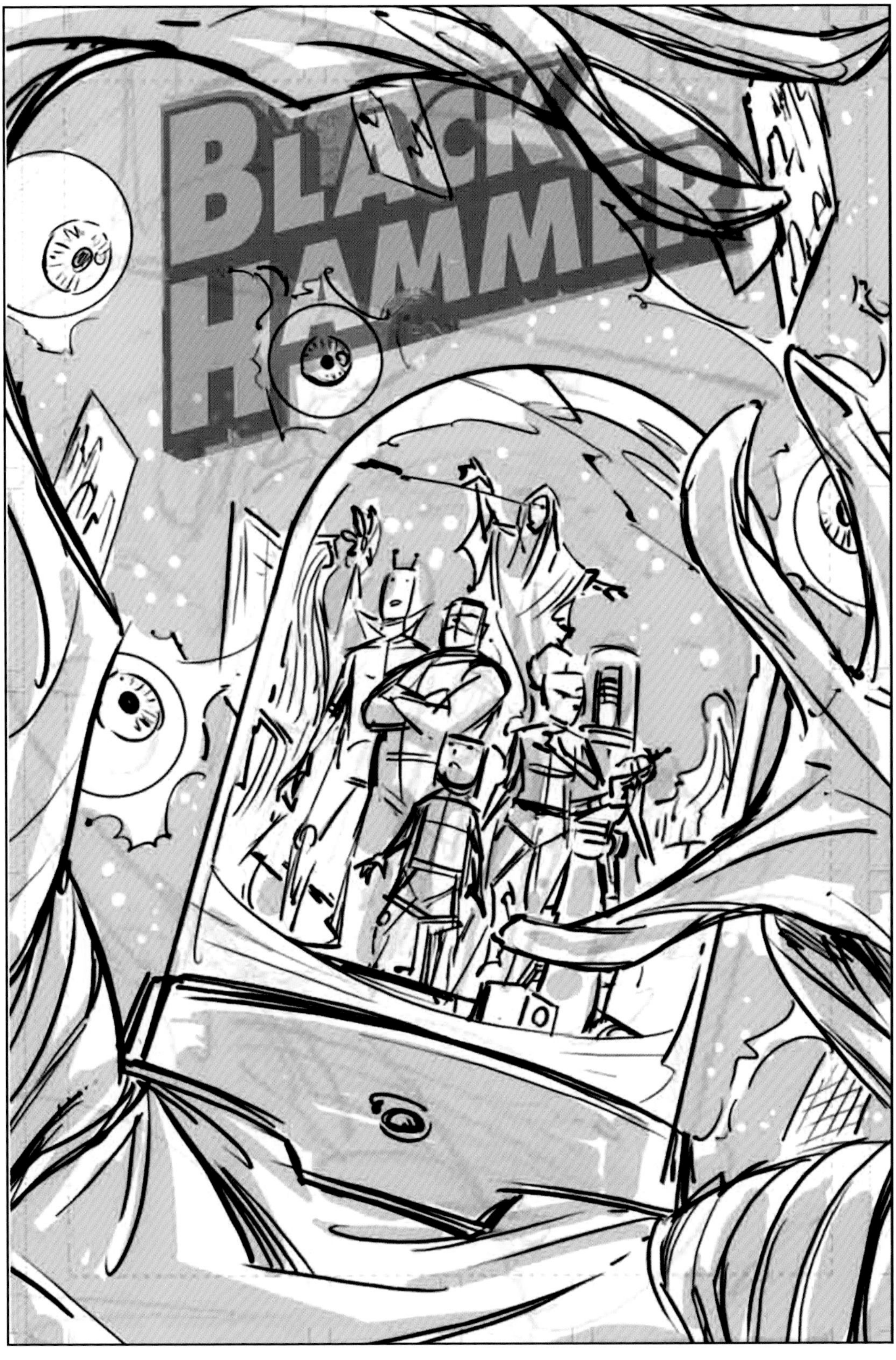
BLACK HAMMER

Black Hammer Visions issue 1 cover sketches by Diego Olortegui.

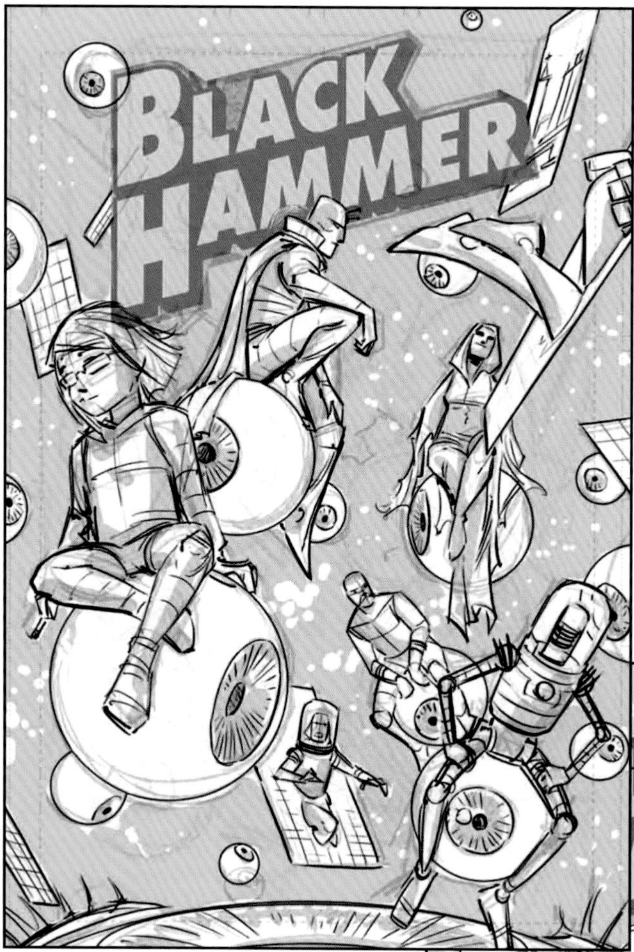
BLACK HAMMER
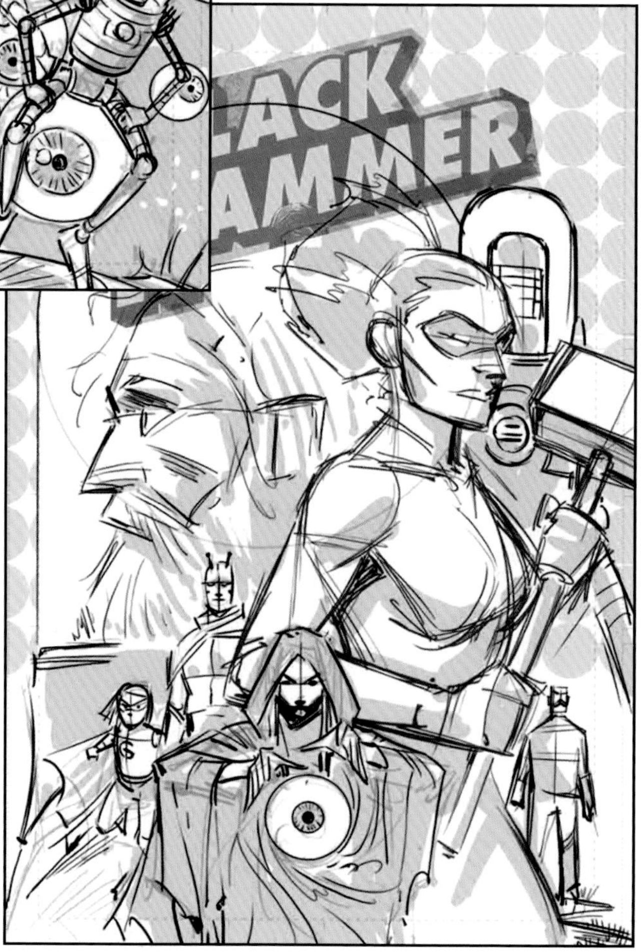
BLACK HAMMER

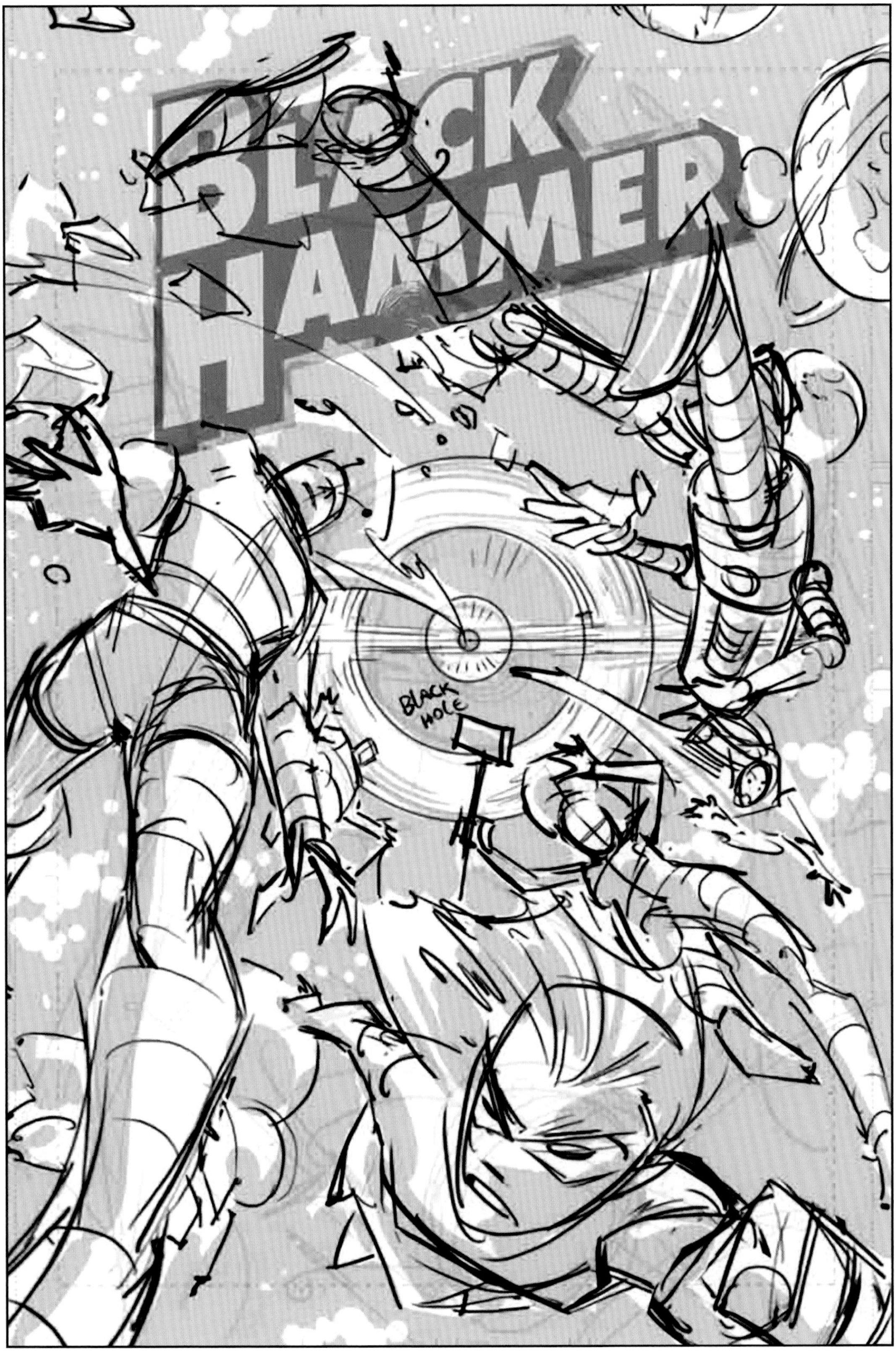
BLACK HAMMER
BLACK HOLE

"If you think there's no room left in your life for another superhero comic, *Black Hammer* might just prove you wrong."—IGN

BLACK HAMMER™

ONCE THEY WERE HEROES, but the age of heroes has long since passed. Banished from existence by a multiversal crisis, the old champions of Spiral City—Abraham Slam, Golden Gail, Colonel Weird, Madame Dragonfly, and Barbalien—now lead simple lives in an idyllic, timeless farming village from which there is no escape! And yet, the universe isn't done with them—it's time for one last grand adventure.

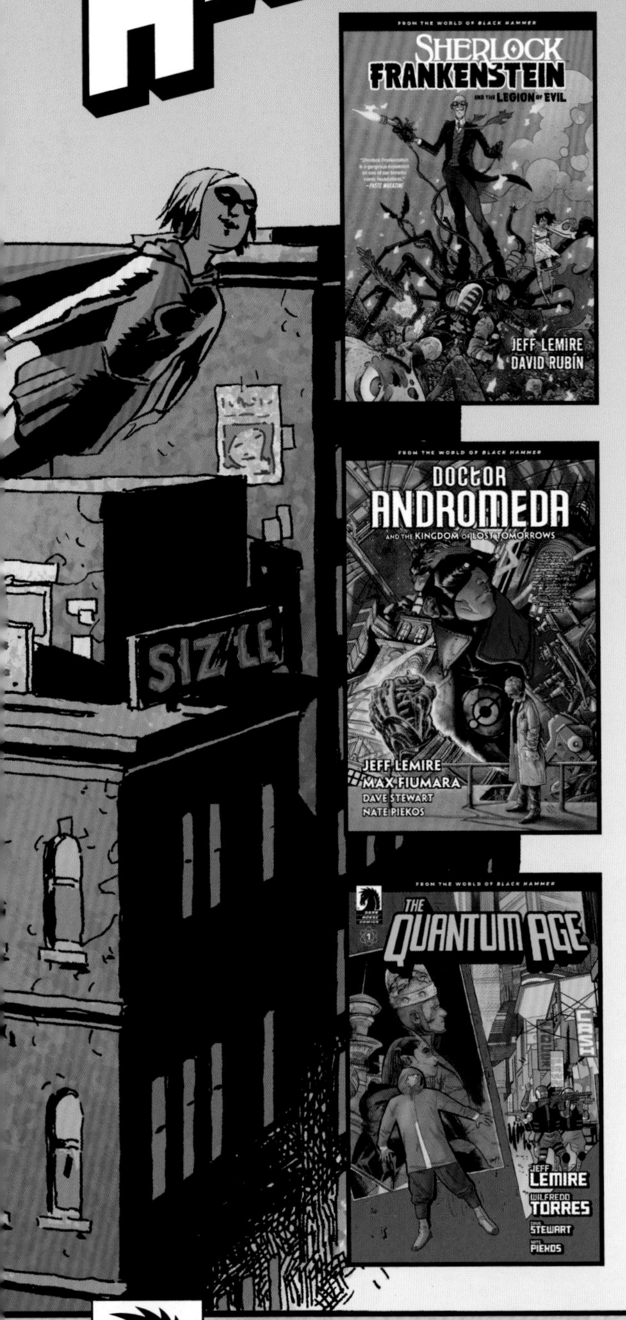

FROM THE WORLD OF BLACK HAMMER
SHERLOCK FRANKENSTEIN
AND THE LEGION OF EVIL
JEFF LEMIRE
DAVID RUBÍN
SIZZLE
FROM THE WORLD OF BLACK HAMMER
DOCTOR ANDROMEDA
AND THE KINGDOM OF LOST TOMORROWS
JEFF LEMIRE
MAX FIUMARA
DAVE STEWART
NATE PIEKOS
FROM THE WORLD OF BLACK HAMMER
THE QUANTUM AGE
JEFF LEMIRE
WILFREDO TORRES
DAVE STEWART
NATE PIEKOS

BLACK HAMMER
Written by Jeff Lemire
Art by Dean Ormston

THE WORLD OF BLACK HAMMER LIBRARY EDITION VOLUME 1
978-1-50671-995-5 • $49.99

THE WORLD OF BLACK HAMMER LIBRARY EDITION VOLUME 2
978-1-50671-996-2 • $49.99

VOLUME 1: SECRET ORIGINS
978-1-61655-786-7 • $14.99

VOLUME 2: THE EVENT
978-1-50670-198-1 • $19.99

VOLUME 3: AGE OF DOOM PART ONE
978-1-50670-389-3 • $19.99

VOLUME 4: AGE OF DOOM PART TWO
978-1-50670-816-4 • $19.99

BLACK HAMMER LIBRARY EDITION VOLUME 1
978-1-50671-073-0 • $49.99

BLACK HAMMER LIBRARY EDITION VOLUME 2
978-1-50671-185-0 • $49.99

SHERLOCK FRANKENSTEIN & THE LEGION OF EVIL
Written by Jeff Lemire • Art by David Rubín
This mystery follows a reporter determined to find out what happened to her father, the Black Hammer. All answers seem to lie in Spiral City's infamous insane asylum, where some dangerous supervillain tenants reside, including Black Hammer's greatest foe—Sherlock Frankenstein!
978-1-50670-526-2 • $19.99

DOCTOR ANDROMEDA & THE KINGDOM OF LOST TOMORROWS
Written by Jeff Lemire • Art by Max Fiumara
This dual-narrative story set in the world of *Black Hammer* chronicles the legacy of a Golden-Age superhero wishing to reconnect with his estranged son, whom he hoped would one day take the mantle of Doctor Andromeda.
978-1-50672-329-7 • $19.99

THE QUANTUM AGE: FROM THE WORLD OF BLACK HAMMER
Written by Jeff Lemire • Art by Wilfredo Torres
A thousand years in the future, a collection of superheroes, inspired by the legendary heroes of Black Hammer Farm, must band together to save the planet from an authoritarian regime, while a young Martian struggles to solve the riddle of what happened to the great heroes of the twentieth century.
VOLUME 1
978-1-50670-841-6 • $19.99

BLACK HAMMER: STREETS OF SPIRAL
Jeff Lemire, Dean Ormston, Emi Lenox, and others
A Lovecraftian teen decides she will do anything to make herself "normal," a bizarre witch guides her guests through her house of horrors, and an all-star slate of guest artists illustrate a bizarre adventure with Colonial Weird on the farm. Also features a complete world guide to the *Black Hammer* universe and its characters!
978-1-50670-941-3 • $19.99

BLACK HAMMER '45: FROM THE WORLD OF BLACK HAMMER
Jeff Lemire, Ray Fawkes, Matt Kindt, and Sharlene Kindt
During the Golden Age of superheroes, an elite Air Force crew called the Black Hammer Squadron bands together to combat the Nazis, a host of occult threats, and their ultimate aerial warrior the Ghost Hunter.
978-1-50670-850-8 • $17.99

BLACK HAMMER/JUSTICE LEAGUE: HAMMER OF JUSTICE!
Written by Jeff Lemire • Art by Michael Walsh
A strange man arrives simultaneously on Black Hammer Farm and in Metropolis, and both worlds are warped as Starro attacks! Batman, Green Lantern, Flash, Wonder Woman, Superman, and more crossover with Golden Gail, Colonel Weird, and the rest of the Black Hammer gang!
978-1-50671-099-0 • $29.99

COLONEL WEIRD—COSMAGOG: FROM THE WORLD OF BLACK HAMMER
Written by Jeff Lemire • Art by Tyler Crook
978-1-50671-516-2 • $19.99

DARK HORSE BOOKS

AVAILABLE AT YOUR LOCAL COMICS SHOP OR BOOKSTORE
TO FIND A COMICS SHOP IN YOUR AREA, VISIT COMICSHOPLOCATOR.COM.
For more information or to order direct, visit darkhorse.com.